An Anthology of
Henry George's Thought

The Henry George
Centennial Trilogy

Volume One: *An Anthology of Henry George's Thought*
                ISBN 1–878822–81–0

Volume Two: *An Anthology of Tolstoy's Spiritual Economics*
                ISBN 1–878822–91–8

Volume Three: *An Anthology of Single Land Tax Thought*
                ISBN 1–878822–92–6

An Anthology of Henry George's Thought

Volume I
of the Henry George
Centennial Trilogy

Kenneth C. Wenzer

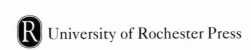 University of Rochester Press

First published 1997

University of Rochester Press
34–36 Administration Building, University of Rochester
Rochester, New York, 14627, USA
and at P.O. Box 9, Woodbridge, Suffolk IP12 3DF, UK

ISBN 1–878822–81–0

Library of Congress Cataloging-in-Publication Data

George, Henry, 1839–1897.
    [Selections. 1997]
    An anthology of Henry George's thought / edited by Kenneth C.
Wenzer.
        p.   cm.—(Henry George centennial trilogy ; v. 1)
    Includes bibliographical references.
    ISBN 1–878822–81–0 (alk. paper)
    1. George, Henry, 1839–1897. 2. Economists—United States.
3. Single tax. 4. Free trade. I. Wenzer, Kenneth C., 1950–
II. Title. III. Series: George, Henry, 1839–1897. Works. 1997.
HB119.G4A25   1997
330′.092—dc21   96–47170
                                                                          CIP

British Library Cataloguing-in-Publication Data

A catalogue record for this book
is available from the British Library

Typeset by Cornerstone Composition Services
This publication is printed on acid-free paper
Printed in the United States of America

For
Steven, Joshua, Sharon,
and
the Henry George Foundation
of America

Contents

Preface

For almost three decades Henry George (1839–1897) was one of the most famous social radicals, not only in the United States, but throughout the English-speaking world. With many others, he sought to regenerate a world beset by ungovernable transformation, in particular its most heartless off-spring, unrestrained industrial capitalism and rampant urbanization. But George's portrayal of material and spiritual suffering, as illustrated in his most famous work, *Progress and Poverty*, is as impassioned as that as any visionary writer.

He espoused a singular type of radicalism, commonly labeled the "single tax." Virtually unknown today, it was a composite of left-wing ideas, American ideals, and religious values. But though George's political economy may seem a compound of disparate elements to the reader of a later time, he and his followers perceived it as a harmonious whole. Millenarian in spiritual fervor, Georgists simultaneously held both conservative and radical ideas—for instance, a potent belief in God and community owner-ship of land. His life of probity along with his religious devotion defined him for tens of thousands as the father of a new spiritual utopia. Further-more, George and his moral and redemptive social economics were a reflection of each other—and of late nineteenth-century America: of her grandiose dreams, as well as her shortcomings.

I intend here neither a biography of George nor a detailed presentation of his ideology. The reader is urged to consult the bibliography for further reading suggestions. In a short introductory essay, however, I do outline George's basic world view and present those who were influenced by his charisma and teachings.

This anthology is the first addition to George's published works in nearly a century. His seven extant books still do not fully answer some questions inherent in his political economy. In this new presentation of his speeches, articles, and correspondence he more completely addresses such issues as landownership, confiscation, how much ground rent the state should take, the role of the single tax, ideological differences with the socialists, his internationalism, and the nature of his social radicalism. Various selections have been divided topically into chapters, though there is some overlapping of subjects. My major mandate for this anthology is to preserve what I consider to be George's most important thoughts with as little intrusion as possible. Each section has a short introduction and where necessary there is approriate annotation. For the most part, George's works speak for themselves.

The primary source is George's *The Standard;* secondarily, the Henry George Papers from the Manuscripts and Archives Section of the New York Public Library. *The Standard* was first printed on January 8, 1887, and the last issue appeared on August 31, 1892. George was at the helm until the last week of 1890. Then William T. Croasdale took command, and finally Louis F. Post. This newspaper has preserved for us the most fertile and active period in George's life, which was also the time of his greatest popularity. In the varous sources, the United Labor Party, the Anti-Poverty Society, the Haymarket Affair, presidential, state, and local elections, and foreign politics come alive. Since George was an astonishingly busy man, writing, speechifying, and traveling, sometimes redundancies and grammatical errors have crept into the articles and speeches. I have opted to modernize spellings but otherwise to edit these works only lightly to retain the tenor of the times. Unquoted titles are mine. Correspondence has been virtually untouched, as it should be in respect for another's heart.

I am happy to acknowledge friends and colleagues whose moral and professional support has been indispensable. At the Henry George Foundation of America: Dr. Steven Cord, Joshua Vincent, and Sharon Feinman. At the Robert Schalkenbach Foundation: Dr. Mason Gaffney and Susan Klinglehoefer. At the Henry George School of Social Sciences: George Collins and Simon Winters. At McKeldin Library (University of Maryland, College Park): Lily Griner, Patricia Heron, Susan Caldwell, and Kevin Hammett. I also thank William Pencak, Lindy Davies, John Blanpied, Laurie Knisley, and Pat Aller for their help. The New York Public Library has proved to be a singular repository and must be acknowleged for allowing me to use this material. Dr. Oscar Johannsen has also kindly given me permission to reprint a number of indicated pamphlets published by the Schalkenbach Foundation. Without the understanding and graciousness of Sean Culhane of the University of Rochester Press this book would have not been possible. As usual, I must applaud Dr. Thomas West of the Catholic University of America for his friendship and scathing editorializing. Despite all this kind assistance I could not, however, have finished this work without my companions, Oliver and Raisonique, nor Clio for her constant presence and love.

Abbreviations
used in notes

GR   General Research Division of The New York Public Library; Astor, Lenox, and Tilden Foundation.

HGP   Henry George Papers, Rare Books and Manuscript Division of The New York Public Library; Astor, Lenox, and Tilden Foundation.

PSS   Lev Nikolaevich Tolstoy, *Polnoe sobranie sochinenii* (Complete works) (Moscow: Gosudarstvennoe izdatel'stvo khudozhestvennoi literatury, 1928–1964).

Chapter 1

An Introductory Essay on George's Philosophy

At least from the time of Plato's *Republic*, people have longed for a simpler and more harmonious world, free of constraints and iniquities. The pursuit of social perfection has taken disparate and apparently incompatible forms, religious and secular, radical and reactionary. Often such thinking imagines the earth as a gift from a God or the gods. Utopians and dreamers believe in an interplay of air, water, and land within a transcendant or immanent system giving birth, providing sustenance, and embracing death. A mankind attuned to these forces will find peace and happiness. The harmony of nature, so utopians insist, can be discovered by observation; but it can also be discerned through introspection, for nature has implanted herself in the psyche. Those who search for a perfected world have recoiled from the injustice of land monopolization, the squalor of cities, the cruelties of factories, and the quickened pace which has atomized society and alienated the individual.

To that utopian vision Henry George committed himself.

Henry George, who had faced hardships himself since his birth in Philadelphia in 1839, turned his attention to the causes of economic need early in life.[1] "Once in daylight . . . there came to me, a thought, a vision, a call . . . every nerve quivered. And there and then I made a vow. . . . It was that impelled me to write" a work that will answer the question: why does industrial progress result not in the abolition of poverty, but in its increase?[2] George's first and best known major effort culminated in 1879: *Progress and Poverty: An Inquiry Into the Cause of Industrial Depressions and of Increase of Want with Increase of Wealth . . . the Remedy*. A letter in 1883 reflects his piety. And "when I had finished the last page . . . I flung myself on my knees and wept like a child. The rest, was in the Master's hands. That is a feeling that has never left: that is constantly with me."[3]

In this tome and others George places in land the origin of wealth, concluding that the "vast majority of mankind, even in [the] richest civilized countries, leave the world as destitute of wealth as they entered it" because injustice and poverty come not of nature, but of vicious forces of production and distribution.[4] George concludes that, despite material progress, even in a free America, "Only in broken gleams and partial light has the sun of Liberty yet beamed among men."[5] The culprit is private property in land, especially its monopolization and speculation. "The idea that land . . . can become subject to such individual ownership as attaches to things that man produces by labor, is as repugnant . . . as the idea that air or sunlight may be so owned."[6] The ownership of land ultimately determines the totality of all relations in society: it is the source of food for the body and fuel for the hearth.[7] To produce their own sustenance, workers apply themselves to others' land in some form, and so turn themselves into slaves lower than any beast of burden.[8] "Our boasted freedom," George says,

> necessarily involves slavery, so long as we recognize private property in land. Until that is abolished, Declarations of Independence and Acts of Emancipation are in vain. So long as one man can claim the exclusive ownership of the land from which others must live, slavery will exist, and as material progress goes on, must grow and deepen![9]

Since land, as a fixed quantity and the primary source of all wealth, is the basis of the "industrial pyramid,"[10] its monopolization creates a concentration of wealth that can be maintained only by force.[11] This artificial scarcity brings in its wake parasitism, speculation, burdensome rents, business depressions, and war.[12] "The Creator showers upon us his gifts—more than enough for all. But like swine scrambling for food, we tread them in the mire . . . while we tear and rend each other!"[13]

George makes a radical distinction between land and the possessions humans really need or enjoy. Property titles acquired by forced appropriation are a criminal fraud since thay have no basis in labor. History has been a sad witness to the subversion of man's equal and natural rights to God's land. Only the individual's labor gives true title to wealth.[14] To "deprive a man of land is as certainly to kill him as to deprive him of blood by opening his veins."[15] George's political economy promoted social equality in land, production, and distribution as a prelude to a perfect cooperative world conformable to the teachings of God.[16] Political economy in George's rendering fought Social Darwinism and laissez-faire liberalism, which claimed that capital and not labor was the creator of wealth.

The remedy for prevailing economic and social evils and the spur to human creativity was to tax ground rents based on the land's assessed unimproved value, rather than on the selling price. Any improvements on the land or on the wealth and personal possessions earned by labor would also be exempt from taxation. "We may safely leave them the shell, if we take the kernel. *It is not necessary to confiscate land; it is only necessary to confiscate rent.*"[17] Those who inefficiently use large holdings will thus be forced to relinquish their excess land and captured rent. Others who can prudently use the ground, agriculturally, industrially, or otherwise will be rewarded. Freed land will be assurance that whoever makes improvements by the exertion of their labor will keep their whole value. Income and capital will accrue for greater production and exchange of wealth will be fostered.

George's ideas have been simplified as the "single tax."[18] The "land belongs equally to all [and since] land values arise from the presence of all [it] should be shared among all."[19] An equal distribution of the land is impossible and unnecessary. A tax based on the value of the land would be enough to make it the common property of the people.[20] This money would go to society, the rightful common owner since the community as a whole creates value.[21] Through public control, the tax collected could respond to individual and societal needs and would be more wisely disbursed by a benign government, or "cooperative association—society,"[22] for "the best government is that which governs least."[23] Although George was unclear as to its specific nature, the state would probably be concerned with minimal administrative and regulative functions, rather than police and military.

The single tax would act as a balancing and stabilizing mechanism between the city and the countryside, in part, by developing a love of a simpler life for people beset by great changes.[24] This use of ground rent tax, the linchpin of his political economy and primary generator of reform, along with unrestricted free trade,[25] would distribute wealth and exchange more equitably: the farmlands would be covered with crops, the cities would prosper, and a new era, not of political and economic corruption but of true freedom and morality conformable to the laws of God, would dawn.[26] Assumed here is that the land would be the safety valve for all economic problems and that the majority of laborers, still imbued with an agricultural consciousness and longing for the land, would return to it.

George's inquiries into the lives of men and his search for an all-encompassing philosophy were essentially ethical and religious with justice for the individual as the cornerstone. His prophetic but progressive vision of God, man, and the land was to be realized in a spiritual republic on a regenerated earth. Through a fiery evangelical fervor and steadfast belief in the perfectibiltiy of man, George believed that his work continued Jesus' revolutionary teachings.[27] The earth is our mother and God is our father and we "are as much children of the soil as are the flowers and the trees."[28] Since harmony reigns in the heavens, we must labor for a perfect concord on earth: our life in the here and now should be emblematic of this spirit. George longs "for the promised Millennium, when each one will be free to follow [his] noblest impulses, unfettered by [present] restrictions and necessities . . . when the poorest and the meanest will have a chance to use all his God-given faculties."[29]

> Into higher, grander spheres desire mounts and beckons, and a star that rises in the east leads . . . [man] on. Lo! the pulses of . . . man [would] throb with the yearnings of the god—he would aid in the process of the suns!. . . . [Man] is the mythic earth tree, whose roots are in the ground, but whose topmost branches may blossom in the heavens![30]

He perceived that his philosophy contained the single unifying factor for people of all religious and political persuasions. His earnest desire that everyone should have equal access to the richness of creation, expressed with such eloquent sincerity, was potent material. George's influence on the Anti-Poverty Society, founded in 1887 and lasting only a year, was enormous. His talks brought thousands to tears with the language of hope.[31] His numerous speeches across the United States were important events for many more thirsting for a better life.

Orations at George's funeral in 1897 speak of "a veritable apostle, crusader, and martyr to God and the realization of His goodness on earth."[32] The man and his works helped to awaken a greater sensitivity to poverty and injustice. Intellectual currents and movements such as progressivism at the turn of the century drew on George for inspiration. Clarence Darrow claimed that *Progress and Poverty* was revolutionary in its attack on monopoly and found in George a prophet of a new age of realizable ideals.[33] Robert La Folette was reported to have said that he did not want to read this work lest it would radically change his social philosophy. John Dewey extolled George as "one of the world's great social philosophers, certainly the greatest which this country has produced."[34]

Not only the United States but the British Isles were touched by George's sincerity.[35] George Bernard Shaw claimed that George had converted him and many others to a greater social awareness in the "Great Socialist revival."[36] Australia and New Zealand enacted land reforms in response to George.[37] Many of their cities still tax buildings less than land, although others, in true Georgist spirit, asssess only the latter. Even in far-off Imperial Russia the name Henry George was familiar to the intelligentsia, who were grappling with a solution to the suffering of the peasant and the maldistribution of the land. By the time of George's influence, serfdom was gone, but chattel slavery had been replaced by land slavery—the peasants were still eking-out a bare subsistence, if they were fortunate to be spared from exploitation.

One of the more concerned nobles was Lev Nikolaevich Tolstoy. In his search for universal absolutes, purer spiritual values, and a solution to society's moral and economic problems, the famed novelist avidly read Confucius, Jean-Jacques Rousseau, Charles Dickens, John Ruskin, Henry David Thoreau, Walt Whitman, Edward Bellamy (the author of *Looking Backward*), and the abolitionist William Lloyd Garrison to name but a few. But Henry George most fired his imagination, and he was instrumental in publishing George's works in Russian.[38] On February 24, 1885, Tolstoy wrote to his collaborator, Victor G. Chertkov:

> I was sick for a week but consumed by George's latest [*Social Problems*] and the first book *Progress and Poverty*, which produced a strong and joyous impression on me. . . . This book is wonderful, but it is beyond value, for it destroys all the cobwebs of Spencer-Mill political economy—it is like the pounding of water and acutely summons people to a moral consciousness of the cause and even defines the cause. There is weakness in it, as with anything created by man, but there is a genuine humanitarian thought and heart, not scientific trash. . . . I see in him a brother, one of those who according to the teachings of the Books of the Apostles [has more] love [for people] than for his own soul.[39]

Still mesmerized by *Progress and Poverty*, Tolstoy in a letter the next day advised Prince L. D. Urusov, an avid Tolstoyan, to read it. George is "a marvelous writer—a writer, who will usher in an epoch."[40] Nine years later, on November 24, 1894, Tolstoy wrote to Ernest Crosby, an American disciple:

> The more I know of him [George], the more I esteem him, and am astonished at the indifference of the civilized world to his work.
> If the new Tsar [Nicholas II] would ask me what I would advise him to do, I would say to him: use your autocratic power to abolish the land property in Russia and to introduce the single tax system; and then give up your power and [grant] the people a liberal constitution.
> I write this to you, because I know that you are one of the coworkers of H. George, and that you . . . [believe in] his ideas.
> I wish you success in your work.[41]

By 1908, two years before his death, Tolstoy had become obsessed with George's single tax, regarding it as vital for the moral and economic regeneration not only of his homeland, but of the world. This *idée fixe* is amply illustrated in the following correspondence.

> I read through your letter and I find your thoughts about land to be correct. The land is God's. It should not and cannot belong to anyone.

All people have an equal right to it and the only concern is how to distribute it.... Many people like you truthfully say that the land cannot be anyone's property. Genuine property is determined only by labor and people must work in harmony on it. Many truly understand that to distribute the land among the people is important and wise. These matters were resolved in a very just form by the American scholar Henry George.... [Whoever uses the land] would pay ... to society i.e., to the government for community needs.... There will be no domestic taxes or foreign duties, i.e., there will not be requisitions or taking anything away from people's work, because all taxes will be replaced by this land payment. Henry George was wise concerning this. ... The injustice of landownership is now becoming as obvious to people as what occurred fifty years ago when the evil of serfdom became blatant. It could not last long, and when the time came, it was abolished. The slavery of people and the stealing from their labor through landownership cannot long remain in the same manner.[42]

For over a century, a single tax movement in the United States and abroad has been devoted much in the same manner as Tolstoy to the alleviation of economic and social injustice. George's philosophy still inspires the hearts of a small but active body of men and women attracted to its simple reverence for nature, its exaltation of the individual, its lack of compromise with injustice, and its minimalist solution to social ills.

Notes

1. There are a number of biographies of George. Among the standard works are: Henry George, Jr., *Henry George*, American Men and Women of Letters Series, ed. Daniel Aaron (New York: Chelsea House, 1981) and Charles A. Barker, *Henry George* (New York: Oxford University Press, 1955).
2. George to Father Dawson, Feb. 1, 1883, Reel #3, HGP. See pages 243–244.
3. *Ibid.*
4. Henry George, *The Science of Political Economy* (New York: Robert Schalkenbach Foundation, 1992), 312.
5. Henry George, "The American Republic: Its Dangers and Possibilities," in *Our Land and Land Policy*, Vol. 8 of *The Complete Works of Henry George* (New York: Doubleday, Page & Co., 1904), 178.
6. Henry George, *A Perplexed Philosopher* (New York: Robert Schalkenbach Foundation,1988), 175.
7. Henry George, *Progress and Poverty* (New York: Robert Schalkenbach Foundation, 1992), 295 and "The Land Question," in *The Land Question* (New York: Robert Schalkenbach Foundation, 1935), 27–28.
8. George, *Progress*, 284–285.
9. *Ibid.*, 357.

10. *Ibid.*, 269.
11. Henry George, *Protection or Free Trade* (New York: Robert Schalkenbach Foundation, 1992), 326; *Progress*, 295, 326, 517–518, 541, and 544; and "Our Land," in *Our Land*, 86.
12. George, "Land Question," in *Land Question*, 22, 39–40, and 81; George, "Thy Kingdom Come," in *Our Land*, 283–287; *Progress*, 370, 379–382, 528, 542–543, and 549–550; and "Peace," *The Standard*, Sept. 21, 1889, GR.
13. George, *Progress*, 550. See pages 10–14.
14. George, "Salutatory," *The Standard* , Jan. 8, 1887, GR. See pages 26–27.
15. George, "The Condition of Labor: An Open Letter to Pope Leo XIII," in *Land Question*, 26.
16. George, *Protection*, 8 and *Science*, 451–452.
17. George, *Progress*, 405. Emphasis in original.
18. George, "Justice the Object-Taxation the Means," in *Our Land*, 297–321.
19. George, "Land and Taxation," in *Our Land*, 230.
20. George, "The Land for the People" (New York: Robert Schalkenbach Foundation, n.d.), 6. See also George, "The Single Tax: What It Is and Why We Urge It" (New York: Robert Schalkenbach Foundation, n.d.) for a succinct view of the benefits of the single tax. See pages 67–69.
21. George, "Condition of Labor," in *Land Question*, 9–10 and Steven B. Cord, *Henry George: Dreamer or Realist?* (Philadelphia: University of Pennsylvania Press, 1965), 63.
22. George, "Land Question," in *Land Question*, 83–84.
23. George, "American Republic," in *Our Land* , 172; "Land and Taxation," in *Our Land*, 229; and *Progress*, 454–457.
24. John L. Thomas, *Alternative America: Henry George, Edward Bellamy, Henry Demarest Lloyd, and the Adversary Tradition* (Cambridge: Belknap Press, 1983), 123.
25. George, "To Workingmen," in *Our Land*, 265–276.
26. George, *Perplexed Philosopher*, 209–210; *Progress*, 433–453; "Our Land," in *Our Land*, 111–115; "Land Question," in *Land Question*, 80–86; and "Condition of Labor," in *Land Question*, 16–17. See also George, "The Study of Political Economy," in *Our Land*, 153.
27. George, "Anti-Poverty: The Society Musters to Welcome Judge Maguire," *The Standard*, Oct. 8, 1887, GR. See pages 28–29.
28. *Ibid.*, "Justice the Object," in *Our Land*, 303.
29. George to Annie Fox, June 5, 1862, #1, HGP. See pages 238–241. Elsewhere, George predicts that the age of material deprivation and enslavement, which Moses foresaw on Mt. Pisgah, will give way to an era of prosperity, peace, and love ("Moses," New York: Robert Schalkenbach Foundation, n. d.). See pages 14–25.
30. George, *Progress*, 136–137.
31. His fiery disciple, the excommunicated Catholic priest Dr. Edward McGlynn was also an imposing speaker for the cause. McGlynn held that "there is a marriage by nature sanctioned . . . and given a sacramental value by . . . the teaching of Christ, between land and labor . . . between the children of this

footstool of God and their Father" (Rev. Edward McGlynn, "Anti-Poverty: The People's Answer to the Papal Court," *The Standard*, June 4, 1887, GR). The single tax, according to McGlynn, would lay the basis of true justice as a precursor of pure love, where everyone would be "endowed not merely with the power of knowing Him, but with the royal liberty of a child of God" (*Ibid.*, "Anti-Poverty: A Crowded Meeting Ratifies the Syracuse Platform," *The Standard*, Aug. 27, 1887, GR). Also see Stephen Bell, *Rebel, Priest, and Prophet: A Biography of Dr. Edward McGlynn* (New York: Robert Schalkenbach Foundation, 1968). See pages 221–234 for more details.

32.   Edmund Yardley, ed., "Address of John Sherwin Crosby," in *Addresses at the Funeral of Henry George* (Chicago: The Public Publishing Company, 1905), 47.

33.   Clarence Darrow, "Henry George," *Everyman* (Sept.-Oct., 1913); 17–22.

34.   John Dewey, in George R. Geiger, *The Philosophy of Henry George* (New York: The Macmillan Co., 1933), xiii.

35.   See George, Jr., *Henry George*, 522–542 and Geiger, *Philosophy of Henry George*, 381–424.

36.   George Bernard Shaw, "Geo. Bernard Shaw's Tribute to the Work of Henry George," in *The Single Tax Review*, Apr. 15, 1905, 26–28.

37.   Barker, *Henry George*, 594–595.

38.   Lev Nikolaevich Tolstoy, *PSS*, 83: 483. Most of George's works were translated into Russian by Tolstoy's friend S. D. Nikolaev. All translations from Russian into English are mine unless otherwise indicated.

39.   Tolstoy to V. F. Chertkov, Feb. 24, 1889, *PSS*, 85: 144. *Social Problems* was read before *Progress and Poverty*.

40.   Tolstoy to L. D. Urusov, Feb. 25, 1894, *PSS*, 63: 212. According to one of Tolstoy's Russian biographers, it was the introduction to *Progress and Poverty* that produced "the strongest and most favorable impression," especially those lines in which George declares: "I propose to beg no question, to shrink from no conclusion, but to follow truth wherever it may lead. Upon us is the responsibility of seeking the law, for in the very heart of our civilization today women faint and little children moan. . . . If the conclusion that we reach run counter to our prejudices, let us not flinch; if they challenge institutions that have long been deemed wise and natural, let us not turn back" N. N. Gusev, *Lev Nikolaevich Tolstoi: materiali k biografii s 1881 po 1885 god* (L. N. Tolstoy: material for a biography from 1881 to 1885)(Moscow: Izdatel'stvo "Nauka," 1970), 387.

41.   Tolstoy to Ernest Crosby, Nov. 24, 1894, in R. F. Christian, ed., *Tolstoy's Letters, 1880–1910*, vol. 2 (New York: Charles Scribner's Sons, 1978), 512. Economic progress was unthinkable without an inheritance tax, a tax on the wealthy, and the application of Georgist ideas (Tolstoy, *PSS*, 53: 97–98).

42.   Tolstoy to Rgotinov, Aug. 29, 1908, *PSS*, 78: 215.

Chapter 2

Exhortative Works

George's expertise on the platform rivaled his literary style. It was a rare combination of eloquence and personality that propelled him to great popularity in the English-speaking world and an eminent place in the late nineteenth century.

In an age before radio, movies, and television, people craved entertainment and knowledge, especially in isolated rural areas with marginal means of transportation and communication. Their primary way to reach the outside world was to hitch a horse, jump into the wagon, drive for many torturous miles, and spend an evening in the nearest town hall or church. The Chautauqua lectures, for instance, became legendary. Speakers famed throughout the country, now lucky to be found in a footnote or two, enthralled audiences on subjects of all kinds. After the turn of the century, the voice of William Jennings Bryan spoke for the conscience of many Americans.

A generation earlier it was Henry George. His rhetoric moved people not only in the United States but in Australia, Ireland, and Britain, calling his listeners and readers to compassion for the poor and to the establishment of an economy that would be also a spiritual commonwealth. It was this mixture of realizable social reform, devoutness, and concern for the welfare of all, that made him so compelling.

These writings and foreign and domestic speeches are representative of George's inner strength and guilelessness coupled with a vision of a nobler civilization. "Ode to Liberty" contains probably the most elegant lines in *Progress and Poverty*. George summons Liberty to fulfill herself in a free economy and society—a Golden Age of perfection. "Moses," probably George's most famous speech, evokes the ancient leader and lawgiver but as the founder of a perfected freedom and the brotherhood of people under the fatherhood of God. The goals of the "Salutatory," which appeared in the first issue of *The Standard* in 1887, are self-evident, but we have still not reached them. The other selections give the reader a fairly good idea of George's dislike for class divisions, his call for the improvement of society, his belief in the primacy of individual rights, and his vision of Man and God working together for a more just world. With missionary fervor George invited his audience to "see the cat."[1] Finally, I include one letter from a reader of *The Standard* to illustrate his emotional power over people.

"Ode to Liberty"[2]

We honor liberty in name and in form. We set up her statues and sound her praises. But we have not fully trusted her. And with our growth so grow her demands. She will have no half service!—Liberty! it is a word to conjure with, not to vex the ear in empty boastings. For Liberty means Justice, and Justice is the natural law—the law of health and symmetry and strength, of fraternity and cooperation.

They who look upon Liberty as having accomplished her mission when she has abolished hereditary privileges and given men the ballot, who think of her as having no further relations to the everyday affairs of life, have not seen her real grandeur—to them the poets who have sung of her must seem rhapsodists, and her martyrs fools! As the sun is the lord of life, as well as of light; as his beams not merely pierce the clouds, but support all growth, supply all motion, and call forth from what would otherwise be a cold and inert mass all the infinite diversities of being and beauty, so is Liberty to mankind. It is not for an abstraction that men have toiled and died; that in every age the witnesses of Liberty have stood forth, and the martyrs of Liberty have suffered.

We speak of Liberty as one thing, and of virtue, wealth, knowledge, invention, national strength and national independence as other things. But, of all these, Liberty is the source, the mother, the necessary condition. She is to virtue what light is to color; to wealth what sunshine is to grain; to knowledge what eyes are to sight. She is the genius of invention, the brawn of national strength, the spirit of national independence. Where Liberty rises, there virtue grows, wealth increases, knowledge expands, invention multiplies human powers, and in strength and spirit the freer nation rises among her neighbors as Saul amid his brethren—taller and fairer. Where Liberty sinks, there virtue fades, wealth diminishes, knowledge is forgotten, invention ceases, and empires once mighty in arms and arts become a helpless prey to freer barbarians!

Only in broken gleams and partial light has the sun of Liberty yet beamed among men, but all progress hath she called forth.

Liberty came to a race of slaves crouching under Egyptian whips, and let them forth from the House of Bondage. She hardened them in the desert and made of them a race of conquerors. The free spirit of the Mosaic Law took their thinkers up to heights where they beheld the unity of God, and inspired their poets with strains that yet phrase the highest exaltations of thought. Liberty dawned on the Phoenician coast, and ships passed the Pillars of Hercules to plow the unknown sea. She shed a partial light on Greece, and marble grew to shapes of ideal beauty, words became the instruments of subtlest thought, and against the scanty militia of free cities the countless hosts of the Great King broke like surges against a rock.[3] She cast her beams on the four-acre farms of Italian husbandmen, and born of her strength a power came forth that conquered the world. They glinted from shields of German warriors, and Augustus wept his legions.[4] Out of the night that followed her eclipse, her slanting rays fell again on free cities, and a lost learning revived, modern civilization began, a new world was unveiled; and as Liberty grew, so grew art, wealth, power, knowledge, and refinement. In the history of every nation we may read the same truth. It was the strength born of Magna Charta that won Crecy and Agincourt.[5] It was the revival of Liberty from the despotism of the Tudors that glorified the Elizabethan Age. It was the spirit that brought a crowned tyrant to the block[6] that planted here the seed of a mighty tree. It was the energy of ancient freedom that, the moment it had gained unity, made Spain the mightiest power of the world, only to fall to the lowest depth of weakness when tyranny succeeded liberty. See, in France, all intellectual vigor dying under the tyranny of the Seventeenth Century to revive in splendor as Liberty awoke in the Eighteenth, and on the enfranchisement of French peasants in the Great Revolution, basing the wonderful strength that has in our time defied defeat.

Shall we not trust her?

In our time, as in times before, creep on the insidious forces that, producing inequality, destroy Liberty. On the horizon the clouds begin to lower. Liberty calls to us again. We must follow her further; we must trust her fully. Either we must wholly accept her or she will not stay. It is not enough that men should vote; it is not enough that they should be theoretically equal before the law. They must have liberty to avail themselves of the opportunities and means of life; they must stand on equal terms with reference to the bounty of nature. Either this, or Liberty withdraws her light! Either this, or darkness comes on, and the very forces that progress has evolved turn to powers that work destruction. This is the universal law. This is the lesson of the centuries. Unless its foundations be laid in justice the social structure cannot stand.

Our primary social adjustment is a denial of justice. In allowing one man to own the land on which and from which other men must live, we have made them his bondsmen in a degree which increases as material progress goes on. This is the subtle alchemy that in ways they do not realize is extracting from the masses in every civilized country the fruits of their weary toil; that is instituting a harder and more hopeless slavery in place of that which has been destroyed; that is bringing political despotism out of political freedom, and must soon transmute democratic institutions into anarchy.

It is this that turns the blessings of material progress into a curse. It is this that crowds human beings into noisome cellars and squalid tenement houses; that fills prisons and brothels; that goads men with want and consumes them with greed; that robs women of the grace and beauty of perfect womanhood; that takes from little children the joy and innocence of life's morning.

Civilization so based cannot continue. The eternal laws of the universe forbid it. Ruins of dead empires testify, and the witness that is in every soul answers, that it cannot be. It is something grander than Benevolence, something more august than Charity—it is Justice herself that demands of us to right this wrong. Justice that will not be denied; that cannot be put off—Justice that with the scales carries the sword. Shall we ward the stroke with liturgies and prayers? Shall we avert the decrees of immutable law by raising churches when hungry infants moan and weary mothers weep?

Though it may take the language of prayer, it is blasphemy that attributes to the inscrutable decrees of Providence the suffering and brutishness that come of poverty; that turns with folded hands to the All-Father and lays on Him the responsibility for the want and crime of our great cities. We degrade the Everlasting. We slander the Just One. A merciful man would have better ordered the world; a just man would crush with his foot such an ulcerous ant hill! It is not the Almighty, but we who are responsible for the vice and misery that fester amid our civilization. The Creator showers upon us his gifts—more than enough for all. But like swine scrambling for food, we tread them in the mire—tread them in the mire, while we tear and rend each other!

In the very centers of our civilization today are want and suffering enough to make sick at heart whoever does not close his eyes and steel his nerves. Dare we turn to the Creator and ask Him to relieve it? Supposing the prayer was heard, and at the behest with which the universe sprang into being there should glow in the sun a greater power; new virtue fills the air; fresh vigor the soil; that for every blade of grass that now grows two should spring up, and the seed that now increases fifty-fold should increase a hundredfold! Would poverty be abated or want relieved? Manifestly no! Whatever benefit would accrue would be but temporary. The new powers streaming through the material universe could be utilized only through land. And land, being private property, the classes that now monopolize the bounty of the Creator would monopolize all the new bounty. Landowners would alone be benefited. Rents would increase, but wages would still tend to the starvation point!

This is not merely a deduction of political economy; it is a fact of experience. We know it because we have seen it. Within our own times, under our very eyes, that Power which is above all, and in all, and through all; that Power of which the whole universe is but the manifestation; that Power which maketh all things, and without which is not anything made that is made, has increased the bounty which men may enjoy, as truly as though the fertility of nature had been increased. Into the mind of one came the thought that harnessed steam for the service of mankind.[7] To the inner ear of another was whispered the secret that compels the lightning to bear a message around the globe.[8] In every direction have the laws of matter been revealed; in every department of industry have arisen arms of iron and fingers of steel, whose effect upon the production of wealth has been precisely the same as an increase in the fertility of nature. What has been the result? Simply that landowners get all the gain. The wonderful discoveries and inventions of our century have neither increased wages nor lightened toil. The effect has simply been to make the few richer; the many more helpless!

Can it be that the gifts of the Creator may be thus misappropriated with impunity? Is it a light thing that labor should be robbed of its earnings while greed rolls in wealth—that the many should want while the few are surfeited? Turn to history, and on every page may be read the lesson that such wrong never goes unpunished; that the Nemesis that follows injustice never falters nor sleeps! Look around today. Can this state of things continue? May we even say, "After us the deluge!" Nay; the pillars of the state are trembling even now, and the very foundations of society begin to quiver with pent-up forces that glow underneath. The struggle that must either revivify, or convulse in ruin, is near at hand, if it be not already begun.

The fiat has gone forth! With steam and electricity, and the new powers born of progress, forces have entered the world that will either compel us to a higher plane or overwhelm us, as nation after nation, as civilization after civilization, have been overwhelmed before. It is the delusion which precedes destruction that sees in the popular unrest with which the civilized world is feverishly pulsing only the passing effect of ephemeral causes. Between democratic ideas and the aristocratic adjustments of society there is an irreconcilable conflict. Here in the United States, as there in Europe, it may be seen arising. We cannot go on permitting men to vote and forcing them to tramp. We cannot go on educating boys and girls in our public schools and then refusing them the right to earn an honest living. We cannot go on prating of the inalienable rights of man and then denying the inalienable right to the bounty of the Creator. Even now, in old bottles the new wine begins to ferment, and elemental forces gather for the strife!

But if, while there is yet time, we turn to Justice and obey her, if we trust Liberty and follow her, the dangers that now threaten must disappear, the forces that now menace will turn to agencies of elevation. Think of the powers now wasted; of the infertile fields of knowledge yet to be explored; of the possibilities of which the wondrous inventions of this century give us but a hint. With want destroyed; with greed changed to noble passions; with the fraternity that is born of equality taking the place of the jealousy and fear that now array men against each other; with mental power loosened by conditions that give to the humblest comfort and leisure; and who shall measure the heights to which our civilization may soar? Words fail the thought! It is the Golden Age of which poets have sung and high-raised seers have told in metaphor! It is the glorious vision which has always haunted man with gleams of fitful splendor. It is what he saw whose eyes at Patmos were closed in a trance.[9] It is the culmination of Christianity—the City of God on earth, with its walls of jasper and its gates of pearl! It is the reign of the Prince of Peace!

"Moses"[10]

There is in modern thought a tendency to look upon the prominent characters of history as resultants rather than as initiatory forces. As in an earlier stage the irresistible disposition is to personification, so now it is to reverse this process, and to resolve into myths mighty figures long enshrined by tradition.

Yet, if we try to trace to their sources movements whose perpetuated impulses eddy and play in the currents of our times, we at last reach the individual. It is true that "institutions make men," but it is also true that "in the beginnings men make institutions."

In a well-known passage Macaulay[11] has described the impression made upon the imagination by the antiquity of that church, which, surviving dynasties and empires, carries the mind back to a time when the smoke of sacrifice rose from the Pantheon and camelopard[12] and tiger bounded in the Flavian amphitheater. But there still exist among us observances—transmitted in unbroken succession from father to son—that go back to a yet more remote past. Each recurring year brings a day on which, in every land, there are men who, gathering about them their families, and attired as if for a journey, eat with solemnity a hurried meal. Before the walls of Rome were traced, before Homer sung, this feast was kept, and the event to which it points was even then centuries old.[13]

That event signals the entrance upon the historic stage of a people on many accounts remarkable—a people who, though they never founded a great empire nor built a great metropolis, have exercised upon a large portion of mankind an influence, widespread, potent, and continuous; a people who have for nearly two thousand years been without country or organized nationality, yet have preserved their identity and faith through all vicissitudes of time and fortune—who have been overthrown, crushed, scattered; who have been ground, as it were, to very dust, and flung to the four winds of heaven; yet who, though thrones have fallen, and empires have perished, and creeds have changed, and living tongues have become dead, still exist with a vitality seemingly unimpaired—a people who unite the strangest contradictions; whose annals now blaze with glory, now sound the depths of shame and woe.

The advent of such a people marks an epoch in the history of the world. But it is not of that advent so much as of the central and colossal figure around which its traditions cluster that I propose to speak.

Three great religions place the leader of the Exodus upon the highest plane they allot to man. To Christendom and to Islam, as well as to Judaism, Moses is the mouthpiece and lawgiver of the Most High; the medium, clothed with supernatural powers, through which the Divine Will has spoken. Yet this very exaltation, by raising him above comparison, may prevent the real grandeur of the man from being seen. It is amid his brethren that Saul stands taller and fairer.

On the other hand, the latest school of Biblical criticism asserts that the books and legislation attributed to Moses are really the product of an age subsequent to that of the prophets. Yet to this Moses, looming vague and dim, of whom they can tell us almost nothing, they, too, attribute the beginning of that growth which flowered after centuries in the humanities of Jewish law, and in the sublime conception of one God, universal and eternal, the Almighty Father.

But whether wont to look on Moses in this way or in that, it may be sometimes worth our while to take the point of view in which all shades of belief or disbelief may find common ground, and accepting the main features of Hebrew record and tradition, consider them in the light of history as we know it, and of human nature as it shows itself today. Here is a case in which sacred history may be treated as we would treat profane history without any shock to religious feeling. Nor can the keenest criticism resolve Moses into a myth. The fact of the Exodus presupposes such a leader.

To lead into freedom a people long crushed by tyranny; to discipline and order such a mighty host; to harden them into fighting men, before whom warlike tribes quailed and walled cities went down; to repress discontent and jealousy and mutiny; to combat reactions and reversions; to turn the quick, fierce flame of enthusiasm to the service of a steady purpose, required some towering character—a character blending in highest expression the qualities of politician, patriot, philosopher, and statesman.

Such a character in rough but strong outline the tradition shows us—the union of the wisdom of the Egyptians with the unselfish devotion of the meekest of men. From first to last, in every glimpse we get, this character is consistent with itself, and with the mighty work which is its monument. It is the character of a great mind, hemmed in by conditions and limitations, and working with such forces and materials as were at hand—accomplishing, yet failing. Behind grand deed, a grander thought. Behind high performance the still nobler ideal.

Egypt was the mold of the Hebrew nation—the matrix, so to speak, in which a single family, or, at most, a small tribe grew to a people as numerous as the American people at the time of the Declaration of Independence. For four centuries, according to the Hebrew tradition—that is to say, for a period longer than America has been known to Europe—this growing people, coming from a patriarchal family, from a roving, pastoral life, had been placed under the dominance of a highly-developed and ancient civilization—a civilization whose fixity is symbolized by monuments that rival in endurance the everlasting hills—a civilization so ancient that the Pyramids, as we now know, were hoary with centuries ere Abraham looked upon them.

No matter how clearly the descendants of the kinsmen who came into Egypt at the invitation of the boy-slave become prime minister, maintained the distinction of race, and the traditions of a freer life, they must have been powerfully affected by such a civilization; and just as the Hebrews of today are Polish in Poland, German in Germany, and American in the United States, so, but far more clearly and strongly, the Hebrews of the Exodus must have been essentially Egyptian.

It is not remarkable, therefore, that the ancient Hebrew institutions show in so many points the influence of Egyptian ideas and customs. What *is* remarkable is the dissimilarity. To the unreflecting nothing may seem more natural than that a people, in turning their backs upon a land where they had been long oppressed, should discard its ideas and institutions. But the student of history, the observer of politics, knows that nothing is more unnatural. Habits of thought are even more tyrannous than habits of the body. They make for the masses of men a mental atmosphere out of which they can no more rise than out of the physical atmosphere. A people long used to despotism may rebel against a tyrant; they may break his statutes and repeal his laws, cover with odium that which he loved, and honor that which he hated; but they will hasten to set up another tyrant in his place. A people used to superstition may embrace a purer faith, but it will be only to degrade it to their old ideas. A people used to persecution may flee from it, but only to persecute in their turn when they get power.

For "institutions make men." And when amid a people used to institutions of one kind, we see suddenly arise institutions of an opposite kind, we know that behind them must be that active, that initiative force—the men who in the beginnings make institutions.

This is what occurs in the Exodus. The striking differences between Egyptian and Hebrew polity are not of form but of essence. The tendency of the one is to subordination and oppression; of the other, to individual freedom. Strangest of recorded births! from out the strongest and most splendid despotism of antiquity comes the freest republic. From between the paws of the rock-hewn Sphinx rise the genius of human liberty, and the trumpets of the Exodus throb with the defiant proclamation of the rights of man.

Consider what Egypt was. The very grandeur of her monuments, that after the lapse, not of centuries but of millennia, seem to say to us, as the Egyptian priests said to the boastful Greeks, "Ye are children!" testify to the enslavement of the people—are the enduring witnesses of a social organization that rested on the masses an immovable weight. That narrow Nile valley, the cradle of the arts and sciences, the scene, perhaps, of the greatest triumphs of the human mind, is also the scene of its most abject enslavement. In the long centuries of its splendor, its lord, secure in the possession of irresistible temporal power, and securer still in the awful sanctions of a mystical religion, was as a god on earth, to cover whose poor carcass with a tomb befitting his state hundreds of thousands toiled away their lives. For the classes who came next to him were all the sensuous delights of a most luxurious civilization, and high intellectual pleasures which the mysteries of the temple hid from vulgar profanation. But for the millions who constituted the base of the social pyramid there was but the lash to stimulate their toil, and the worship of beasts to satisfy the yearnings of the soul. From time immemorial to the present day the lot of the Egyptian peasant has been to work and to starve that those above him might live daintily. He has never rebelled. The spirit for that was long ago crushed out of him by institutions which make him what he is. He knows but to suffer and to die.

Imagine what opportune circumstances we may, yet to organize and carry on a movement resulting in the release of a great people from such a soul-subduing tyranny, backed by an army of half a million highly-trained soldiers, required a leadership of most commanding and consummate genius. But this task, surpassingly great though it was, is not the measure of the greatness of the leader of the Exodus. It is not in the deliverance from Egypt, it is in the constructive statesmanship that laid the foundations of the Hebrew commonwealth that the superlative grandeur of that leadership looms up. As we cannot imagine the Exodus without the great leader, neither can we account for the Hebrew polity without the great statesman. Not merely intellectually great, but morally great—a statesman aglow with the unselfish patriotism that refuses to grasp a scepter or found a dynasty.

The lessons of modern history, the manifestations of human nature that we behold around us, would teach us to see in the essential divergence of the Hebrew polity from that of Egypt the impress of a master mind, even if Hebrew tradition had not testified both to the influence of such a mind, and to the constant disposition of accustomed ideas to reassert themselves in the minds of the people. Over and over again the murmurings break out; no sooner is the back of Moses turned than the cry, "These be thy gods, O Israel!" announces the setting up of the Egyptian calf; while the strength of the monarchical principle shows itself in the inauguration of a king as quickly as the far-reaching influence of the great leader is somewhat spent.

It matters not when or by whom were compiled the books popularly attributed to Moses; it matters not how much of the code there given may be the survivals of more ancient usage or the amplifications of a later age; its great features bear the stamp of a mind far in advance of people and time, of a mind that beneath effects sought for causes, of a mind that drifted not with the tide of events but aimed at a definite purpose.

The outlines that the record gives us of the character of Moses—the brief relations that wherever the Hebrew Scriptures are read have hung the chambers of the imagination with vivid pictures—are in every way consistent with this idea. What we know of the life illustrates what we know of the work. What we know of the work illumines the life.

It was not an empire such as had reached full development in Egypt, or existed in rudimentary patriarchal form in the tribes around, that Moses aimed to found. Nor was it a republic where the freedom of the citizen rested on the servitude of the helot, and the individual was sacrificed to the state.[14] It was a commonwealth based upon the individual—a commonwealth whose ideal it was that every man should sit under his own vine and fig tree, with none to vex him or make him afraid, a commonwealth in which none should be condemned to ceaseless toil; in which, for even the bond slave, there should be hope; in which, for even the beast of burden, there should be rest. A commonwealth in which, in the absence of deep poverty, the manly virtues that spring from personal independence should harden into a national character—a commonwealth in which the family affections might knit their tendrils around each member, binding with links stronger than steel the various parts into the living whole.

It is not the protection of property, but the protection of humanity, that is the aim of the Mosaic Code. Its sanctions are not directed to securing the strong in heaping up wealth so much as to preventing the weak from being crowded to the wall. At every point it interposes its barriers to the selfish greed that, if left unchecked, will surely differentiate men into landlord and serf, capitalist and workman, millionaire and tramp, ruler and ruled. Its Sabbath day and Sabbath year secure, even to the lowliest, rest and leisure. With the blast of the jubilee trumpets the slave goes free, the debt that cannot be paid is cancelled, and a redivision of the land secures again to the poorest his fair share in the bounty of the common Creator.[15] The reaper must leave something for the gleaner; even the ox cannot be muzzled as he treadeth out the corn. Everywhere, in everything, the dominant idea is that of our homely phrase—"Live and let live!"

And the religion with which this civil policy is so closely intertwined exhibits kindred features—from the idea of the brotherhood of man springs the idea of the fatherhood of God. Though the forms may resemble those of Egypt, the spirit is that which Egypt had lost. Though a hereditary priesthood is retained, the law in its fullness is announced to all the people. Though the Egyptian rite of circumcision is preserved, and Egyptian symbols reappear in all the externals of worship, the tendency to take the type for the reality is sternly repressed. It is only when we think of the bulls and the hawks, of the deified cats and sacred ichneumons of Egypt,[16] that we realize the full meaning of the command—"Thou shalt not make to thyself any graven image!"

And if we seek beneath form and symbol and command, the thought of which they are but the expression, we find that the great distinctive feature of the Hebrew religion, that which separates it by such a wide gulf from the religions amid which it grew up, is its utilitarianism, its recognition of divine law in human life. It asserts, not a God whose domain is confined to the far-off beginning or the vague future, who is over and above and beyond men, but a God who in his inexorable laws is here and now; a God of the living as well as of the dead; a God of the market place as well as of the temple; a God whose judgments wait not another world for execution, but whose immutable decrees will, in this life, give happiness to the people that heed them and bring misery upon the people that forget them. Amid the forms of splendid degradation in which a once noble religion had in Egypt sunk to petrifaction, amid a social order in which the divine justice seemed to sleep, I AM was the truth that dawned upon Moses. And in his desert contemplation of nature's flux and reflux, the death that bounds her life, the life she brings from death, always consuming yet never consumed— I AM was the message that fell upon his inner ear.

The absence in the Mosaic Books of any reference to a future life is only intelligible by the prominence into which this truth is brought. Nothing could have been more familiar to the Hebrews of the Exodus than the doctrine of immortality. The continued existence of the soul, the judgment after death, the rewards and punishments of the future state, were the constant subjects of Egyptian thought and art. But a truth may be hidden or thrown into the background by the intensity with which another truth is grasped. And the doctrine of immortality, springing as it does from the very depths of human nature, ministering to aspirations which become stronger and stronger as intellectual life rises to higher planes and the life of the affections becomes more intense, may yet become so incrusted with degrading superstitions, may be turned by craft and selfishness into such a potent instrument for enslavement, and so used to justify crimes at which every natural instinct revolts, that to the earnest spirit of the social reformer it may seem like an agency of oppression to enchain the intellect and prevent true progress; a lying device with which the cunning fetter the credulous.

The belief in the immortality of the soul must have existed in strong forms among the masses of the Hebrew people. But the truth that Moses brought so prominently forward, the truth his gaze was concentrated upon, is a truth that has often been thrust aside by the doctrine of immortality, and that may perhaps, at times, react on it in the same way. This is the truth that the actions of men bear fruit in this world, that though on the petty scale of individual life wickedness may seem to go unpunished and wrong to be rewarded, there is yet a Nemesis that with tireless feet and pitiless arm follows every national crime, and smites the children for the father's transgression; the truth that each individual must act upon and be acted upon by the society of which he is a part, that all must in some degree suffer for the sin of each, and the life of each be dominated by the conditions imposed by all.

It is the intense appreciation of this truth that gives the Mosaic institutions so practical and utilitarian a character. Their genius, if I may so speak, leaves the abstract speculations where thought so easily loses and wastes itself, or finds expression only in symbols that become finally but the basis of superstition, in order that it may concentrate attention upon the laws which determine the happiness or misery of men upon this earth. Its lessons have never tended to the essential selfishness of asceticism, which is so prominent a feature in Brahmanism and Buddhism, and from which Christianity and Islamism have not been exempt. Its injunction has never been, "Leave the world to itself that you may save your own soul," but rather, "Do your duty in the world that you may be happier and the world be better." It has disdained no sanitary regulation that might secure the health of the body. Its promise has been of peace and plenty and length of days, of stalwart sons and comely daughters.

It may be that the feeling of Moses in regard to a future life was that expressed in the language of the Stoic, "It is the business of Jupiter, not mine";[17] or it may be that it partook of the same revulsion that shows itself in modern times, when a spirit essentially religious has been turned against the forms and expressions of religion, because these forms and expressions have been made the props and bulwarks of tyranny, and even the name and teachings of the Carpenter's Son perverted into supports of social injustice— used to guard the pomp of Caesar and justify the greed of Dives.[18]

Yet, however such feelings influenced Moses, I cannot think that such a soul as his, living such a life as his—feeling the exaltation of great thoughts, feeling the burden of great cares, feeling the bitterness of great disappointments—did not stretch forward to the hope beyond; did not rest and strengthen and ground itself in the confident belief that the death of the body is but the emancipation of the mind; did not feel the assurance that there is a power in the universe upon which it might confidently rely, through wreck of matter and crash of worlds. Yet the great concern of Moses was with the duty that lay plainly before him; the effort to lay the foundations of a social state in which deep poverty and degrading want should be unknown—where men released from the meaner struggles that waste human energy should have opportunity for intellectual and moral development.

Here stands out the greatness of the man. What was the wisdom and stretch of the forethought that in the desert sought to guard in advance against the dangers of a settled state, let the present speak.

In the full blaze of the nineteenth century, when every child in our schools may know as common truths things of which the Egyptian sages never dreamed; when the earth has been mapped and the stars have been weighed; when steam and electricity have been pressed into our service, and science is wresting from nature secret after secret—it is but natural to look back upon the wisdom of three thousand years ago as the man looks back upon the learning of the child.

And yet, for all this wonderful increase of knowledge, for all this enormous gain of productive power, where is the country in the civilized world in which today there is not want and suffering—where the masses are not condemned to toil that gives no leisure, and all classes are not pursued by a greed of gain that makes life an ignoble struggle to get and to keep? Three thousand years of advance, and still the moan goes up, "They have made our lives bitter with hard bondage, in mortar and in brick, and in all manner of service!" Three thousand years of advance! and the piteous voices of little children are in the moan.

We progress and we progress; we girdle continents with iron roads and knit cities together with the mesh of telegraph wires; each day brings some new invention; each year marks a fresh advance—the power of production increased, and the avenues of exchange cleared and broadened. Yet the complaint of "hard times" is louder and louder; everywhere are men harassed by care, and haunted by the fear of want. With swift, steady strides and prodigious leaps, the power of human hands to satisfy human wants advances and advances, is multiplied and multiplied. Yet the struggle for mere existence is more and more intense, and human labor is becoming the cheapest of commodities. Beside glutted warehouses human beings grow faint with hunger and shiver with cold; under the shadow of churches festers the vice that is born of want.

Trace to its root the cause that is thus producing want in the midst of plenty, ignorance in the midst of intelligence, aristocracy in democracy, weakness in strength—that is giving to our civilization a one-sided and unstable development, and you will find it something which this Hebrew statesman three thousand years ago perceived and guarded against. Moses saw that the real cause of the enslavement of the masses of Egypt was, what has everywhere produced enslavement, the possession by a class of the land upon which and from which the whole people must live. He saw that to permit in land the same unqualified private ownership that by natural right attaches to the things produced by labor, would be inevitably to separate the people into the very rich and the very poor, inevitably to enslave labor—to make the few the masters of the many, no matter what the political forms; to bring vice and degradation, no matter what the religion.

And with the foresight of the philosophic statesman who legislates not for the need of a day, but for all the future, he sought, in ways suited to his times and conditions, to guard against this error. Everywhere in the Mosaic institutions is the land treated as the gift of the Creator to His common creatures, which no one had the right to monopolize. Everywhere it is, not your estate, or your property, not the land which you bought, or the land which you conquered, but "the land which the Lord thy God giveth thee"—"the land which the Lord lendeth thee." And by practical legislation, by regulations to which he gave the highest sanctions, he tried to guard against the wrong that converted ancient civilizations into despotisms—the wrong that in after centuries ate out the heart of Rome, that produced the imbruting serfdom of Poland and the gaunt misery of Ireland, the wrong that is today crowding families into single rooms in this very city and filling our new States on the other side of the Atlantic with tramps. He not only provided for the fair division of the land among the people, and for making it fallow and common every seventh year, but by the institution of the jubilee he provided for a redistribution of the land every fifty years, and made monopoly impossible.

I do not say that these institutions were, for their ultimate purpose, the very best that might even then have been devised, for Moses had to work, as all great constructive statesmen have to work, with the tools that came to his hand, and upon materials as he found them. Still less do I mean to say that forms suitable for that time and people are suitable for every time and people. I ask, not veneration of the form, but recognition of the spirit.

Yet how common it is to venerate the form and to deny the spirit. There are many who believe that the Mosaic institutions were literally dictated by the Almighty, yet who would denounce as irreligious and "communistic" any application of their spirit to the present day. And yet today how much we owe to these institutions! This very day the only thing that stands between our working classes and ceaseless toil is one of these Mosaic institutions. Nothing in political economy is better settled than that under conditions which now prevail the working classes would get no more for seven days' labor than they now get for six, and would find it as difficult to reduce their working hours as now.

Let the mistakes of those who think that man was made for the Sabbath, rather than the Sabbath for man, be what they may; that there is one day in the week that the working man may call his own, one day in the week on which hammer is silent and loom stands idle, is due, through Christianity, to Judaism—to the code promulgated in the Sinaitic wilderness. And who that considers the waste of productive forces can doubt that modern society would be not merely happier but richer, had we received as well as the Sabbath day the grand idea of the Sabbath year, or adapting its spirit to our changed conditions, secured in another way an equivalent reduction of working hours?

It is in these characteristics of the Mosaic institutions that, as in the fragments of a Colossus, we may read the greatness of the mind whose impress they bear—of a mind in advance of its surroundings, in advance of its age; of one of those star souls that dwindle not with distance, but, glowing with the radiance of essential truth, hold their light while institutions and languages and creeds change and pass.

That the thought was greater than the permanent expression it found, who can doubt? Yet from that day to this that expression has been in the world a living power.

From the free spirit of the Mosaic Law sprang that intensity of family life that amid all dispersions and persecutions has preserved the individuality of the Hebrew race; that love of independence that under the most adverse circumstances has characterized the Jew; that burning patriotism that flamed up in the Maccabees and bared the breasts of Jewish peasants to the serried steel of Grecian phalanx[19] and the resistless onset of Roman legion; that stubborn courage that in exile and in torture held the Jew to his faith. It kindled that fire that has made the strains of Hebrew seers and poets phrase for us the highest exaltations of thought; that intellectual vigor that has over and over again made the dry staff bud and blossom. And passing outward from one narrow race it has exerted its power wherever the influence of the Hebrew Scriptures has been felt. It has toppled thrones and cast down hierarchies. It strengthened the Scottish Covenanter[20] in the hour of trial, and the Puritan amid the snows of a strange land. It charged with the Ironsides at Naseby;[21] it stood behind the low redoubt on Bunker Hill.

But it is in example as in need that such lives are helpful. It is thus that they dignify human nature and glorify human effort, and bring to those who struggle hope and trust. The life of Moses, like the institutions of Moses, is a protest against that blasphemous doctrine, current now as it was three thousand years ago—that blasphemous doctrine preached oft-times even from Christian pulpits—that the want and suffering of the masses of mankind flow from a mysterious dispensation of providence, which we may lament, but can neither quarrel with nor alter. Let him who hugs that doctrine to himself, him to whom it seems that the squalor and brutishness with which the very centers of our civilization abound are not his affair, turn to the example of that life. For to him who will look, yet burns the bush; and to him who will hear, again comes the voice, "The people suffer: who will lead them forth?"

Adopted into the immediate family of the supreme monarch and earthly god; standing almost at the apex of the social pyramid which had for its base those toiling millions; priest and prince in a land where prince and priest might revel in all delights—everything that life could offer to gratify the senses or engage the intellect was open to him.

What to him the wail of them who beneath the fierce sun toiled under the whips of relentless masters? Heard from granite colonnade or beneath cool linen awning, it was mellowed by distance to monotonous music. Why should he question the Sphinx of Fate,[22] or quarrel with destinies the high gods had decreed? So had it always been, for ages and ages; so must it ever be. The beetle rends the insect, and the hawk preys on the beetle; order on order, life rises from death and carnage, and higher pleasures from lower agonies. Shall the man be better than nature? Soothing and restful flows the Nile, though underneath its placid surface finny tribes wage cruel war, and the stronger eat the weaker. Shall the gazer who would read the secrets of the stars turn because under his feet a worm may writhe?

Theirs to make bricks without straw; his a high place in the glorious procession that with gorgeous banners and glittering emblems, with clash of music and solemn chant, winds its shining way to dedicate the immortal edifice their toil has reared. Theirs the leek and the garlic; his to sit at the sumptuous feast. Why should he dwell on the irksomeness of bondage, he for whom the chariots waited, who might at will bestride the swift coursers of the Delta, or be borne on the bosom of the river with oars that beat time to songs? Did he long for the excitement of action?—there was the desert hunt, with steeds fleeter than the antelope and lions trained like dogs. Did he crave rest and ease?—there was for him the soft swell of languorous music and the wreathed movements of dancing girls. Did he feel the stir of intellectual life?—in the arcana of the temples he was free to the lore of ages; an initiate in the select society where were discussed the most engrossing problems; a sharer in that intellectual pride that centuries after compared Greek philosophy to the babblings of children.

It was no sudden ebullition of passion that caused Moses to turn his back on all this, and to bring the strength and knowledge acquired in a dominant caste to the lifelong service of the oppressed. The forgetfulness of self manifested in the smiting of the Egyptian shines through the whole life. In institutions that molded the character of a people, in institutions that to this day make easier the lot of toiling millions, we may read the stately purpose.

Through all that tradition [we have been] given the same grand passion—the unselfish desire to make humanity better, happier, and nobler. And the death is worthy of the life. Subordinating to the good of his people the natural disposition to found a dynasty, which in his case would have been so easy, he discards the claims of blood and calls to his place of leader the fittest man. Coming from a land where the rites of sepulcher were regarded as all-important, and the preservation of the body after death was the passion of life; among a people who were even then carrying the remains of their great ancestor, Joseph, to rest with his fathers, he yet conquered the last natural yearning and withdrew from the sight and sympathy of men to die alone and unattended, lest the idolatrous feeling, always ready to break forth, should in death accord him the superstitious reverence he had refused in life.

"No man knoweth of his sepulcher unto this day." But while the despoiled tombs of the Pharaohs mock the vanity that reared them, the name of the Hebrew who, revolting from their tyranny, strove for the elevation of his fellow men, is yet a beacon light to the world.

Leader and servant of men! Lawgiver and benefactor! Toiler toward the promised land seen only by the eye of faith! Type of the high souls who in every age have given to earth its heroes and its martyrs, whose deeds are the precious possession of the race, whose memories are its sacred heritage! With whom among the founders of empire shall we compare him?

To dispute about the inspiration of such a man were to dispute about words. From the depths of the unseen such characters must draw their strength; from fountains that flow only from the pure in heart must come their wisdom. Of something more real than matter; of something higher than the stars; of a light that will endure when suns are dead and dark; of a purpose of which the physical universe is but a passing phase, such lives tell.

"Salutatory"[23]

I begin the publication of this paper in response to many urgent requests, and because I believe that there is a field for a journal that shall serve as a focus for news and opinions relating to the great movement, now beginning, for the emancipation of labor by the restoration of natural rights.

The generation that abolished chattel slavery is passing away, and the political distinctions that grew out of that contest are becoming meaningless. The work now before us is the abolition of industrial slavery.

What God created for the use of all should be utilized for the benefit of all; what is produced by the individual belongs rightfully to the individual. The neglect of these simple principles has brought upon us the curse of widespread poverty and all the evils that flow from it. Their recognition will abolish poverty, will secure to the humblest independence and leisure, and will lay a broad and strong foundation on which all other reforms may be based. To secure the full recognition of these principles is the most important task to which any man can address himself today. It is in the hope of aiding in this work that I establish this paper.

I believe that the Declaration of Independence is not a mere string of glittering generalities. I believe that all men are really created equal, and that the securing of those equal natural rights is the true purpose and test of government. And against whatever law, custom or device that restrains men in the exercise of their natural rights to life, liberty, and the pursuit of happiness I shall raise my voice.

Confident in the strength of truth, I shall give no quarter to abuses and ask none from their champions. The political corruption that shames our democracy, the false theories that assume that a nation's prosperity lies in shutting itself in from free intercourse with other nations, the stupid fiscal system that piles up hundreds of millions of dollars in our treasury vaults while we are paying interest on an enormous debt; the aping of foreign nations that insists upon standing armies and navies modeled on aristocratic plans; the judicial system that offers a mockery of justice on one side and condones evildoing on the other; the false philanthropy that gives a dole while it denies a right; the lip worship of a just God and the heart worship of the Golden Calf—all these are to my mind parts of one connected whole whose foundations are in the denial of the equal rights of man to the use of Nature's bounty; and in attacking and exposing them as opportunity may offer, I shall render easier the exposure and abolition of the great wrong from which they primarily spring.

I shall endeavor to conduct this paper by the same rules on which a just man would regulate his conduct. I shall not wittingly give currency to an untruth, and, if I inadvertently do so, will endeavor to repair the wrong.

I shall endeavor to be fair to opponents and true to friends. I do not propose to make everything that shall appear here square to my own theories, but will be willing to give place to views which may differ from my own when they are so stated as to be worthy of consideration. I hope to make this paper the worthy exponent and advocate of the great party yet unnamed that is now beginning to form,[24] but at the same time to make its contents so varied and interesting as to insure for it a general circulation.

I ask for *The Standard* the active aid of all who wish to see such a paper firmly established. . . .

"Anti-Poverty: Religion Marching Hand in Hand with Politics"[25]

. . . The difference between the new party that is now coming to the front, the party that is as Mr. Glackin has said, destined to control this great Republic and to write its policy on our laws and institutions, differs from the other parties that exist today in this, that it has a belief, that it has a faith. We know what we want ("Hear, hear!"), and we know how to get it. (Deafening applause and a voice, "We will get it!")

Policy! We have nothing whatever to do with policy. Our policy is the right. (Applause) The Pole Star of justice is the star by which we steer, and we are moving on our path with an ardor, a strength and a determination that are born of a religious conviction. (Applause) Truly has it been said that this is a new crusade. Of all great wars and uprisings of men to murder one another of which history tells us, those great uprisings of Europe in which the flower of her youth were hurled on Asia were, in their inception at least, the noblest.

It was with the cry, "God wills it! God wills it," that the flower of the youth and chivalry of Europe were hurled on Asia to win back the Holy Land from the Turk. False views of religion, superstition deep and dark, lay at the base of that great movement; but there also lay at its base something of that spirit that links him to God—the enthusiasm for what was to the man who felt its power a high and a noble cause.

And now again, in this nineteenth century, on this new continent, and in our ranks, goes up the cry, "God wills it! God wills it!" (Great applause) And again that enthusiasm that would take men and women to death can if need be will fill hearts and fire tongues. Greater and nobler though is our crusade, its aim is not to rescue from the infidel the tomb wherein the dead Christ has lain, but to rescue from vice and want and misery the living images of Christ (applause); to take out of the squalor and degradation those little children of whom the Master said, "Let them come unto me," of whom the

Master said, "It were better for a man that he should have a millstone tied around his neck and be thrown into the sea than that he should offend one of those little ones." (Great applause)

Aye, we know it! The fullness of time has come. "God wills it! God wills it," and because He wills it we go on to victory. (Applause) What matters it whether it be today or tomorrow or next week, what matters it who falls from our ranks, what matters it who turns back, this movement must and will go on. (Deafening applause) . . .

"Anti-Poverty:
The Society Musters to Welcome Judge Maguire"[26]

. . . This is no political movement in the ordinary acceptation of the term. This is a deeply religious movement. (Applause) This audience—the way people have flocked to this hall— the way all over the state in which they crowd to hear the words of the priest of the people (great applause) prove that today, as eighteen centuries ago, when the real truths of Christianity are preached, the common people hear them gladly. In this is the strength of this great movement. This is the sign in which it goes on conquering and to conquer. One of the greatest of patriots, of philanthropists, one of the greatest of moral teachers, the great Italian, Mazzini,[27] said in the last generation that all movements for social reform must be utterly hopeless so long as they do not take hold of the religious sentiment of men; that to fight power and wealth and organization, to break up a system founded on selfishness and appealing to selfishness, it is utterly idle to call upon men in the name of their own personal interests; that something deeper, something stronger, must be appealed to; and in the religious sentiment of men, in the sentiment of sympathy with their fellows, in their love for their God, He is the only power that can reform the world and rescue our civilization from what will otherwise prove its certain destruction. (Cheers) Here today in the United States of America, in the city of New York, that world conquering power has been aroused. It is the same power that placed the cross above the temples of the Caesars. It is the great power preached through the whole earth, by the mouths of the poor and enslaved, the doctrine that revolutionized the world and made modern civilization possible. (Cheers) And now it comes again, another and a greater crusade, the mightiest of revolutions, the movement that aims at nothing less than the abolishing of poverty; the movement that aims at nothing less than the placing of all men upon a footing of equality (cheers); the movement that aims at nothing less than the regeneration of the world. (Great cheering) It is an honor, it is a privilege that I feel to the bottom of my heart that I am permitted to take part in it;

and every man, and every woman, and every child who joins with us may feel the same joy and the same pride. (Great applause) . . .

"For Cleveland and for Freedom: The Single Tax Men to the Front"[28]

. . . It is fifty-five years since a William Lloyd Garrison[29] was first announced to speak in New York. (Great applause) The meeting was well advertised. It was denounced by the newspapers, by the most respectable citizens, by the most influential politicians. Wealth, conservatism, and influence joined in the cry that such a wretch should not be permitted to speak in New York. Five thousand men with tar and feathers, and ropes and clubs, went to that meeting place to greet William Lloyd Garrison. Only that they could not recognize him, a William Lloyd Garrison would not have addressed us tonight. (Applause) What was his crime? It was that he stood for freedom. (Applause) Unknown, uninfluential, a poor printer, the genius of freedom came to him and called him to follow and to speak for her! (Applause) The young man obeyed her mandate, accepted her cross, followed her path. It brought him into prison, it brought to him hatred, obloquy, insult. A price was put upon his head, and mobs hunted him through American cities because he asserted the brotherhood of man and the dignity of labor. Churches denounced him because he preached, as applicable there and then, the gospel of liberty and fraternity that One they pretend to worship preached eighteen hundred years before in Galilee. He was accused of the crime of wanting to rob men of property that they had bought—property in men! (Applause) But he proclaimed, without thought of abatement or compromise. A freedom led him on. To him it was given to see the accomplishment of his work; to hear cursing changed to praises. Today in Boston, where that man was once hated and threatened and maligned and mobbed—in the finest avenue of the city, stands the statue of William Lloyd Garrison. (Applause) And (turning to Mr. Garrison) we of New York have welcomed you tonight, son of that father, not only for your own sake, but because you bear a name that liberty has made her own—a name that the world over is linked with a great struggle for freedom. It is fitting that you should be here and join with us in this movement that has for its object the destruction of industrial slavery, the breaking away of all the fetters that bind and enslave and impoverish men. (Applause) We are the abolitionists of this day and generation. Not merely abolitionists as to our mode of procedure, which is the abolition of one tax after another until no tax is left, but the tax which stifles no industry, oppresses no enterprise, hampers no natural right, takes from no one the earnings of hand or brain, but simply takes for common use what the common growth creates. (Applause) Not merely because we stand on the side of freedom in the struggle now beginning for industrial freedom! (Applause) But because, like the abolitionists of the last generation, we recognize the common brotherhood of man, the common fatherhood of God! Because we would restore to all men—not to one class, but to all—that liberty with which their Creator has endowed them. As your father stood for freedom so with us do you stand for freedom now! (Great applause)

Let us go forward with courage, taking heart of hope from the lessons of the past, taking faith and determination from what we have seen with our own eyes, and what we see today. Let us go forward striving for quick success, doing our best to bring it on; but with a confidence that nothing can shake; that, no matter what the morrow may bring forth, we are on a side that must ultimately triumph—the side of truth, and hope and righteousness! (Applause) Let us go on in the campaign doing our best, not merely to strike away commercial restrictions, but to destroy the superstition that turns to restriction for what freedom alone can give—to bring to our children, if it may be not to ourselves, that happy day when liberty from her Western home shall indeed enlighten the world—when there shall be work for all, plenty for all, leisure for all. (Great applause)

"Thy Kingdom Come"[30]

We have just joined in the most solemn, the most sacred, the most catholic of all prayers: "Our Father which art in Heaven!" To all of us who have learned it in our infancy, it oft calls up the sweetest and most tender emotions. Sometimes with feeling, sometimes as a matter of course, how often have we repeated it! For centuries, daily, hourly, has that prayer gone up. "Thy kingdom come!" Has it come? Let this Christian city of Glasgow answer—Glasgow, that was to "Flourish by the preaching of the Word." "Thy kingdom come!" Day after day, Sunday after Sunday, week after week, century after century, has that prayer gone up; and today, in this so-called Christian city of Glasgow, 125,000 human beings—so your medical officer says—125,000 children of God are living whole families in a single room. "Thy kingdom come!" We have been praying for it and praying for it, yet it has not come. So long has it tarried that many think it never will come. Here is the vital point in which what we are accustomed to call the Christianity which overran the ancient world—that Christianity which, beneath a rotten old civilization, planted the seeds of a newer and a higher [one]. We have become accustomed to think that God's kingdom is not intended for this world; that, virtually, this is the devil's world, and that

God's kingdom is in some other sphere, to which He is to take good people when they die—as good Americans are said when they die to go to Paris. If that be so, what is the use of praying for the coming of the kingdom? Is God—the Christian's God, the Almighty, the loving Father of whom Christ told—is He such a monster as a god of that kind would be; a god who looks on this world, sees its sufferings and its miseries, sees high faculties aborted, lives stunted, innocence turned to vice and crime, and heartstrings strained and broken, yet having it in his power, will not bring that kingdom of peace, and love, and plenty, and happiness? Is God, indeed, a self-willed despot, whom we must coax to do the good He might?

But, think of it. The Almighty—and I say it with reverence—the Almighty could not bring that kingdom of Himself. For, what is the kingdom of God; the kingdom that Christ taught us to pray for? Is it not in the doing of God's will, not by automata, not by animals who are compelled, but by intelligent beings made in His image; intelligent beings clothed with free will, intelligent beings knowing good from evil. Swedenborg never said a deeper nor a truer thing, nor a thing more compatible with the philosophy of Christianity, than when he said God had never put anyone into hell; that the devils went to hell because they would rather go to hell than go to heaven.[31] The spirits of evil would be unhappy in a place where the spirit of good reigned; wedded to injustice, and loving injustice, they would be miserable where justice was the law. And, correlatively, God could not put intelligent beings having free will into conditions where they *must* do right without destroying that free will. Nay! Nay! "Thy kingdom come!"—when Christ taught that prayer He meant, not merely that men must idly phrase these words, but that for the coming of that kingdom they must work as well as pray!

Prayer! Consider what prayer is. How true is the old fable! The wagoner, whose wagon was stuck in the rut, knelt down and prayed to Jove to get it out. He might have prayed till the crack of doom, and the wagon would have stood there. This world—God's world—is not that kind of a world in which the repeating of words will get wagons out of mire or poverty out of slums. He who would pray with effect must work!

"Our Father which art in Heaven." Not a despot, ruling by his arbitrary fiats, but a Father, a loving Father, *our* Father; a Father for us all—that was Christ's message. He is our Father and we are His children. But there are men, who, looking around on the suffering and injustice with which, even in so-called Christian countries, human life is full, say there is no Father in heaven, there can be no God, or He would not permit this. How superficial is that thought! What would we as fathers do for our children? Is there any man, who, having a knowledge of the world and the laws of human life, would so surround his boy with safeguards that he could do no evil and could suffer no pain? What could he make by that course of education? A pampered animal, not a self-reliant man! We are, indeed, His children. Yet let one of God's children fall into the water, and if he has not learned to swim he will drown. And if he is a good distance from land and near no boat or anything on which he may get, he will drown anyhow, whether he can swim or not. God the Creator *might* have made men so that they could swim like the fishes, but how could He have made them . . . like the fishes and yet have adapted this wonderful frame of ours to all the purposes which the intelligence that is lodged within it requires to use it for? God can make a fish; He can make a bird; but could He, His laws being what they are, make an animal that might at once swim as well as a fish and fly as well as a bird? That the intelligence which we must recognize behind nature is almighty does not mean that it can contradict itself and stultify its own laws. No; we are the children of God. What God is, who shall say? But every man is conscious of this, that behind what he sees there must have been a Power to bring that forth; that behind what he knows there is an intelligence far greater than that which is lodged in the human mind, but which human intelligence does in some infinitely less degree resemble.

Yes; we are His children. We in some sort have that power of adapting things which we know must have been exerted to bring this universe into being. Consider those great ships for which this port of Glasgow is famous all over the world; consider one of those great ocean steamers, such as the *Umbria*, or the *Etruria*, or the *City of New York*, or the *City of Paris*. There, in the ocean which such ships cleave, are the porpoises, there are the whales, there are the dolphins, there are all manner of fish. They are today just as they were when Caesar crossed to this island, just as they were before the first ancient Briton launched his leather-covered boat. Man today can swim no better than man could swim then, but consider how by his intelligence he has advanced higher and higher, how his power of making things has developed, until now he crosses the great ocean quicker than any fish. Consider one of those great steamers forcing her way across the Atlantic Ocean, four hundred miles a day, against a living gale. Is she not in some sort a product of a godlike power—a machine in some sort like the very fishes that swim underneath? Here is the distinguishing thing between man and the animals; here is the broad and impassable gulf. Man among all the animals is the only maker. Man among all the animals is the only one that possesses that godlike power of adapting means to ends. And is it possible that man possesses the power of so adapting means to ends that he can cross the Atlantic in six days, and yet does not possess the power of abolishing the conditions that crowd thousands of families into one room? When we consider the achievements of man and then look upon the misery that exists today in the very centers of wealth, upon the ignorance, the weakness, the injustice, that characterize our highest civilization, we may know of a surety that it is not the fault of God; it is the fault of man. May we not know that in that very power God has given to His children here, in that power of rising higher, there is involved—and necessarily involved—the power of falling lower?

"Our Father!" "*Our* Father!" *Whose?* Not *my* Father—that is not the prayer. "Our Father" not the father of any sect, of any class, but the Father of all men. The All-Father, the equal Father, the loving Father. He it is we ask to bring the kingdom. Aye, we ask it with our lips! We call him "Our Father," the All, the Universal Father, when we kneel down to pray to Him. But that He is the All-Father—that He is all men's Father we deny by our institutions. The All-Father who made the world, the All-Father who created man in His image, and put him upon the earth to draw his subsistence from its bosom; to find in the earth all the materials that satisfy his wants, waiting only to be worked up by his labor! If He is the All-Father, then are not all human beings, all children of the Creator, equally entitled to the use of His bounty? And, yet, our laws say that this God's earth is not here for the use of all His children, but only for the use of a privileged few? There was a little dialogue published in the United States, in the West, some time ago. Possibly you may have seen it. It is between a boy and his father, when visiting a brickyard. The boy looks at the men making bricks, and he asks who those dirty men are, why they are making up the clay, and what they are doing it for. He learns, and then he asks about the owner of the brickyard. "He does not make any bricks; he gets his income from letting the other men make bricks." Then the boy asks about what title there is to the bricks, and is told that it comes from the men having made them. Then he wants to know how the man who owns the brickyard gets his title to the brickyard—whether he made it? "No, he did not make it," the father replies, "God made it." The boy asks, "Did God make it for him?" Whereat his father tells him that he must not ask questions such as that, but that anyhow it is all right, and it is all in accordance with God's law. Then the boy, who of course was a Sunday-school boy, and had been to church, goes off mumbling to himself that God so loved the world that He gave His only begotten Son to die for all men; but that He so loved the owner of this brickyard that he gave him not merely his only begotten Son but the brickyard too.

This has a blasphemous sound. But I do not refer to it lightly. I do not like to speak lightly of sacred subjects. Yet it is well sometimes that we should be fairly shocked into thinking. Think of what Christianity teaches us; think of the life and death of Him who came to die for men! Think of His teachings, that we are all the equal children of an Almighty Father, who is no respector of persons, and then think of this legalized injustice—this

denial of the most important, most fundamental rights of the children of
God, which so many of the very men who teach Christianity uphold; nay,
which they blasphemously assert is the design and the intent of the Creator
himself. Better to me, higher to me, is the atheist, who says there is no
God, than the professed Christian, who, prating of the goodness and the
Fatherhood of God, tells us in words as some do, or tells us indirectly as
others do, that millions and millions of human creatures—(at this point a
child was heard crying)—don't take the little thing out—that millions
and millions of human beings, like that little baby, are being brought into
the world daily by the creative fiat, and no place in this world provided for
them. Aye! tells us that, by the laws of God, the poor are created in order
that the rich may have the unctuous satisfaction of dealing out charity to
them—tells us that a state of things like that which exists in this city of
Glasgow, as in other great cities on both sides of the Atlantic, where little
children are dying every day, dying by hundreds of thousands, because,
having come into this world—those children of God, with His fiat, by His
decree—they find that there is not space on the earth sufficient for them to
live; and are driven out of God's world because they cannot get room enough,
cannot get air enough, cannot get sustenance enough. I believe in no such
God. If I did, though I might bend before him in fear, I would hate him in
my heart. Not room enough for the little children here! Look around any
country in the civilized world; is there not room enough and to spare? Not
food enough? Look at the unemployed labor, look at the idle acres, look
through every country and see natural opportunities going to waste. Aye!
that Christianity that puts on the Creator the evil, the injustice, the suffering,
the degradation that are due to man's injustice, is worse, far worse, than
atheism. That is *the* blasphemy, and if there be a sin against the Holy Ghost,
that is the unpardonable sin!

Why, consider—"Give us this day our daily bread." I stopped in a hotel
last week—a hydropathic establishment.[32] A hundred or more guests sat
down to table together. Before they ate anything, a man stood up, and
thanking God, asked Him to make us all grateful for His bounty. So at every
mealtime such an acknowledgment is made over well-filled boards. What
do men mean by it? Is it mockery, or what?

If Adam, when he got out of Eden, had sat down and commenced to
pray, he might have prayed till this time without getting anything to eat
unless he went to work for it. Yet food *is* God's bounty. He does not bring
meat all cooked, nor vegetables all prepared, nor lay the plates, not spread
the cloth. What He gives are the opportunities of producing these things—of
bringing them forth by labor. His mandate is—it is written in the Holy Word,
it is graven on every fact in nature—that by labor we shall bring forth these
things. Nature gives to labor and to nothing else. What God gives are the

natural elements that are indispensable to labor. He gives them, not to one, not to some, not to one generation, but to *all*. They are His gifts, His bounty to the whole human race. And yet in all our civilized countries what do we see? That a few men have appropriated these bounties, claiming them as theirs alone, while the great majority have no legal right to apply their labor to the reservoirs of nature and draw from the Creator's bounty. And thus it comes that all over the civilized world that class that is called peculiarly the "laboring class" is the poor class, and that men who do no labor, who pride themselves on never having done honest labor and on being descended from fathers and grandfathers who never did a stroke of honest labor in their lives, revel in a superabundance of all the things that labor brings forth.

Mr. Abner Thomas, of New York, a strick orthodox Presbyterian—and the son of that Dr. Thomas, famous in America if not here, the pastor of a Presbyterian church in Philadelphia, and the author of a commentary on the Bible that is still a standard work—wrote a little while ago an allegory, called "A Dream." Dozing off in his chair, he imagined that he was ferried over the River of Death, and, taking the straight and narrow way, came at last within sight of the Golden City. A fine looking old-gentleman angel opened the wicket, inquired his name, and let him in; warning him, at the same time, that it would be better if he chose his company in heaven, and did not associate with disreputable angels.

"What!" said the newcomer, "is not this heaven!"

"Yes," said the warden, "but there are a lot of tramp angels here now."

"How can that be?" said Mr. Thomas, in his dream. "I thought everybody had plenty in heaven."

"It used to be that way some time ago," said the warden; "and if you wanted to get your harp polished or your wings combed, you had to do it yourself. But matters have changed since we adopted the same kind of property regulations in heaven as you have in civilized countries on earth, and we find it a great improvement, at least for the better class."

Then the warden told the newcomer that he had better decide where he was going to board.

"I don't want to board anywhere," said Thomas; "I would much rather go over to that beautiful green knoll and lie down."

"I would not advise you to do so," said the warden; "the angel who owns that knoll does not like to encourage trespassing. Some centuries ago, as I told you, we introduced the system of private property in the soil of heaven. So we divided the land up. It is all private property now."

"I hope I was considered in that division?" said Thomas.

"No," said the warden, "you were not; but if you go to work, and are saving, you can easily earn enough in a couple of centuries to buy yourself a nice piece. You get a pair of wings free as you come in, and you will have no difficulty in hypothecating[33] them for a few days' board until you find work. But I would advise you to be quick about it, as our population is constantly increasing, and there is a great surplus of labor. Tramp angels are, in fact, becoming quite a nuisance."

"What shall I go to work at?" said Thomas.

"Our principal industries," responded the warden, "are the making of harps and crowns and the growing of flowers; but there are many opportunities for employment in personal service."

"I love flowers," said Thomas, "and I will go to work growing them. There is a beautiful piece of land over there that nobody seems to be using. I will go to work on that."

"You can't do that," said the warden. "That property belongs to one of our most far-sighted angels, who has got very rich by the advance of land values, and who is holding that piece for a rise. You will have to buy it or feu it[34] before you can work on it, and you can't do that yet."

And so the story goes on to describe how the roads of heaven, the streets of the New Jerusalem, were filled with disconsolate tramp angels, who had pawned their wings, and were outcasts in heaven itself.

You laugh, and it *is* ridiculous. But there is a moral in it that is worth serious thought. Is not the ridiculousness in our imagining of the application to God's heaven of the same rules of division that we apply to God's earth, even while we pray that His will may be done on earth as it is done in heaven?

Really, if you come to think of it, it is impossible to imagine heaven treated as we treat this earth, without seeing that, no matter how salubrious were its air, no matter how bright the light that filled it, no matter how magnificent its vegetable growth, there would be poverty, and suffering, and a division of classes in heaven itself, if heaven were parcelled out as we have parcelled out the earth. And, conversely, if men in this life were to act towards each other as we must suppose the inhabitants of heaven to do, would not this earth be a very heaven? "Thy kingdom come." No one can think of the kingdom for which the prayer asks without feeling that it must be a kingdom of justice and equality—not necessarily of equality in condition, but of equality in opportunity. And no one can think of it without seeing that a very kingdom of God might be brought on this earth if men would but seek to do justice—if men would but acknowledge the essential principle of Christianity, that of doing to others as we would have others do to us, and of recognizing that we are all here equally the children of the one Father, equally entitled to share His bounty, equally entitled to live our lives and develop our faculties, and to apply our labor to the raw material that He has provided. Aye! and when a man sees that, then there arises that hope of the coming of the kingdom that carried the Gospel through the streets of Rome, that carried it into pagan lands, that made it, against the most ferocious persecution, the dominant religion of the world. Early Christianity did not mean, in its prayer for the coming of Christ's kingdom, a kingdom in heaven, but a kingdom on earth. If Christ had simply preached of the other world, the high priests and the Pharisees would not have persecuted Him, the Roman soldiery would not have nailed His hands to the cross. Why was Christianity persecuted? Why were its first professors thrown to wild beasts, burned to light a tyrant's gardens, hounded, tortured, put to death, by all the cruel devices that a devilish ingenuity could suggest? Not that it was a new religion, referring only to the future. Rome was tolerant of all religions. It was the boast of Rome that all gods were sheltered in her Pantheon; it was the boast of Rome that she made no interference with the religions of peoples she conquered. What was persecuted was a great movement for social reform—the Gospel of Justice—heard by common fishermen with gladness, carried by laborers and slaves into the Imperial City. The Christian revelation was the doctrine of human equality, of the fatherhood of God, of the brotherhood of man. It struck at the very basis of that monstrous tyranny that then oppressed the civilized world; it struck at the fetters of the captive, at the bonds of the slave, at that monstrous injustice which allowed a class to revel on the proceeds of labor, while those who did the labor fared scantily. That is the reason why early Christianity was persecuted. And when they could no longer hold it down, then the privileged classes adopted and perverted the new faith, and it became, in its very triumph, not the pure Christianity of the early days, but a Christianity that, to a very great extent, was the servitor of the privileged classes. And, instead of preaching the essential fatherhood of God, the essential brotherhood of man, its high priests engrafted on the pure truths of the Gospel the blasphemous doctrine that the All-Father is a respecter of persons, and that by His will and on His mandate is founded that monstrous injustice which condemns the great mass of humanity to unrequited hard toil. There has been no failure of Christianity. The failure has been in the sort of Christianity that has been preached.

Nothing is clearer than that if we are all children of the universal Father, we are all entitled to the use of His bounty. No one dare deny that proposition. But the men who set their faces against its carrying out say, virtually: "Oh, yes! that is true; but it is impracticable to carry it into effect!" Just think of what this means: This is God's world, and yet such men say that it is a world in which God's justice, God's will, cannot be carried into effect. What a monstrous absurdity, what a monstrous blasphemy! If the loving God does reign, if His laws are the laws not merely of the physical but of the moral universe, there must be a way of carrying His will into effect, there must be a way of doing equal justice to all His creatures. . . .

"Welcomed Home: Henry George Arrives in Good Health and High Spirits"[35]

Very noticeable at my meetings this time was the number of clergymen, especially clergymen of that church, or of that body (they prefer that term), to which our good friend, Thomas G. Shearman,[36] belongs—the Congregationalists (applause), who were present and took part, and who invited me to fill their pulpits whenever there was an opportunity. To me this was extremely gratifying. This movement, I find it everywhere the same as I found it in my own case—this movement is at the bottom a religious movement. (Applause)

I care nothing whatever for creeds—religion lies beneath creeds. (Applause). I care nothing whatever, how much or how little any man may think he knows of that power which is above all, through all, and in all. (Applause) But the essence of religion is the desire to do something for others than oneself (applause), is the feeling that in working for the good of mankind one is working on the side of that great power that is all good; is the faith that beneath what is false is something that is true, and beneath all that fluctuates is something that is firm.

I find everywhere, wherever I go, that the men who are with us and are of us, the men who in our slang phrase, for such it has become, that expresses so much, have really "seen the cat" (applause) are in their hearts religious men (applause), have for their motive a religious motive, and consequently are imbued with a strength that cannot be swerved from its purpose. (Applause)

"In Liverpool: The Financial Reform Meeting at the Liverpool Rotunda"[37]

... Mr. Henry George, on rising, was greeted with prolonged cheering, again and again renewed. When silence was at last obtained he said: It is a deep pleasure for me to be here tonight, the guest of the Liverpool Financial Reform Association, and to speak at my last meeting in England with my honored countrymen, [including] William Lloyd Garrison of Massachusetts. (Cheers) You are right, Mr. Garrison. The true republic, the American Republic that we hope for and pray is not yet here. (Hear, hear) A poor thing is a republic where the tramp jostles the millionaire, where liberty is mocked by a paternal system of interference with human rights, where, under the pretext of protecting labor, labor is robbed! (Cheers) And here, in the motherland, in the United States, in Australia and New Zealand, we of the

English tongue find the same difficulties confronting us. Liberty is not yet here; but, thank God, she is coming. (Cheers) Not merely the American Republic, not merely the Republic of the Southern Cross, not merely the Republic of Great Britain and Ireland is it that we see in the future, but that great republic that some day is to confederate the English speaking people everywhere (loud cheers) that is to bring a grander "Roman peace" to the world. (A voice: More than that.) Aye, more than that—that is to bring civilization as much higher, as much better than what we call a Christian civilization, as this is higher and better than barbarism. And already, in meetings such as this, it seems to me that I feel an earnest [presentiment] of the coming time when we of one blood and one speech are also to be one. (Cheers)

For the same principles, for the same great cause that we stand in the United States we stand here. And in a little over a week from now I will be standing on an American platform speaking to men whose hearts are beating in the same cause in which we are engaged here. (Cheers) Our little local politics may differ; our greater politics are one and the same. We have the same evils to redress, the same truth to propagate, the same end to seek. And that end, what is it but liberty? (Hear, hear) He who listens to the voice of Freedom, she will lead and lead him on. Before I was born, before our friend there was born, there was in a southern city of the United States a young printer bearing the name William Lloyd Garrison (Cheers) He saw around him the iniquity of negro slavery. (Hear, hear) The voice of the oppressed cried to him and would not let him rest, and he took up the cross. He became the great apostle of human liberty, and today in American cities that once hooted and stoned him there are now statues raised to William Lloyd Garrison. He began as a protectionist. As he moved on he saw that liberty meant something more than simply the abolition of chattel slavery. He saw that liberty also meant, not merely the right to freely labor for oneself, but the right to freely exchange one's production, and, from a protectionist, William Lloyd Garrison became a free trader. (Cheers) And now, when the first is gone, the second comes forward, to take one further step to realize that for perfect freedom there must also be freedom in the use of natural opportunities. (Hear, hear, and cheers)

We have come . . . to the same point by converging lines. Why is freedom of trade good? Simply that trade—exchange—is but a mode of production. Therefore, to secure full free trade we must also secure freedom to the natural opportunities of production. (Hear, hear) Our production— what is it? We produce from what? From land. All human production consists but in working up the raw materials that we find in nature—consists simply in changing in place, or in form, that matter which we call land. To free production there must be no monopoly of the natural element. Even in our methods we agree primarily on this essential point—that everyone ought to be free to exert his labor, to retain or to exchange its fruits, unhampered by restrictions, unvexed by the tax gatherer. (Hear, hear) . . .

Chattel slavery, thank God, is abolished at last. Nowhere, where the American flag flies, can one man be bought, or sold, or held by another. (Cheers) But a great struggle still lies before us now. Chattel slavery is gone; industrial slavery remains. The effort, the aim of the abolitionists of this time is to abolish industrial slavery. (Cheers) The free trade movement in England was a necessary step in this direction. The men who took part in it did more than they knew. Striking at restrictions in the form of protection, aiming at emancipating trade by reducing tariffs to a minimum for revenue only, they aroused a spirit that yet goes further. There sits, in the person of my friend, Mr. Briggs,[38] one of the men of that time, one of the men who, not stopping, has always aimed at a larger freedom, one of the men who today hails what we in the United States call the single tax movement, as the natural outcome and successor of the movement which Richard Cobden led.[39] (A voice: "Three cheers for Mr. Briggs," and cheers) And here, in your Financial Reform Association, you have the society that has best preserved the best spirit of that time, that has never cried "Hold!" [and] that has always striven to move forward to a fuller and a brighter day. (Hear, hear) In the United States, carried away by the heat of the great struggle, we allowed protection to build itself up. We have to now make the fight that you have partially won over here; but, in making that fight, we make the fight for full and absolute free trade. I don't believe that protection can ever be abolished in the United States until a majority of the people have been brought to see the absurdity and the wickedness of all tariffs, whether protective or for revenue only (hear, hear); have been brought to realize the deep truth of the fatherhood of God and the brotherhood of man; have been led to see what Mr. Garrison has so eloquently said, that the interests of mankind are harmonious, not antagonistic, that one nation cannot profit at the expense of another, but that every people is benefited by the advance of other peoples—(cheers)—until we shall aim at a free trade that will enable the citizen of England to enter the ports of the United States as freely as today, the citizen of Massachusetts crosses into New York. (Cheers)

The English Speaking People
Have you ever thought of the position that this English-speaking race of ours is going to hold in the next century? Here, the motherland—this little island. Put it alongside the United States, Canada, Australia, or South Africa; how small it is. Our outposts are now so planted, every sea knows so well our commerce, our millions are so many, that in the next century this English-speaking people will be to the world of that time a mightier power than Rome was to the civilized world of the past. (Cheers) What is the cause

of this, what is the reason of it? Why is it that English is spoken on the North American continent by so many millions of people, and not French or Spanish? Why is it that it is English that is being taught in the public schools of South Africa, of Australia, of New Zealand? (A voice: "They are the public robbers of the world," and laughter) Robbers they have been, but it is not by virtue of their robbery. Spain was even a more unconscionable robber. No! I will tell you why. It is simply because there has been more freedom; it is simply because the English people have had less of a paternal government than the people of the continent. (Cheers) It is not because her colonies were fostered—it is because they were neglected, that they grew up. (Laughter) That is today our strength, and that will give us strength in the future. What we want today to bring us all together is, not union under one government that shall assume to govern, but that absolute freedom of intercourse that shall entwine all interests, that absolute freedom of inter-course that shall establish a daily ferry from this side of the Atlantic to the other side of the Atlantic, that shall make everyone belonging to any of these nations, wherever he may be on the territory of another, feel as though he were at home. (Cheers) That is what we strive for—for the freedom of all, for self-government to all (hear, hear)—and for as little government as possible. (Laughter and cheers) We don't believe that tyranny is a thing alone of kings and monarchs; we know well that majorities can be as tyrannous as aristocracies (hear, hear); we know that mobs can persecute as well as crowned heads. (Hear, hear) What we ask for is freedom—that in each locality, large or small, the people of that locality shall be free to manage the affairs that pertain only to that locality (hear, hear, and cheers); that each individual shall be free to manage the affairs that relate to him; that government shall not presume to say of whom he shall buy or to whom he shall sell, shall not attempt to dictate to him in any way, but shall confine itself to its proper function of preserving the public peace, of preventing the strong from oppressing the weak, of utilizing for the public good all the revenues that belong of right to the public, and of managing those affairs that are best managed by the whole. (Cheers) Our doctrine is the doctrine of freedom, our gospel is the gospel of liberty, and we have faith in it, why should we not? (Cheers)

The Old Argument
The People who say that such terrible things would follow the institution of the single tax are simply like the people who had predicted terrible things to follow the building of railroads and the abolition of chattel slavery. Why I remember, and Mr. Garrison well remembers, the day when in the United States all the arguments that are used in this country against the single tax were used against the abolition of chattel slavery, even down to the "poor

widow argument." We used to be told—I was only a boy then—we used to be told, when William Lloyd Garrison, father of this man, was the best denounced man on two continents, that it might be well if we could find the people who originally brought these slaves from Africa, to make them give them up. "But," it was urged, "these negroes are owned by people who paid their money for them. (Laughter) Would you take away from a man without any compensation the property that he bought?" (Laughter) Then we used to be told, as you are told now, about that hard working mechanic. "Here is a hard working laboring man. He has toiled early and late, and he has bought a slave to help him. Are you going to take a man's slave without compensation and rob him of the products of his labor?" (Laughter) So they say today of the English mechanic, or English laborer, who has bought himself a little bit of land. And then we used to be told: "Here is a man who worked hard and saved his money, and he invested in half-a-dozen slaves. He died, and those slaves are the only means of subsistence the widow has to support his orphan children. Would you emancipate those slaves, and let that poor widow and those little orphans starve to death?" (Laughter)

Slavery and Slavery

It is the old, old story! And no wonder, for property in land is just as absurd, just as monstrous as property in human beings. (Hear, hear, and cheers) What difference does it make whether you enslave a man by making his flesh and blood the property of another, or whether you enslave him by making the property of another that element on which and from which he must live if he is to live at all? (A voice: "None whatever!" and cheers) Why, in those old days slave ships used to set out from this town of Liverpool for the coast of Africa to buy slaves. They did not bring them to Liverpool; they took them over to America. Why? Because you people were so good, and the Englishmen who had got to the other side of the Atlantic, and had settled there, were so bad? Not at all. I will tell you why the Liverpool ships carried slaves to America and did not bring them back to England. Because in America population was sparse and land was plentiful. Therefore to rob a man of his labor—and that is what the slaveowner wanted the slave for—you had got to catch and hold the man. That is the reason the slaves went to America. The reason they did not come here, the reason they were not carried over to Ireland was that here population was relatively dense, land was relatively scarce and could easily be monopolized, and to get out of the laborer all that his labor could furnish, save only wages enough to keep him alive—even the slaveowner had to give this—it was only necessary to own land.

What is the difference, economically speaking, between the slaves of South Carolina, Missouri, Mississippi, and Georgia and the free peasantry of Ireland or the agricultural laborer of England? (Cheers) Go to one of those slave states in the slave days, and there you would find a planter, the owner of five hundred slaves, living in elegant luxury, without doing a stroke of work, having a fine mansion, horses, [and a] carriage—all the things that work produces, but doing none of it himself. The people who did the work were living in negro huts, on coarse food; they were clothed in coarse raiment. If they ran away, he had the privilege of chasing them back, tying them up and whipping them and making them work. Come to this side of the Atlantic, in a place where you saw the same state of development. There you found also five hundred people living in little cabins, eating coarse food, clothed in coarse raiment, working hard, yet getting only enough of the things that work produces to keep them in good times, when bad times came having to appeal to the world for charity. But you found among those little cabins, too, the lordly mansion of the man who did no work. (Hear, hear, and groans) You found the mansion; you did not often find the man. (Laughter and cheers) As a general rule he was off in London, or in Paris, enjoying himself on the fruits of their labor. (Hear, hear) He had no legal right to make them work for him. Oh! no. If they ran away he could not put bloodhounds on their track and bring them back and whip them; but he had, in hunger, in starvation, a ban dog[40] more swift, more keen, more sure than the bloodhound of the south. (Cheers) The slaveowner of the south—the owner of men—had to make those men work for him. He went to all that trouble. The landlord of Ireland did not have to make men work for him. He owned the land, and without land men cannot work; and so men would come to him—equal children of the Creator, equal citizens of Great Britain—would come to him, with their hats in their hands, and beg to be allowed to live on his land, to be allowed to work and to give to him all the produce of their work, except enough to merely keep them alive, and thank him for the privilege. . . .

The Single Tax Marches Onward[41]

. . . Even Mark Twain's new book *A Connecticut Yankee in King Arthur's Court*, shows to whoever merely turns its leaves the growth and diffusion of our ideas, for from almost every other illustration gleams either a paw of the cat, the head of the cat, or the full, fair body of the cat. And every day and wherever I go I hear of men who have never identified themselves with our organizations or made any public sign, who are thoroughgoing single tax men. When time and opportunity are ripe and single tax principles do come into practical issue, the sudden burst of strength which they will show will seem like the rush of the Conemaugh flood.

"Publisher's Notes"[42]

"I love *The Standard* dearly," writes a lady from the Pacific Coast, sending an order for a dozen recruit subscriptions. "I love *The Standard* dearly. But dearly as I love it, and anxious as I am for its success, if the object of these recruit subscriptions were merely to get new subscribers for *The Standard* I shouldn't send them. I couldn't afford it." And then our friend goes on to tell us that what she feels she cannot afford for the paper, she is perfectly certain she [could do] for the cause. "I want to make converts," she writes. "I want to bring people to see the truth as I see it. I want to hasten the coming of God's kingdom upon earth. And scanty as are my means I cannot afford not to spend money for such a purpose."

Do you catch our friend's idea? Do you see the thought in her mind? She has learned to look upon this paper of ours not as an end, but as a means—as an instrument to be used in doing her work.

And, good readers of *The Standard*, this is just the sort of interest we want you to take. *The Standard* is your paper, published to aid you in your work, and can never fill its proper sphere of usefulness until you utilize it to the utmost. It can do good work for you if you will use it; its force will largely go to waste if you do not.

Have you ever considered what the duty is that you owe to the cause in which you are interested? It is very simple. The problem before us is to turn public opinion our way—to make people think as we do. We must make our converts one by one, and we must do this largely by individual effort, each one of us striving to bring into the fold his own little band of converts. Our antipoverty societies, our tax reform associations, our land and labor clubs, our political organizations, our *Standard*, our tracts and other literature are all the only means to this end—instruments which we can use to advantage if we will, or suffer to lie idle if we prefer. To win success each one of us must make himself a center of individual effort—must feel himself responsible for bringing in the men and women in his neighborhood and whom he knows.

Ah! if we would only do this, how soon would our triumph come. If each one of us would but number his friends and swear that he would know no rest and abate no effort until every one of them should be brought to our side! Who is there among us who couldn't attack a least half a dozen? And with each new convert fired in turn with the same missionary zeal, making himself the center of a new circle of effort—with the leaven of thought spreading and working more and more, day by day, through the whole lump of humanity—a single year would bring the victory.

Friends, the work is your work; the responsibility for its doing rests upon you; not one of you can evade his share. The tools lie ready to your hands. Will you use them?

Notes

1. Expression coined by George for those who regard the single tax as a basis for social reform.
2. "Ode to Liberty" is a pamphlet issued by the Robert Schalkenbach Foundation and reprinted here with permission. This speech was originally delivered in San Francisco on July 4, 1877 as "The American Republic." It was later incorporated in chapter five ("The Central Truth") of Book X in *Progress and Poverty*. See its "Centennial Edition" (New York: Robert Schalkenbach Foundation), 546–552.
3. A reference to the Persian King Darius I (549–485? B.C.), who led two unsuccessful expeditions against the Greek city states.
4. Reference to the defeat of Augustus' (63 B.C.–14 A.D.) Roman legions commanded by Varus by the Germans under Arminus in 9 A.D.
5. Crecy (1346) was a major victory for the English over the French during the Hundred Years War. The English longbow was the major factor. Agincourt (1415) was also another battle between the victorious English and the French.
6. Charles I (1600–1649). Stuart king of England whose Catholic sympathies and bitter struggle with Parliament led to the Puritan Revolution. He was convicted of treason and beheaded by Cromwell's government.
7. A reference to James Watt (1736–1819), the Scottish inventor of the steam engine.
8. The telegraph, invented by Samuel F. B. Morse (1791–1872).
9. St. John the Divine wrote the Revelation at Patmos, an Aegean island.
10. "Moses" is a pamphlet issued by the Robert Schalkenbach Foundation and reprinted here with permission. It was the opening address delivered in San Francisco before the Young Men's Hebrew Association in June 1878. It is considered to be one of George's most eloquent speeches. See Barker, *Henry George*, 248–250. Cecil B. De Mille, the brother-in-law of George's daughter Anna, had the cast of the movie *Moses* read it as part of their preparation for its filming.
11. Thomas Babington Macaulay (1800–1859), noted English historian, author, poet, and Whig parliamentarian. His most famous work was *The History of England from the Accession of James the Second*.
12. An obsolete word for a giraffe.
13. The Feast of Passover.
14. An ancient Spartan serf owned by the state and assigned to a landowner.
15. A year every half-century when debts were forgiven and slaves were freed (Lev. 25.8–55).
16. A carnivorous animal with similar features and habits to that of a weasel, but the size of a cat.
17. The Stoics were a school of philosophy founded by Zeno of Citium (ca. 200 B.C.). Among their beliefs, the putting aside of emotions was paramount.
18. A rich man of parable (Luke 16.19–31).
19. The Maccabees were a Jewish family (2nd and 1st centuries B.C.) who led the opposition to Syrian overlordship and Hellenizing influences. A phalanx was

a body of heavily-armed soldiers in compact formation with shields and spears, effectively used by Alexander the Great to repulse charges.

20. Scottish people bound by oath to defend Presbyterianism with the signing of the Covenant of 1638.

21. Ironsides refers to Cromwell himself or his army who fought during the Puritan Revolution against the Royalists. Naseby was a major victory for the Round-heads in 1645, which led to the surrender of Charles I.

22. Refers to a mythological beast who killed travelers who failed to answer a riddle. It was solved by Oedipus.

23. *The Standard*, Jan. 8, 1887, GR. This short notice in the first issue of *The Standard* succinctly presents George's goal.

24. The United Labor Party was founded in 1886 and disbanded in 1888.

25. *The Standard*, Sept. 10, 1887, GR. An excellent example of George's fiery oratory that captivated his audiences.

26. *The Standard*, Oct. 8, 1887, GR. Here politics and faith are mixed into a harmonious whole. Judge James Maguire was a friend and supporter of George. As congressman he attempted to introduce George's reforms in Congress in 1894.

27. Giuseppe Mazzini (1805–1872) was a freedom fighter instrumental in the Italian unification (Risorgimento) and a writer known for revolutionary political idealism.

28. *The Standard*, Sept. 1, 1888, GR. George historically links his cause with abolition.

29. The father was a famous abolitionist, who lived from 1805 to 1879. The son was a friend and supporter of George.

30. *The Standard*, June 22, 1889, GR. This speech is also to found in *Our Land and Land Policy*, 279–293. It was immensely popular in Scotland.

31. Emmanuel Swedenborg (1688–1772). Swedish religious thinker and mystic. Followers founded the Church of the New Jerusalem.

32. Hydropathy was also known as "the water cure." The patient undergoes daily baths wrapped in wet sheets for over an hour.

33. A pledge to a creditor as security.

34. Feu (or fee) has a number of definitions: a) an inherited estate of land without limitation to any particluar class of heirs (fee simple) or limited to a class of heirs (fee tail), b) an estate or territory held by a feudal lord on condition of service, or c) to have full ownership in land.

35. *The Standard*, Aug. 3, 1889, GR. Here George displays his compassion for mankind and universality shorn of particular religions.

36. A well-known lawyer and friend of George who coined the term "Single Tax" in 1887.

37. *The Standard*, Aug. 10,1889, GR. George's indgnation against suffering and his internationalism is displayed here.

38. Thomas Briggs of London was a friend and supporter of George.

39. Richard Cobden (1804–1865) was an English statesman influential in diplomatic affairs and in the repeal of the Corn Laws which permitted greater import of grain to ease food prices.

40. A dog kept tied or chained to serve as a watchdog or retained because of its ferocity.
41. *The Standard*, Dec. 14, 1889, GR. An outstanding example of George's faith and optimism.
42. *The Standard*, Apr. 7, 1888, GR. A reponse to the infectiousness of George as man and philosopher.

Chapter 3

A Clarification of the Single Tax and Property

Henry George was the leading proponent of the "single tax," yet today even many knowledgeable historians fail to understand these two words or connect them with George. The following selections should enlighten those who are unaware of the single tax, and clarify his meanings for those with some exposure to George's published works.

Although George at first reluctantly accepted the term single tax (coined by Thomas Shearman) as an apt description of the raison d'être of his political economy, after a time he defended it. But interpretation of methods and goals led to dissent among adherents, a familiar characteristic of all movements. One of the selections here demonstrates how George handles differences of opinion. Of special interest is the incorporation of the single tax into the political platform of the United Labor Party and George's demonstration that the principles underlying the land tax are rooted in English history.

Sometimes George became enthusiastic about his ideas. Although consistent in his belief about noncompensation to landowners, he was, as a rule, reticent about this point. In moments of a well-charged speech, however, he emphasized turning land over to the people with absolutely no compensation to the monopolizers of the soil. The spirit of indignation and rebellion, especially when he spoke overseas, could seize this normally even-tempered man of letters.

Goals of *The Standard*[1]

The Standard advocates the abolition of all taxes upon industry and the products of all industry, and the taking by taxation upon land values irrespective of improvements, of the annual rental value of all those various forms of natural opportunities embraced under the general term, Land.

We hold that to tax labor or its products is to discourage industry.

We hold that to tax land values to their full amount will render it impossible for any man to exact from others a price for the privilege of using those bounties of nature in which all living men have equal right of use; that it will compel every individual controlling natural opportunities to either utilize them by the employment of labor, or abandon them to others; that it will thus provide opportunities of work for all men, and secure to each the full reward of his labor; and that as a result involuntary poverty will be abolished, and the greed, intemperance and vice that spring from poverty and the dread of poverty will be swept away.

Commentary on the Term "Single Tax"[2]

. . . The term single tax does not really express all that a perfect name would convey. It only suggests the fiscal side of our aims. And in reality the single tax is not a tax at all. Since it is a tax in form, the term is useful as suggesting method. Before we adopted this name, people, even intelligent people, insisted on believing that we proposed to divide the land up: and many a time have I met a man who after informing me that he had read *Progress and Poverty*, and was familiar with my ideas, would continue; "But what I don't understand is, how, after you have once divided land up equally, you propose to keep it divided." Since we have used the term single tax this sort of misinterpretation seems to have almost entirely disappeared, and I think no little of the great progress we have made is owing to the fact that in our name we have kept before the public the idea that the practical measures we proposed consisted simply of a reform in taxation.

Not only is single tax to my mind preferable to the term land rent tax [for it links us] to those great Frenchmen [the Physiocrats], ahead of their time, who, over a century ago, proposed the *impôt unique* as the great means for solving social problems and doing away with poverty, but that it far more fully expresses our aim.[3] What we want to do is not merely to impose a certain kind of tax, but to get rid of other taxes. Our proper name, if it would not seem too high flown, would be "freedom men," or "liberty men," or "natural order men," for it is on establishing liberty, on removing restrictions, on giving natural order full play, and not on any mere fiscal change that we base our hopes of social reconstruction.

. . . At a [recent] meeting which William Lloyd Garrison and myself addressed in Tremont Temple, Boston, [he spoke] of our cause as a continuation of that to which he gave his early manhood and prime. For we are abolitonists, not merely in that we aim at the extension of human freedom, but in that our methods consist of abolishing restrictions, not of creating new machinery.

This idea is more fully expressed in the term single tax than it would be in land rent tax or any other such phrase. We want as few taxes as possible, as little restraint as is conformable to that perfect law of liberty which will allow each individual to do what he pleases without infringement of the equal right of others.

"The Land for the People: Speech by Henry George in Ashton-Under-Lyne, England"[4]

The Israelites and the Manna

Why, you remember how it is written, that in the journey of the Israelites across the desert, manna was sent down to feed them. If that desert had been divided up like England, who would have owned the manna?—(Hear, hear) Though enough and to spare came down, how could the common Israelites, who had no legal right to use a square inch of that desert, have got any manna. Why, only by selling their labor. They might have sold their labor to the rich Israelites, gathering up the manna, and got in return part of the manna they gathered. That would not have been enough for them. Then they might have given in return for more manna all they brought out from Egypt. When that was exhausted, how then? Why, here would have been great heaps of manna, and there would have been Israelites wanting manna; and then the "mannaed" class in all probability would have talked about the overproduction of manna. (Laughter)

Now, labor produces all wealth. That is perfectly clear. What, then, is the basis of the right of property? There is only one basis, and it is a curious thing that if you look through all the apologists for the rights of property in things that are not produced by labor you will find that they all came to that basis. The sure foundation of the right of ownership is in the right of each individual to himself, the right to use his own powers and to enjoy what he can obtain fairly by them. It is a natural principle that the man who produces a thing—that is, brought it forth from its natural reservoir and fitted it for the satisfaction of human wants—has the right of ownership in it, and to it the sacred right of property attaches. What a man produces is and ought to be his—his against all the world, to use, give away, sell, bequeath, to make any use of that he pleases, so long, of course, as he does not use it to injure others. This is the foundation of the right of property. Now the right of a man to himself to the produce of his labor in itself condemns the right of any one to ownership in the earth. If he has the right to what his labor produces would he not be robbed if anyone were to take a part of it from him as a return for the privilege of allowing him to breathe the air, or to warm himself by the sun? Does he not do the same thing when he takes part of the produce of that same labor for the right to use the earth? [It has been stated] that there have been classes in the past who, if they had thought of it, no doubt would have made air and water property. But, the reason they did not was perfectly plain.

"Taxing Land Values"[5]

. . . As to the effect upon the general interests of society of substituting the tax on land values for other taxes three claims can be made, [that is] they would tend to create:

1. Great governmental and social economies.
2. A great increase in the production of wealth.
3. A just equalization in the distribution of wealth.

1. The substitution of taxation upon the single item of land values for all the various taxes now imposed would be an enormous governmental and social economy. We should save the salaries and perquisites and official expenses of the horde of functionaries, national, state, and municipal, who are now engaged in assessing and collecting all these other taxes, or in doing things directly or indirectly necessitated by the cumbrous system. We should get rid of them all, from those fee-paid local officials who in a single term expect a fortune, and those federal collectors whose places are deemed of more importance than the governorship of sovereign states, down to the officials who are busied in seeing whether cigar boxes are stamped and peddlers are provided with licenses, or in searching the trunks and persons of passengers as they land. We should save the cost of trying and imprisoning offenders; we should save, too, the cost of all the devices—some of them very expensive—that are resorted to evade revenue laws, for it is obvious that all these expenses must ultimately be borne by consumers.

The tax upon land values is of all taxes that which combines the maximum of certainty with the minimum of expense. "Land lies out of doors;" it cannot be hid or disguised, and its value is easily ascertained. Any competent real estate dealer can . . . [determine] the value per front foot of any lot on Broadway. But, to ascertain the value of the building on it, it will be necessary to get an expert to make an examination; while, if that building be filled with goods, it is impossible for any outsider to [ascertain] their value. A tax upon the value of land can be collected to the last cent by a tax collector sitting in his office. Deducting the very small percentage, which would be all that would be required to pay the expenses of the periodical assessment and the receipt of taxes, the people in their collective capacity would thus get the benefit of all that was paid in taxes by individual people.

But the saving that would result is by no means to be estimated by the reduction in the cost and direct incidents of collecting revenues. It is the great vice of taxes that distribute themselves in added prices that, beyond the official tax gatherers, they create a long line of virtual tax gatherers, and that each man in the line not only takes the tax, but his profit on the tax, and in many cases enables [him] to take a great deal more. How strongly the "whisky ring" opposed the reduction of the whisky tax and the match manufacturers the abolition of the tax on matches is well known. And so with all indirect taxes. The difficulty is not usually in imposing them, but in abolishing them. Let a bill be introduced in Congress to abolish the tax on any of the long list of things taxed, and straightway there will appear in the lobby some one to protest and logroll against it, a sure proof that somebody besides the government is making money from the tax—that is to say, that the tax is taking from the people at large a good deal more than the government is getting from it. That this system, which engages great private interests in keeping up rather than in putting down taxation, fosters governmental extravagance and corruption is clear.

Now, by abolishing all other taxes in favor of the tax upon land values we should not only save very largely in the ways thus pointed out, but by the greater simplicity that would be given to government, we should save the political demoralization which the present system entails. It is "the money in politics" that makes our politics so corrupt, that puts honesty and patriotism at a disadvantage, and gives us traders and jobbers where we ought to have statesmen. That there is so much money in politics arises principally from the great number of officers which our present system of taxation necessitates, and from the great number of pecuniary interests which it concerns in the running of government. And beyond all this is the effect upon morals. Nearly all the taxes which we propose to abolish become, in one way or another, taxes upon conscience, and by setting a premium on bribery, forgery and fraud, foster political corruption and social demoralization.

Now, in view of the great economies which in all these various ways would result from the substitution of a tax on land values for all other taxes, is it not clear that the change would be of the greatest benefit, and would conduce largely to the general prosperity? Beside such "civil service reform" as this, the little picayune measure, good though it may be in itself, on which men like George William Curtis[6] have been spending so much time and talent, is as a minnow to a whale.

2. The present system, which taxes buildings and improvements, capital in all its forms, and in most of our states in all its shadows, is a system of direct discouragement to production, a system which fines the man who creates wealth just in proportion as he creates wealth. Instead of acting on the principle that the man who makes two blades of grass grow where one grew before is a public benefactor, our system of taxation treats him as a public enemy. If a man clothes a barren waste with grain and fruit trees, if he drains a swamp or opens a mine, if he puts up a house where none stood before, or erects a factory, or turns wood or iron into a ship, if he gets him[self] a library with which to store and exercise his mind, or a telescope with which to sweep the heavens, or a laboratory in which to seek out the laws of nature's combinations; if out of his savings he lays by a provision for his declining days; if by his energy and thrift he accumulates capital with which to assist and organize and provide the tools for industry—down comes the tax gatherer to make him pay for having done these things! Is not this as absurd as it is unjust? Is it not in direct contravention to the plainest dictates of enlightened public policy? Do we not all want more wealth? Why, then, should we tax and fine the production of wealth?

Some of the southern states have recently passed laws exempting cotton manufactories from taxation for a term of years, and the result has been the erection of a number of cotton factories, for the capitalists who thus invest their money can calculate on dividing as profits what otherwise they would have had to pay as taxes. Are not these states wise in this? Do not these cotton factories create new industries, add to the wealth of the neighborhoods in which they are erected, and enrich the whole state? But if this be wise, would it not be still wiser to make the exemption permanent instead of a term of [one] year? And if it be wise to exempt cotton factories, would it not be wiser still to exempt all sorts of factories, all forms of capital, all kinds of wealth—houses and goods, horses and cattle, railroads and telegraphs? Is not the state the richest that has the most of these things? Why, then, should the state tax them? Is not the stupid system that does tax them too absurd for any rational defense? The people of New York want cheaper house rents. Is it not stupid, then, to put taxes on buildings, which necessarily will diminish the erection of buildings, and, unlike the tax on land values, must inevitably be collected from tenants in higher rents?

But the direct obstacles to production, which this system imposes, are not the worse. All the indirect taxes which pass from hand to hand, increasing the cost of commodities, are taxes against production, which increase as they go. This barbarous tariff of ours, that raises an artificial barrier around our coasts is more difficult for commerce to surmount than would be the Andes or the Himalayas, takes from the people much more than is received by the government, and, by its action and reaction on prices, hampers every exertion of industry, from the building of a railroad to the shingling of a woodshed or the making of a shirt.

Now, it is clear that to abolish all the taxes that thus hamper industry, would be to vastly stimulate production and increase the general wealth. But this is only one side of it. To put taxation on the value of land would also be to remove obstacles to production. For the speculative value, which now attaches to land as soon as it becomes probable that it will be needed for use is a direct check to production. To get the vacant lot on which to put up a house, even on the outskirts of any one of our large cities, costs as much as or more than ordinarily does the house. Before he can strike a plowshare into virgin soil, the farmer, unless he will go far beyond where his labor can be exerted to most advantage, is obliged to pay out a large part of his capital, to embarrass himself with a mortgage, or to agree to give up a large share of his produce as rent. The result is to fill the land with tramps; to crowd our centers even in the best of times with men who are willing to work, anxious to work, but unable to find opportunity to work—and thus to produce an unnatural competition, which in all occupations tends to force wages down to the minimum on which men can live, and which workingmen are driven to resist by what President Glackin, in his address to the Anti-Poverty Society on last Sunday night, styled the resort to brute force. The result is to crowd people together too closely in the cities, to scatter them too far apart in the country. To say nothing of the moral, social and intellectual disadvantages which result from this unnatural distribution of population, there is a great obstacle put in the way of improvement, a manifest waste of productive forces.

The measure we propose, which would utterly destroy the speculative value of land, and would reduce the selling value of land to but a nominal figure, would remove this obstacle and prevent this waste. No one would care to take up land that he could not use, or to hold land unless it was put to its most valuable use. The homes of our farmers would be closer together, the poorer classes of our cities would no longer be compelled to herd in tenement houses, and the capitalist who proposed to erect a factory would no longer have to pay out so much of his capital for a site. Instead of that, he would pay the annual rental value of the land in taxes, but this would be in lieu of all other taxation. Thus, the effect of this measure would be to throw open to labor and capital the means of production while relieving production from taxation. And the result of thus opening to labor the natural opportunities for its employment . . . would be to set to work every man willing to do so; to do away with that unnatural competition which comes from a glutted labor market. It would be to create a demand for commodities that would set every wheel of industry in motion, and stimulate the forces of production to their utmost.

Clearly this would greatly promote the general prosperity and greatly add to the general wealth.

3. All taxes which increase prices are necessarily taxes in favor of monopoly, since the more capital it requires to go into any business, or to make any improvement, the smaller the number of those who can do so. And, besides this general characteristic of the taxes we would abolish, many of these taxes are specially designed to foster monopolies. It is, moreover, evident that when a large part of the produce of the labor and capital of the community is taken in rent by those who do nothing to aid in production (for landowners as landowners in no wise aid production), there is not merely created an unnecessary and unnatural inequality in the distribution of wealth, but this primary inequality gives rise to a tendency to further inequality. "Unto him that hath shall be given, and from him that hath not shall be taken away," is the expression of a universal law. To take from one and give to another is, both by decreasing the relative power of the other, to put them upon an unequal footing in treating of future divisions. If we trace [the origins of] the majority of great fortunes, we shall find it in monopolies of some kind—the primary and most important of all being the monopoly of the land. It is not because capital gets an undue proportion of the wealth that it helps to produce (though capital in some of its aggregations involve monopoly), that, in spite of all the enormous advances which invention and improvement and the growth of population have made, and still are making, in productive power, labor gets but such a scant living, and wages tend constantly to the minimum that will support life. With the advance of the arts and the progress of society, interest—which measures the return to capital—does not increase, but tends rather to diminish. It is rent which goes up, and up, and up. To divert to common uses this great fund which, though drawn from the production of the whole community, now goes to but a portion of the community, would be to turn into a promoter of equality what is now a promoter of inequality. To release capital from taxation, to lift the burden which now rests upon improvement and production, to destroy speculative land values, and throw open land to those who would use it, would open opportunities for labor in every direction and send wages up. In all industries laborers would get a fairer proportion than now of the value their labor creates.

There can be no dispute that in the three ways thus outlined the effect of substituting a tax on land values for all the other taxes by which our public revenues are now raised would be most beneficial to the general interests of society. It would greatly simplify and cheapen government; it would greatly increase the production of wealth; it would do away with the gross inequalities in the distribution of wealth which are now so painfully apparent. And whoever will further consider the matter will see that improvement in one of these directions would react to produce improvement in others—as, for instance, greater equality in the distribution of wealth would, by increasing intelligence and stimulating invention, vastly multiply the forces of production, and, by raising the standard of morals, render government both purer and abler, and diminish the economic wastes which immorality entails.

With relation to the factors of production and the primary distribution of the produce, society is divided for purposes of economic investigation into three classes—landowners, capitalists, and laborers. Of these it is evident that the change would be to the advantage of the capitalists and laborers, and to the disadvantage of the landowners. But it is only in the abstract that such a distinction can be clearly made in any country, and especially in such a country as ours. We have, it is true, a considerable class of laborers who are neither capitalists nor landowners; but we have few capitalists who are not laborers, for in the economic use of the term the managing head of any great industrial enterprise is as truly a laborer as is any workman in his employ; and we have probably no landowners who are not either laborers or capitalists, for, in the strict definition of the term, buildings and improvements are capital, not land. A very great number of our people combine the characters of landowner, capitalist and laborer, and there are certainly a large majority who combine at least two of these characters. This, while all would profit in the general social gains, it is only in the character of landowner that against these general gains anyone could set individual loss. Therefore, the proposition to concentrate taxes on land values should as a matter of mere individual interest, commend itself even to landowners whose interests as landowners do not exceed their interests as capitalists or laborers, or both.

With reference to the ownership of land and with regard to actual facts, our people may be divided into three classes—those who own land which they do not themselves use, those who own land which they use, and those who own no land. The latter class may contain some capitalists, but is mainly composed of laborers—farm hands, manual laborers, operatives, mechanics, clerks, professional men, etc., who depend for their living upon the earnings of their labor. This is the class which it is most important to consider, not merely for sentimental reasons, but because, since they constitute the base of the social pyramid, whatever improves or depresses their condition will affect all the rest. Now, it is manifest that to take taxes off capital and improvement and production and exchange would be greatly to benefit all of those who live by their earnings, whether of hand or of head. It is manifest also that it would benefit all who live partly by the earnings of their capital—storekeepers, merchants, manufacturers, etc.—and that by increasing the net productiveness of capital it would benefit those whose incomes are drawn from capital alone.

Take now the case of those to whom the opponents of the single tax are so fond of referring—the farmers who till their own acres, and the men who own their homesteads in which they live. It is true that the change we propose would diminish the selling value of the land (but merely of the bare land, not of the buildings or improvements), and if fully carried out would virtually destroy it. But it would in no wise diminish the usefulness of their land; it would in no wise diminish, but would in fact increase, their incomes. They would pay under this system less taxes than they pay now. The clerk or mechanic or business or professional man who owns a house and lot in which he lives might pay more taxes on his lot than now, but in return for this he would escape the taxes now levied on his house and its contents, and, through the medium of indirect taxation, upon everything that his family consumes. And so with the farmer. Our present system of taxation falls with peculiar severity upon the farming class. Not only is improved land all over the United States taxed higher than unimproved land of the same quality, but the taxes which so largely raise the prices of all the farmer has to buy do not, and cannot, so long as we are exporters of agricultural produce, raise the prices of what the farmer has to sell. And, further than this, to put taxation solely upon land values would shift the weight of taxation from the sparsely settled agricultural districts to those populous centers where land has a real and a high value. As it would destroy the speculative value of land, the result would be that many farmers would have no taxes at all to pay, for, no matter what might be the value of his improvements, no farmer would have more taxes to pay than could be collected from unimproved land equal to his in quality and situation. Manifestly it would be a very great relief for the farmer to abolish all the taxes which now fall upon his improvements and his consumption, and substitute for them a tax upon the value of bare land, which is always higher in populous centers than in agricultural districts, and in sparsely settled agricultural districts hardly exists at all, except as the result of speculation. And from the effects upon the diffusion of population the farmer would greatly gain. Just as the city population would gain from the destruction of the system which now builds tenement houses amid vacant lots, so would the agricultural communities gain in productive power and social enjoyment when settlement should become closer, from the fact that there would no longer be any inducement for any one to take up or hold more land than he could use.

Further than this, it must be remembered that, although the selling price of land would diminish, this, since it would affect all land, would not affect the exchange value of the homestead lot or farm, as compared with other homestead lots or farms. It would be, to the man who wants for himself and his family the security of a home in which to live, or land to cultivate, a purely nominal and intangible loss. To offset there would be great and actual gains; and, as his children grew up, it would be very much easier for them to get homesteads or farms of their own.

The only people who would really lose would be those whose incomes are mainly drawn from the rent, not of buildings, but of land, and those who are holding land in the expectation of future profit from the high prices that in time those who want to use it will be compelled to pay them. But there are few, if any, individuals who belong exclusively to this class. In varying degrees all our large landholders are also capitalists, and would gain as capitalists though they might lose as landowners. And, if in some cases the relative loss exceeded the relative gain, it would only be (and this, if necessary, might be made certain by some provision as to widows, etc.) in the case of those who could readily stand the loss without being really hurt. In any large view it will always be found that the true interests of all individuals coincide with the best interests of society.

To put all taxes on land values would be to remove all burdens from capital and labor; to free industry, and energy, and thrift from restriction or fine; to take away the incentives to speculation in land, and to throw open natural opportunities to those who would use them, without, as now, compelling them to pay a heavy premium to some nonuser. From the freedom of operation which would thus be given to productive forces there would result an enormous increase in the production of wealth. The fund from which all incomes must be drawn would be vastly augmented. And at the same time there would come about a great equalization in distribution; for that freedom of operation which is essential to the largest production of wealth is also essential to its fairest distribution.

To one who has never thought over the matter it may seem preposterous to say that in a simple change in the methods of taxation lies the fundamental cure for pauperism and low wages and all the social difficulties which afflict modern society. Yet, to all who will carefully think over it this will [readily] appear. When it is considered what is really involved in this simple change, such great effects do not seem disproportionate to the cause. For, to remove taxation from the production and accumulation of wealth, and to put it on the appropriation of that element which is the raw material of wealth, would be to remove obstructions to the natural play of social forces—obstructions which produce in the social organism just such effects as bandages and ligatures that impede the circulation of the blood would produce in the human body. It would conform our most important social adjustments to the supreme law of justice; for the right to land is common and equal while the right to the products of labor is individual and exclusive; [these] are correlative propositions too manifest to need discussion.

"The Land for the People"[7]

The Land Question is not merely a question between farmers and the owners of agricultural land. It is a question that affects every man, every woman, and every child. The Land Question is simply another name for the great labor question, and the people who think of the Land Question as having importance simply for farmers forget what land is.

If you would realize what land is, think of what men would be without land. If there were no land, where would be the people? Land is not merely a place to graze cows or sheep upon, to raise corn or raise cabbage. It is the indispensable element necessary to the life of every human being. We are all land animals; our very bodies come from the land, and to the land they return again.

Whether a man dwells in the city or in the country, whether he be a farmer, a laborer, a mechanic, a manufacturer, or a soldier, land is absolutely necessary to his life. No matter what his occupation may be, if he is engaged in productive labor, that productive labor, if you analyze it, is simply the application of human exertion to land, the changing in place or in form of the matter of the universe.

We speak of productive work. What is productive work? We make things. How do we make them? Man does not create them. Man cannot create something out of nothing. All the things that we call making are producing; bringing forth, not creating.

Men produce coal by going down under the ground, hewing out the coal, and bringing it to the surface of the earth; they produce fish by going to the lough,[8] or river, or ocean and pulling the fish out; they produce houses by bringing together timber and stones and iron into the shape and form of a house; they produce cloth by taking the wool of a sheep or the fibers of a plant and bringing them together in a certain connection; they produce crops by opening the ground and putting in seed and leaving it there for the germinating influences of nature—always a bringing forth, never a creation, so that human exertion, that is to say labor upon land, is the only way that man has of bringing forth those things which his needs require and which are necessary to enable him to sustain life. Land and labor—these are the two necessary and indispensable factors to the production of wealth.

Now as to the rights of ownership—as to that principle which enables a man to say of any certain thing—"This is mine; it is my property"—where does that come from? If you look you will see that it comes from the right of the producer to the thing which he produces. What a man makes he can justly claim to be his. Whatever any individual, by the exercise of his powers, takes from the reservoirs of nature, molds into shapes fitted to satisfy human needs, that is his; to that a just and sacred right of property attaches. That is a right based on the right of the individual to improvement, the right to the enjoyment of his own powers, to the possession of the fruits of his exertions. That is a sacred right, to violate which is to violate the sacred command, "Thou shalt not steal." There is the right of ownership. Now that right, which gives by natural and Divine laws, the thing produced to him whose exertion has produced it, which gives to the man who builds a house the right to that house, to the man who raises a crop the right to that crop, to the man who raises a domestic animal a right to that domestic animal—how can that right attach to the reservoirs of nature? How can that right attach to the earth itself?

We start out with these two principles, which I think are clear and self-evident: that which a man makes belongs to him, and can by him be given or sold to anyone that he pleases. But that which existed before man came upon the earth, that which was not produced by man, but which was created by God—that belongs equally to all men. As no man made the land, so no man can claim a right of ownership in the land. As God made the land, and as we know both from natural perception and from revealed religion, that God the Creator is no respecter of persons, that in His eyes all men are equal, so also do we know that He made this earth equally for all the human creatures that He has called to dwell upon it. We start out with this clear principle that as all men are here by the equal permission of the Creator, as they are all here under His laws equally requiring the use of land, as they are all here with equal right to live, so they are all here with equal right to the enjoyment of His bounty.

We claim that the land of Ireland, like the land of every country, cannot justly belong to any class, whether that class be large or small; but that the land of Ireland, like the land of every other country, justly belongs in usufruct[9] to the whole people of that country equally, and that no man and no class of men can have any just right in the land that is not equally shared by all others.

We say that all the social difficulties we see here, all the social difficulties that exist in England or Scotland, all the social difficulties that are growing up in the United States—the lowness of wages, the scarcity of employment, the fact that though labor is the producer of wealth, yet everywhere the laboring class is the poor class—are all due to one great primary wrong, that wrong which makes the natural element necessary to all, the natural element that was made by the Creator for the use of all, the property of some of the people, that great wrong that in every civilized country disinherited the mass of men of the bounty of their Creator. What we aim at is not the increase in the number of a privileged class, not making some thousands of earth owners into some more thousands. No, no; what we aim at is to secure the natural and God-given right to the humblest in the community—to secure to every child born in Ireland, or in any other country, his natural right to the equal use of his native land.

How can we secure that? We cannot secure it by dividing the land up equally, by giving each man or each family an equal piece. That is a device that might suit a rude community, provided that, as under the Mosaic Code, those equal pieces be made unalienable, so that they could never be sold away from the family. But under our modern civilization where industry is complex, where land in some places is very valuable and in other places of but little value, where it is constantly changing in relative value, the equal division of the land could not secure equality.

The way to secure equality is plain. It is not by dividing the land; it is by calling upon those who are allowed possession of pieces of land giving special advantage to pay to the whole community, the rest of the people, aye, and including themselves—to the whole people, a fair rent or premium for that privilege, and using the fund so obtained for the benefit of the whole people. What we would do would be to make the whole people the general landlord, to have whatever rent is paid for the use of land to go, not into the pockets of individual landlords, but into the treasury of the general community, where it could be used for the common benefit.

Now, rent is a natural and just thing. For instance, if we in this room were to go together to a new country and we were to agree that we should settle in that new country on equal terms, how could we divide the land up in such a way as to insure and to continue equality? If it were proposed that we should divide it up into equal pieces, there would be in the first place this objection, that in our division we would not fully know the character of the land; one man would get a more valuable piece than the other. Then as time passed the value of different pieces of land would change, and further than that if we were once to make a division and then allow full and absolute ownership of the land, inequality would come up in the succeeding generation. One man would be thriftless, another man, on the contrary, would be extremely keen in saving and pushing; one man would be unfortunate and another man more fortunate; and so on. In a little while many of these people would have parted with their land to others, so that their children coming after them into the world would have no land. The only fair way would be this—that any man among us should be at liberty to take up any piece of land, and use it, that no one else wanted to use; that where more than one man wanted to use the same piece of land, the man who did use it should pay a premium which, going into a common fund and being used for the benefit of all, would put everybody upon a plane of equality. That would be the ideal way of dividing up the land of a new country.

The problem is how to apply that to an old country. True, we are confronted with this fact all over the civilized world, that a certain class have got possession of the land, and want to hold it. Now one of your distinguished leaders, Mr. Parnell[10] in his Drogheda speech some years ago, said there were only two ways of getting the land for the people. One way was to buy it, the other was to fight for it. I do not think that is true. I think that Mr. Parnell overlooked at that time a most important third way, and that is the way we advocate.

That is what we propose by what we call the single tax. We propose to abolish all taxes for revenue in place of all the taxes that are now levied, to impose one single tax, and that a tax upon the value of land. Mark me, upon the value of land alone—not upon the value of improvements, not upon the value of what the exercise of labor has done to make land valuable, that belongs to the individual; but upon the value of the land itself, irrespective of the improvements, so that an acre of land that has not been improved will pay as much tax as an acre of like land that has been improved. So that in a town a house site on which there is no building shall be called upon to pay just as much tax as a house site on which there is a house.

I said that rent is a natural thing. So it is. Where one man, all rights being equal, has a piece of land of better quality than another man, it is only fair to all that he should pay the difference. Where one man has a piece of land and others have none, it gives him a special advantage; it is only fair that he should pay into the common fund the value of that special privilege granted him by the community. That is what is called economic rent.

But over and above the economic rent there is the power that comes by monopoly, there is the power to extract a rent, which may be called monopoly rent. On this island that I have supposed we go and settle on, under the plan we have proposed each man should pay annually to the special fund in accordance with the special privilege the peculiar value of the piece of land he held, and those who had land of no peculiar value should pay nothing. That rent that would be payable by the individual to the community would only amount to the value of the special privilege that he enjoyed from the community. But if one man owned the island, and if we went there and you people were fools enough to allow me to lay claim to the ownership of the island and say it belonged to me, then I could charge a monopoly rent; I could make you pay me every penny that you have earned, save just enough for you to live; and the reason I could not make you pay more is simply this, that if you would pay more you would die.

The power to exact that monopoly rent comes from the power to hold land idle—comes from the power to keep labor off the land. Tax up land to its full value and that power would be gone; the richest landowners could not afford to hold valuable land idle. Everywhere that simple plan would compel the landowner either to use his land or to sell out to some one who would; and the rent of land would then fall to its true economic rate—the value of the special privilege it gave would go not to individuals, but to the general community, to be used for the benefit of the whole community. . . . our practical measure for restoring to all men of any country their equal rights in the land of that country is simply to abolish other taxes, to put a tax upon the value of land, irrespective of the improvements, to carry that tax up as fast as we can, until we absorb the full value of the land, and we say that that would utterly destroy the monopoly of land, and create a fund for the benefit of the entire community. How easy a way that is to go from an unjust situation like the present to an ideally just situation may be seen among other things in this. Where you propose to take land for the benefit of the whole people you are at once met by the demands of the landlords for compensation. Now, if you tax them, no one ever heard of such an idea as to compensate a people for imposing tax.

In that easy way the land can again be made the property in usufruct of the whole people, by a gentle and gradual process.

What I ask you here tonight is as far as you can to join in this general movement and push on the cause. It is not a local matter, it is a world-wide matter. It is not a matter that interests merely the people of Ireland, the people of England and Scotland or of any other country in particular, but it is a matter that interests the whole world. What we are battling for is the freedom of mankind; what we are struggling for is for the abolition of that industrial slavery which as much enslaves men as did chattel slavery. It will not take the sword to win it. There is a power far stronger than the sword and that is the power of public opinion. When the masses of men know what hurts them and how it can be cured when they know what to demand, and to make their demand heard and felt, they will have it and no power on earth can prevent them. What enslaves men everywhere is ignorance and prejudice.

If we were to go to that island that we imagined, and if you were fools enough to admit that the land belonged to me, I would be your master, and you would be my slaves just as thoroughly, just as completely, as if I owned your bodies, for all I would have to do to send you out of existence would be to say to you "get off my property." That is the cause of the industrial slavery that exists all over the world, that is the cause of the low wages, that is the cause of the unemployed labor.

How can you remedy it? Only by going to first principles, only by asserting the natural rights of man. You cannot do it by any such scheme as is proposed here of buying out the landlords and selling again to the tenant farmers. What good is that going to do to the laborers? What benefit is it to be to the artisans of the city? And what benefit is it going to be to the farming class in the long run? For just as certain as you do that, just as certain will you see going on here what we have seen going on in the United States, and by the vicissitudes of life, by the changes of fortune, by the differences among men—some men selling and mortgaging, some men acquiring wealth and others becoming poorer—in a little while you will have the reestablishment of the old system. But it is not just in any consideration. What better right has an agricultural tenant to receive any special advantage from the community than any other man? If farms are to be bought for the agricultural tenant, why should not boots for the artisans, shops for the clerks, boats for the fishermen—why should not the government step in to furnish everyone with capital? And consider this with regard to the buying out of the landlords. Why, in Heaven's name, should they be bought out? Bought out of what? Bought out of the privilege of imposing a tax upon their fellow citizens? Bought out of the privilege of appropriating what belongs to all? That is not justice. If, when the people regain their rights, compensation is due to anybody it is due to those who have suffered injustice, not to those who have caused it and profited by it.

"The Single Tax Platform: Adopted by the National Conference of the Single Tax League of the U.S. at Cooper Union, N.Y., Sept. 3, 1890"[11]

We assert as our fundamental principle the self-evident truth enunciated in the Declaration of American Independence, that all men are created equal and are endowed by their Creator with certain inalienable rights.

We hold that all men are equally entitled to the use and enjoyment of what God has created and of what is gained by the general growth and improvement of the community of which they are a part. Therefore, no one should be permitted to hold natural opportunities without a fair return to all for any special privilege thus accorded to him, and that value which the growth and improvement of the community attach to land should be taken for the use of the community.

We hold that each man is entitled to all that his labor produces. Therefore no tax should be levied on the products of labor.

To carry out these principles we are in favor of raising all public revenues for national, state, county, and municipal purposes by a single tax upon land values, irrespective of improvements, and of the abolition of all forms of direct and indirect taxation.

Since in all our states we now levy some tax on the value of land, the single tax can be instituted by the simple and easy way of abolishing, one after another, all other taxes now levied, and commensurately increasing the tax on land values, until we draw upon that one source for all expenses of government, the revenue being divided between local governments, state governments and the general government, as the revenue from direct taxes is now divided between the local and state governments; or, a direct assessment being made by the general government upon the states and paid by them from revenues collected in this manner.

The single tax we propose is not a tax on land, and therefore would not fall on the use of land and become a tax on labor.

It is a tax, not on land, but on the value of land. Thus it would not fall on all land, but only on valuable land, and on that not in proportion to the use made of it, but in proportion to its value—the premium which the user of land must pay to the owner, either in purchase money or rent, for permission to use valuable land. It would thus be a tax not on the use or improvement of land, but on the ownership of land, taking what would otherwise go to the owner as owner, and not as user.

In assessments under the single tax all values created by individual use or improvement would be excluded, and the only value taken into consideration would be the value attaching to the bare land by reason of neighborhood, etc., to be determined by impartial periodical assessments. Thus the farmer would have no more taxes to pay than the speculator who held a similar piece of land idle, and the man who on a city lot erected a valuable building would be taxed no more than the man who held a similar lot vacant.

The single tax, in short, would call upon men to contribute to the public revenues, not in proportion to what they produce or accumulate, but in proportion to the value of the natural opportunities they hold. It would compel them to pay just as much for holding land idle as for putting it to its fullest use.

The single tax therefore, would:

1. Take the weight of taxation off the agricultural districts where land has little or no value irrespective of improvements, and put [it] in towns and cities where bare land rises to a value of millions of dollars per acre.

2. Dispense with a multiplicity of taxes and a horde of tax gatherers, simplify government, and greatly reduce its cost.

3. Do away with the fraud, corruption, and gross inequality insepa-rable from our present methods of taxation, which allow the rich to escape while they grind the poor. Land cannot be hid or carried off, and its value can be ascertained with greater ease and certainty than any other.

4. Give us with all the world as perfect freedom of trade as now exists between the states of our Union, thus enabling our people to share, through free exchanges, in all the advantages which nature has given

to other countries, or which the peculiar skill of other peoples has enabled them to attain. It would destroy the trusts, monopolies, and corruptions which are the outgrowth of the tariff. It would do away with the fines and penalties now levied on anyone who improves a farm, erects a house, builds a machine, or in any way adds to the general stock of wealth. It would leave everyone free to apply labor or expend capital in production or exchange without fine or restriction, and would leave to each the full product of his exertion.

5. It would, on the other hand, by taking for public use that value which attaches to land by reason of the growth and improvement of the community, make the holding of land unprofitable to the mere owner, and profitable only to the user. It would then make it impossible for speculators and monopolies to hold natural opportunities unused or only half used, and would throw open to labor the illimitable field of employment, which the earth offers to man. It would thus solve the labor problem, do away with involuntary poverty, raise wages in all occupations to the full earnings of labor, make overproduction impossible until all human wants are satisfied, render labor-saving inventions a blessing to all, and cause such an enormous production and such an equitable distribution of wealth as would give to all comfort, leisure, and participation in the advantages of an advancing civilization.

With respect to monopolies other than the monopoly of land, we hold that where free competition becomes impossible, as in telegraphs, railroads, water, and gas supplies, etc., such business becomes a proper social function, which should be controlled and managed by and for the whole people concerned, through their proper government, local, state or national, as may be.

"The Single Tax: What It Is and Why We Urge It"[12]

. . . Let us turn to the moral side and consider the question of justice.

The right of property does not rest on human laws; they have often ignored and violated it. It rests on natural laws—that is to say, the law of God. It is clear and absolute, and every violation of it, whether committed by a man or a nation, is a violation of the command, "Thou shall not steal." The man who catches a fish, grows an apple, raises a calf, builds a house, makes a coat, paints a picture, constructs a machine, has, as to any such thing, an exclusive right of ownership which carries with it the right to give, to sell or bequeath that thing.

But who made the earth that any man can claim such ownership of it, or any part of it, or the right to give, sell or bequeath it? Since the earth was not made by us, but is only a temporary dwelling place on which one generation of men follow another; since we find ourselves here, are manifestly here with equal permission of the Creator, it is manifest that no one can have any exclusive right of ownership in land, and that the right of all men to land must be equal and inalienable. There must be an exclusive right of possession of land, for the man who uses it must have secure possession of land in order to reap the products of his labor. But his right of possession must be limited by the equal right of all, and should therefore be conditioned on the payment to the community by the possessor of an equivalent for any special valuable privilege thus accorded him.

When we tax houses, crops, money, furniture, capital or wealth in any of its forms, we take from individuals what rightfully belongs to them. We violate the right of property, and in the name of the State commit robbery. But when we tax ground values, we take from individuals what does not belong to them, but belongs to the community, and which cannot be left to individuals without the robbery of other individuals.

Think what the value of land is. It has no reference to the cost of production, as has the value of houses, horses, ships, clothes, or other things produced by labor, for land is not produced by man, it was created by God. The value of land does not come from the exertion of labor on land, for the value thus produced is a value of improvement. That value attaches to any piece of land means that that piece of land is more desirable than the land which other citizens may obtain, and that they are more willing to pay a premium for permission to use it. Justice therefore requires that this premium of value shall be taken for the benefit of all in order to secure to all their equal rights.

Consider the difference between the value of a building and the value of land. The value of a building, like the value of goods, or of anything properly styled wealth, is produced by individual exertion, and therefore properly belongs to the individual; but the value of land only arises with the growth and improvement of the community, and therefore properly belongs to the community. It is not because of what its owners have done, but because of the presence of the whole great population, that land in New York is worth millions an acre. This value therefore is the proper fund for defraying the common expenses of the whole population; and it must be taken for public use, under penalty of generating land speculation and monopoly which will bring about artificial scarcity where the Creator has provided in abundance for all whom His providence has called into existence. It is thus a violation of justice to tax labor, or the things produced by labor, and it is also a violation of justice not to tax land values.

These are the fundamental reasons for which we urge the Single Tax, believing it to be the greatest and most fundamental of all reforms. We do not think it will change human nature. That, man can never do; but it will bring about conditions in which human nature can develop what is best, instead of, as now in so many cases, what is worse. It will permit such an enormous production as we can now hardly conceive. It will secure an equitable distribution. It will solve the labor problem and dispel the darkening clouds which are now gathering over the horizon of our civilization. It will make undeserved poverty an unknown thing. It will check the soul-destroying greed of gain. It will enable men to be at least as honest, as true, as considerate, and as high-minded as they would like to be. It will remove temptation to lying, false swearing, bribery, and law breaking. It will open to all, even the poorest, the comforts and refinements and opportunities of an advancing civilization. It will thus, so we reverently believe, clear the way for the coming of that kingdom of right and justice, and consequently of abundance and peace and happiness, for which the Master told His disciples to pray and work. It is not that it is a promising invention or cunning device that we look for the Single Tax to do all this; but it is because it involves a conforming of the most important and fundamental adjustments of society to the supreme law of justice, because it involves the basing of the most important of our laws on the principle that we should do to others as we would [expect them to do to us]. . . .

Since we cannot conceive of a heaven in which the equal rights of God's children to their Father's bounty is denied, as we now deny them on this earth, what is the duty enjoined on Christians by the daily prayer: "Thy kingdom come, Thy will be done, *on earth*, as it is in heaven?"

Letter, "My Dear Walker"[13]

With the pressure I find upon me I fear that it will be a long while before I can get leisure to make the detailed review of your paper I would like to. I shall therefore try to point out briefly what I think to be your leading errors. In being brief I shall seem blunt and dogmatic; but you will understand that no disrespect is intended. Let me ask that you will not permit my observations to arouse controversial spirit, but will examine them carefully and one at a time.

To premise:

The assumption which you state and imply through all your reasoning, that the single tax "is a scheme to abolish all existing taxation and substitute therefore a single tax on land values" is incorrect. This, it is true, is as far as some of those who are supporting it in its first stages are prepared now to go, but as understood and advocated by its most active supporters, it is a scheme to abolish private property in land in the method proposed in *Progress and Poverty*. Whether it will do this, or whether it will do this as easily and well as some other plan, may be debatable, but it is not fair to assume that it is a scheme which stops with the supply of existing revenues, or to imply that it looks only to substitution. For we would, and do, strive to have new taxation imposed on this principle.

Nor is it fair to put on my utterances as to the necessity of making land common property any other meaning than that intended by me and obvious in the context of those utterances or to assume that they relate to anything other than the aim of what we now call the single tax.

I do not complain of any conscious misinterpretation of my words or misuse of my propositions. For in place after place your paper shows me that you have failed to take that care in the definition and use of terms, that pains to understand primary propositions before reasoning from them, without which clear thinking is impossible. You even forget what rent in the economic sense is, and confuse it with rent in the ordinary sense; you accept unreservedly a statement of all economists of standing and then go on immediately to show that you do not understand the reason of it; you conclude as to a question of the transfer of taxation without the slightest reference to the principles which govern the incidence of taxation.

In this want of attention to fundamentals is the vice and weakness of your reasoning—the cause of inexactitudes and confusions of thought which have misled you into a very "merry-go-round."

This paper however shows me what I could not get at before, the primary confusion which in all our talks I have not been able to find, and which left me puzzled. What you now show me as to the genesis of your thought is this:

When you first read *Progress and Poverty* you accepted its teachings, (as I can now see, too hurriedly) and advocated taxing land values. It was pointed out to you that to transfer the payment of rates from tenant to landlord would make no difference to either. Without proper examination of the reasons of this, or of the limitations of the answer you had been in the habit of giving to the objection that the landlord could shift taxation, you jumped to the conclusion that what was true of such transference of rates would be equally true of all relief of taxation, and found a reason for this in the power which the control of land gives to force from those who live on it all except a bare subsistence.

This is the backbone of your theory, which you have fortified [just] as an active and subtle mind always fortifies, [but] it [also] accepts error.

Let me begin, so to speak, at the top:

Wherever I speak in *Progress and Poverty*, or elsewhere of the power of landowners to extract from the landless all except the merest subsistence it is plain, (and generally I think, by the immediate context) that I refer to that full and unlimited ownership which gives the power of absolute monopoly—the power of forbidding all use of land.

Thus were there only two men in the world land would have no value, and there would be no such thing as economic rent. But if one of these men [would] be the admitted owner of land of the world, he could extract from the other all he could produce, save the merest subsistence, and would have in fact over him the power of life and death. And so where one man, or a few men, acting in combination owned a country, [and] even with such a sparse population economic rent [would] hardly begin to arise, their ownership would (in proportion as emigration [presents] difficult[ies]), give them the power of extraction over their fellows that the master has over the chattel slave. Under such conditions you would be perfectly right. It would make no difference how taxes were imposed or whether there were any taxes or not. All would come out of what this landlord or landlords could otherwise demand.

But where there is a considerable number of landowners this full power of monopoly does not exist, and such a combination [as] would bring it out by enabling them to act as one is practically impossible.

The natural growth of economic rent does not involve this appropriation of everything. It leaves to labor individual earnings, and to superior qualities their due reward—even in invention and discovery as in the later part of your paper you admirably point out—and though constantly tending to increase with social growth, it does not, I think, ever tend by itself to crowd down wages. But where economic rent is left to individuals, then wherever social growth is going on or is anticipated, the expectation of the future increase of economic rent gives rise to speculation and forestalling which has to a certain extent the effect of combination, and which tends to force down the rent line, to absolutely reduce wages, and to bring out at least some of the powers of monopoly.

Today, in the countries with which we are concerned, there is not that concentration or combination of landownership which gives that absolute power to which I have referred in the sentences you have quoted, and which you evidently have in mind, and improved education and increased facilities of communication have greatly increased the area which it is necessary to control [and] brings out the full powers of land monopoly. The essence and fundamental power of landlordism as we are confronted with it, is its appropriation of economic rent. But our leaving to individuals such a great portion of what you and I agree is the natural provision for the community, without compelling any commensurate return, causes speculative rent to run like a shadow at sunrise, before the advance of economic rent, and enables individuals to hold out of use or at a lower use than others [who] would be glad to [make use of it, even] great quantities of land.

To take rent by taxation or the value of land would destroy all the power there is in landownership as we know it for its pressure would force competition between landowners, and destroy the expectation which has the effect of combination.

Consider: for you shirk this by assuming that the single tax would not go past the point of raising present revenues—what would happen if it were imposed as I would impose it, so as to take practically the whole value of ground as fast as it arose. How would, how could, landowners recoup themselves or be recouped?

And consider this. Would not even a partial application of this tax—any considerable demand by the state for economic rent, (and as is involved in the single tax, its simulacrum speculative rent) in far more rapid degree destroy speculation and break up withholding [?]

Let me now ask you to go back to the beginning as it were and reexamine your fundamental propositions as to the effect of the single tax.

To form a clear idea of the effects of taxation it is necessary to distinguish between: 1) The direct and primary effects of the tax; and, 2) The indirect and secondary effects.

It is in this first part of the subject that your fundamental errors lie. While [discussing] this I shall keep entirely out of mind the indirect and secondary effects. It is necessary first to ascertain the effects of any change, before considering the effects of those effects.

Of Direct and Primary Effects:

Let me lay before you certain propositions which will go to the heart of the matter, asking you to test them one by one.

1. Save where the full power of extraction exists, from the power of forbidding the use of any land, as previously explained, the measure of what the tenant must pay is not his ability to pay, as you assume. You may be worth ten times as much as I, but for a given piece of land as for a given house, horse or jackknife I must pay as much as you. This rent or price is fixed under conditions with which we are concerned by competition.

To say that the landlord cannot raise his rent when taxes are imposed on land values because he is already getting all he can, is true only of the landlord and of ground rent. The reason is this, that the imposition of the tax in no wise lessens the competition of ground landlords. It is not true of building [land]lords and of building rents, for the reason that taxes on buildings do check competition in buildings.

The distinction is the same as between a tax on incomes and a tax on imports. A merchant would have to pay the one because it would in no wise check the competition that limited his prices and so enable him to raise them.

Thus a tax on land values, falling on all land, used or unused, must be paid by the owner; but a tax on buildings or other improvements must be paid by the user. So a tax on land conditioned on the use of land is virtually a tax on use and must be paid by the user.

2. It makes no difference who first pays a tax, the difference is in its incidence, or as to who must be the last payer. If I buy goods in bond, paying the duties myself, or if I buy them clear of duties from the importer, makes no difference. In one case I pay a lower price, in the other a higher price, but in either case I pay the duties.

So it makes no difference whether the user or the owner pays taxes on land and improvements—a tax on land values in no wise checking the competition in land, must fall on the landowner, no matter who first pays it; while a tax on improvements, checking the competition in improvements, must finally be paid by the user, no matter who first pays it.

In the United States the real estate tax, the equivalent of your rates and taxes is collected from the owner. But it would make no difference either to tenant or owner if it were collected from the tenant, as he would pay that much less rent. So in Europe, if the owner paid the rates instead of the tenant, the tenant would pay so much more rent.

The American tax is not conditioned on use, but is assessed on land and improvements irrespective of use. That part, therefore, which is assessed on the improvements falls on the tenant, (or to speak more exactly on the user) and that part which is assessed on the value of the land, on the owner—no matter from whom they are collected.

But your English rates are conditioned on use, and therefore fall on the tenant (or rather user) whether collected from a landlord or from a tenant.

3. But while the landlord could recoup himself in increased rent, if the payment of rates, assessed as now, were transferred from the tenant to him, he could not recoup himself if these rates were abolished, and in their stead a tax on land values, irrespective of use were levied. For a while he would have to pay the tax he would be unable to increase his rent, since a tax on land values imposes no check on the production and maintenance of buildings and the use of land.

The building and land to use being now furnished for a certain sum, with the tenant paying the taxes, would continue to be furnished for that sum, and the taxes being abolished.

Or to take the American case: I pay $1,000 per year for 327 E. 19th Street, my landlady paying the taxes. If the English plan was adopted and I was called on to pay the tax presently assessed, I would pay to my landlady only such a sum of the tax that would make $1,000. But if the taxes on buildings were abolished and the tax on the value of land commensurately increased I would not continue to pay $1,000 per year. For the competition of capital in furnishing buildings would enable me to get the same sort of building for a lower rent, while the competition in land being undiminished I would have no higher ground rent to pay.

The principle is the same as in the case of duties previously supposed. The abolition of the duty would not affect the price of goods sold in bond—the importer could get no more and the purchaser would simply be exempt from the payment of duty he has now to make; and where goods are sold duty paid, the price would be lowered to the extent of the duty.

4. Your distinction between taxes according to the application of revenue derived from them is not good and will not hold.

Whether a revenue raised by import duties would be thrown into the sea, expended in a useless navy, or used for production works, may make much difference in the prosperity of the country, but none in the incidence of the tax. In any case the consumers of the goods must pay it.

5. Your distinction between existing expenditure and fresh expenditure is possibly worse. Consider this:

Here are four countries, alike in all other respects, except that at present:

Country A, (we will suppose) has no taxes and no expenditure.

Country B by general taxation, raises £1,000,000, which is spent for police.

Country C raises £1,000,000 for police and another £1,000,000 for a navy.

Country D raises these two millions, and in addition £1,000,000 for schools.

Next year all four countries decide to come up to the same standard of expenditure to that of D, and to raise this by a tax on land values.

Do you mean to say that in that case, of the four million raised in each country by the same tax—

In country A the landowners must pay the whole four million.

In country B the landowners will only pay three million.

In country C the landowners will only pay two million, and

In country D the landowners will pay nothing at all.

Yet my dear friend, it is precisely this preposterous thing that is involved in your assumption.

6. That the benefit of remitted taxation cannot be retained by the tenant is not the other side of the truth that the burden of a land value tax cannot be shifted by the landlord, it is part of the same truth, resting on the same reasons. Taxes on land values cannot be shifted, because they in no wise check the offering of land for use. But taxes on buildings, etc., can be shifted, because they check competition in offering for consumption of use.

It is only as user that the tenant can get the benefit of the remitted taxation you are speaking of, just as it is only as consumer that the first purchaser of imported goods can benefit by the remission of the duty, then reasons [would arise] which would compel the importer to pass the benefit on to him, compelling him to pass it on to consumers.

In all this I have contented myself with the assertion of the negative, that a tax on land values would not check the competition in offering land for use, and would therefore give the landowners no power of raising their prices or rents so as to recoup themselves for the tax. But something more than this is true, the tax on land values would increase this competition, by making the withholding of land more costly and difficult. As a matter of fact the abolition of taxes on buildings and the transfer of taxation to land values would not merely reduce what the tenant has to pay for the building, but it would to a considerable extent, or perhaps rather, over a considerable area, reduce ground rent.

7. There is evidently in your mind the idea that though the single tax might have the effect at first of forcing unused land into use, and thus for a while open opportunities to labor, yet this effect would cease in a very short time when all land came into use.

This idea will I think disappear when you consider that there is no fixed point in the use of land, but that the use that can be made of land is constantly increasing with social growth and development. When you consider this, it is clear that the potency of the tax on land values in opening land to labor by forcing its use, does not stop with the bringing of all land into some kind of use; but would constantly continue. For as social growth brought out the possibility and the need of higher uses, so would the value increase and the added tax force to such use, by imposing a virtual fine upon holding it for lower uses.

Let me call your particular attention to this, as it is essential to an understanding of what we expect from the single tax.

Of Indirect and Secondary Effects:

Here we come to your "golden error," if I may apply your favorite term to truth confused with error or apprehended out of place. . . .

It is true as you see, that the transference of taxation to land values would add to economic rent, but this is [not] true in the way you see it. It would be an indirect and secondary effect, not a direct and primary effect. It would arise from the greater prosperity which the transference of the tax would cause, not from the transference of the tax itself.

It would be ultimate, not immediate; not taking place at once as you assume, but requiring an interval of time sufficient for the advantage to attach locality, and the competition for the use of that locality to be brought out. During this time the advantage would go to labor not to rent, and insofar as what I may call speculative and monopoly rent were checked, the advantage would remain with labor, since to this extent what would ultimately be taken from labor would consist only of economic rent.

And it is here, through the effect on the general prosperity, that the difference to landowners between throwing away the revenue raised by a tax on land values and using it productively comes in.

It is true that all taxes come out of rent, in this sense—that everything which diminishes prosperity lessens rent or prevents its increase. Taxes on land values take directly from economic rent without lessening its amount, and to all other taxes I think it may be said sweepingly that they diminish prosperity and thus diminish rent or prevent its increase.

To recapitulate:

The result of any tax on land values is to take for public uses a greater or less part of the fund that otherwise goes to the mere owners of land, and this without regard to whether the proceeds of the tax are used to remit existing taxation or for fresh expenditures. Nor is there any way in which landowners can get back what is thus taken.

But the increased prosperity that would follow will have as a secondary effect, the increase of rent. There is no necessity for me to dwell upon this tendency of rent to increase with improved social conditions, for you fully appreciate it—its possibilities really transcend imagination.

With any partial application of the single tax, the diminished proportion of rent left to landowners would tend to become ultimately an increased amount, and if the single tax [were to be] restricted for providing present revenues, [it] would ultimately give the landowners who could hold on (for mere speculative and monopolizing landholders would in the process be shaken off) more than they get at present.

But, observe, that this result will not only require time; but would only be reached by the increased prosperity, by this improvement in social conditions, and that the diminishing, if not the destroying of speculation by restricting rent payments to economic rent, would leave to labor the natural reward of individual exertion.

While we ought to go ahead, as the single tax scheme proposes that we should go ahead, to the point of taking the whole economic rent, each step in the single tax scheme would give a clear gain and a firmer basis for a new advance. Each step would weaken resistance, for the power of expectation would be lessened, and it would take an interval of time before the diminished proportion left to landowners would be increased and prosperity become equal in amount to what they had before. The improved conditions would give to the masses greater desire for social reform and increased power to secure it.

The Single Tax and Land Nationalization
Whether, carried to the ultimate taking of the full economic rent, the single tax or land nationalization would be the best method, I will not now take time to discuss.

The practical question is which affords the easiest line of advance towards that ultimate [goal].

Either method must be a gradual one. You cannot nationalize the land all at once even were you to be willing to buy it. You must do it as you evidently contemplate doing it, here a little and there a little, as in Birmingham.

Now the overwhelming advantage of the single tax method is that it checks speculation and monopoly, and produces a general effect on landholding, while it dispenses with compensation.

The objections to purchase or compensation I have dwelt on at such length in *Progress and Poverty* and elsewhere that I will not speak of that now. But in buying land piecemeal, as in Birmingham you would not be checking speculation in other land, but on the contrary would be encouraging it. And just as with such operations as in Birmingham you add to the beauty of the city or augment public resources you add directly and immediately to the value of the other land which you must buy in the future. Such local and piecemeal measures would produce no affect on the general conditions of labor.

The methods of taxation by which the bulk of our present revenues are raised cost enormously, taking from the people much more than they return to the treasury. Therefore, while I would resort to a tax on land values for new expenditure, and even urge new expenditure for the purpose of popularizing this tax, the greatest relief to the people would be I think by the remission of such existing taxes.

And existing taxation is, (something seen more clearly in other English-speaking countries than in England) greatly corrupting and demoralizing. Now all true and lasting reform, must be at bottom moral reform, and therefore the simplification of government and the doing away with the corruption and demoralizing habits of thought as well as action which the substitution of taxes on land values for shiftable taxes would cause is of enormous importance to my mind. Land nationalization, as you propose it, would on the other hand add to the complexity of government, and under present conditions at least give rise to great corruption. This too may be clearer in the United States, in Canada, or in Australia than it is to you in Birmingham; but I would call to your mind the prices that have been paid by English cities for the land they have bought, the extravagant prices paid by railways, etc.

But the great advantage which the single tax has over land nationalization is that it consorts better with all the traditions and habits of thought of our English-speaking peoples, and enables us to avail ourselves of forces which the scheme of land nationalization cannot enlist.

The proof of this is in what we are doing today in the United States where the dissatisfaction with existing taxation is being pushed by the infusion of the single tax idea not only into a demand for absolute free trade, but into single taxism. The Reform Club of this city [New York] which was originally started by men most bitterly hostile to us, and which is today the most efficient political propaganda organization in the United States is now completely controlled by single tax men, and is doing our work. You may see the same thing in the case of the Financial Reform Association of Liverpool. . . . I have from the very first repeated again and again my conviction that we must expect to carry all the steps in our program up to the last by the aid of men who at the time do not propose to go a step further.

I will now not go into the questioning of interest of such minor points. If this, as I hope it may, will put you on the way to see the true bearings and reasons for the single tax, it will at least bring us into practical harmony.

For even if you continue to think the formal ownership of land the best ultimate method of asserting the common right, you will then at least see this, that it is by the single tax that the point where that can be practically effected can be most easily reached.

I would like to ask you to reread *Progress and Poverty*, for though I have tried to throw this into different form and language you will find all that I have stated here substantially [written] there. And I especially ask you not to go a step further until you clearly see what rent is. [In] truth I think that in trying to understand the socialists, you have confused yourself, which I don't wonder. The truth is that they do not understand themselves. As for Karl Marx, he is the prince of muddleheads.

Letter, "My Dear Sir"[14]

In accordance with your request, I beg to state what method of inquiry seems to me desirable and practicable upon the basis of the resolutions which you left with me. I quite agree with you that the field of inquiry suggested by these resolutions is so wide that you could only undertake to deal with a small part of it.

In making an investigation upon any of these subjects, it would be advisable to take at least one entire county; and it would be very desirable to cover the field in an entire State. The latter would probably be impracticable for your department at present; but you could probably take a few counties in the Eastern and Western States, including some rural counties for the purpose of comparison.

The inquiry which I would suggest would cover:

1. The value of land, exclusive of improvements.

2. The total amount of taxation now levied within each district where the value of the land is ascertained.

3. The probable amount of federal taxation which would be imposed upon the district, in case a direct tax were levied.

4. The probable amount of federal taxation actually collected in the district under the present system of indirect taxation.

In ascertaining the value of land, it would of course be necessary to determine the market value of both improved and unimproved lots at the price which they would fetch, if the existing buildings and improvements were cleared off. This is easy enough in the case of a city or town, but not so easy in the case of farmlands. Of course, all buildings, including barns, and all fences, drains, etc., should be excluded; but the value could not be justly ascertained by taking the selling price of an entire farm and then deducting the cost of these improvements, because the improvements themselves are often misplaced and are almost worthless, though expensive. The true test of value would be the estimated fair price of unimproved portions.

There is scarcely any farm which does not include a considerable amount of unimproved land; but, if such exceptional farms should be met with, a fair basis for appraisal would be the price which could be obtained for a highway running by or through such a farm, if it were thrown into the farm and used for general farm purposes. In preparing returns of the cost of government, as represented by local taxation, the principal items of such cost should be separately stated, as for example, the support of highways, of schools, of jails, etc., the object being to classify public expenses in such a manner that students of your statistics could decide for themselves whether some of these items of public expense could or should be raised by state or county taxation, instead of taxation upon the town or village.

I would further suggest that a county in Massachusetts, another in New York, two in Ohio, and a county here and there in Illinois, Iowa, Wisconsin, Minnesota, and Dakota [Territory] would probably afford a fair basis for these preliminary researches.

Different Interpretations of the Single Tax[15]

During my absence in Europe an able and interesting series of articles by Thomas G. Shearman, meeting certain objections made against the single tax, has been published in *The Standard*. These articles furnished what basis there was, beyond sheer misquotation and misrepresentation, for the notion that *The Standard* had changed its course, and was endeavoring to lower the aims of the movement.

I have sufficiently spoken of this notion and the effort to diffuse it. I wish now to speak of some questions brought up by these articles, and to some extent debated among our friends.

Among the letters received by *The Standard* have been a number debating, and some of them with much ability, the question whether our aim should be to take all, or something less than full economic rent. But as there were some misapprehensions, and as the discussion was largely as to what I held, I have preferred not to give them place until I could say something myself.

Among these communications was one, dated July 19, from the secretary of the Central Single Tax Club of Cleveland, Ohio, enclosing the following resolutions passed by that club:

> Whereas, the question having arisen among single taxers as to the advisability of permitting the holders of land titles to retain a percentage of the economic rent, not to exceed one-tenth, as compensation for collecting said economic rent; therefore be it
> Resolved, that we, the Central Single Tax Club of Cleveland, Ohio, do most emphatically assert our adherence to the principle of taking the entire economic rent for public uses, and protest against anything having the appearance of a compromise with landlordism; and that a copy of these resolutions be sent to *The Standard* for publication.

I, too, would like to take the entire economic rent. But I wish the Cleveland Club had added another resolution explaining how they propose that it shall be done, for it is here that the difficulty comes.

But first as to Mr. Shearman:

Whatever percentage of economic rent he may think will suffice for the necessary expenses of government, he is as good a single tax man as those who wish to take it all. He is for the one single tax, or to speak more precisely, for levying all taxes on one single source of revenue—land value. If that does not constitute a single tax man, what does? In fact it was as a title for the first of his tracts we published, that the term "the single tax," which has been since so generally accepted by our friends, was first used in connection with the movement.

It was I who first used the terms "single tax limited" and "single tax unlimited," which have lately been so much employed. I did so in a speech in New York, some time during last year, in referring to the two sets of men who were working together harmoniously for the single tax—the one with the idea of substituting that means of raising revenue for those now employed, and the other with the idea of not stopping at that, but going further and taking as near as might be the whole value of land for the uses of the community. I spoke, if my memory serves me, of Thomas G. Shearman and John DeWitt Warner[16] as representatives of the single tax men limited, and of myself as a single tax man unlimited. But I went on to say that for practical purposes there was no difference between us, and that the men who only proposed to substitute the single tax for existing taxes were capable of doing as good work for the cause in its present stage as we who, when the time came, proposed to go further.

I then heard no objection to this from the gentlemen who since they have become so suddenly stricken with yearnings for the company of socialists and anarchists have come to look on single tax men limited as protectors of landlords, and schemers to degrade the movement into a "soulless, conscienceless fiscal reform." Nor in speaking so was I departing in the slightest from my original position, or making any bid for an alliance with a political party. I was but repeating what I had said at the first, and had always said, that we must win and would win our decisive battle by the aid of men not at the time willing to go the whole length we wished to go.

In *Progress and Poverty*, book VIII, chapter II, entitled "How equal rights to the land may be asserted and secured," I say:

> We have weighed every objection, and seen that neither on the ground of equity nor expediency is there anything to deter us from making land common property by confiscating rent.
>
> Now, insomuch as the taxation of rent or land values must necessarily be increased just as we abolish other taxes, we may put the proposition into practical form by proposing—
>
> *To abolish all taxation save that upon land values.*

Is it not this that Mr. Shearman proposes to do? So far from having lowered "the pure white banner of the movement" by gladly welcoming to the columns of *The Standard* Mr. Shearman's able articles, or approving of the exclusion from its columns of ranting and misrepresenting attacks upon "Shearmanism," I would have been inconsistent with all I have ever written or declared if I had failed to greet and to treat the single tax men limited as honored coworkers. Nor in drawing the line, as I did, between the single tax men limited and the single tax men unlimited, was the thought in my mind that of differentiating the men I represented from those not willing to go so far. It was that of relieving such men from the idea that in working with us for the single tax they were committing themselves to our whole program. My thought was not merely to assure such men of our understanding on this point, so that they might the more readily join us, and work with us, but to let others understand it.

For there are large classes on whom the advocacy of men who do not go the whole way exerts more influence than that of men who do.

If I may be permitted to offer advice to the Cleveland Single Tax Club, it would be to hold their own individual opinions, but to rescind their resolution at the next meeting. It is a mistake for them to put anything in the way of any limited single tax man joining them. And if they can get any limited single tax man like Thomas G. Shearman it would, in my opinion, be a mistake for them to try to make a single tax man unlimited out of him, if they could. When one dog gets another to help him catch hares, he does not insist that he shall follow in his track. On the contrary the two dogs take somewhat different paths. And they catch more hares because of their divergence.

To insist, if that were possible, that all advocates of the single tax should see the truth at precisely the same angle and to precisely the same extent, and should present it in precisely the same way, would be very stupid. "So many men, so many minds." And the mind that may be impervious to one method of approach is often open to another. As St. Paul saw, mental digestions that may reject the strong meat of the word may receive the milk with avidity. . . .

The only theoretical point worth discussing is as to how near the taking of the whole of economic rent it would be possible [to put into] practice. . . .

This is a point on which I have never been clear. Nor do I think that anyone at present can say with anything like precision how near we may be able [to do so for] public purposes. This uncertainty arises not merely from the fact that we have not had experience to guide us, but also from the fact that the conditions of society and habits of thought must be greatly changed in the greater freedom and better material conditions that must result from the more moderate applications of the single tax principle. I am convinced that with public attention concentrated on one single source of public revenues, and with the public intelligence and public conscience accustomed to look on the payments required from that, not as an exaction from the individual, but as something due in justice from him to the community, we could come much closer to taking the whole of economic rent than might seem possible at present. Yet I regard it as certain that it must always be impossible to take economic rent exactly, or to take it all, without at the same time taking something more [and encroaching on what should be justly left to] the individual. If the members of the Cleveland Club will attempt to formulate any plan for taking full economic rent, no more, no less, they will find that they can no more do it than they can draw a theoretically true circle, or make a line that will fulfill the geometrical definition. Theoretical perfection pertains to nothing human. The best we can do in practice is to approach the ideal. And the best the members of the Cleveland Club or anyone else could do in this regard would be to formulate some plan that should take *about* the whole of economic rent—that is to say, which should compensate for taking something too much from some individuals by taking something too little from others.

But would they consider that the taking of too much from some individuals would be fairly compensated for in this way? Would they not, rather, when they came to think of it, regard such compensation very much as they would regard the cutting out of a coat or a pair of boots, on the principle that undue tightness in some places should be compensated for by undue looseness in others—or the administration of justice on the theory that the conviction of innocent men compensated for the escape of guilty men? Would they not in this case, just as they would in the case of a coat or a pair of boots, or the administration of justice, prefer that the errors should be on the safe side? And would they not deem the safe side, the side of the individual? Is it not better that the state should, on the whole, get something less than its exact due than that individuals should be compelled to pay more than they ought to be called on to pay? If so, we must in any case leave a margin.

This I have always seen. What that margin should be I have never attempted to formulate, and have never put it at ten per cent or at any other per cent. What I have always stated as our aim was that we should take the whole of economic rent "as near as might be."

As we advance in the application of the single tax, speculative land values will rapidly disappear, and land will become less and less valuable to the mere owner, while remaining just as valuable to the user. Mere landlords will thus steadily tend to disappear, and land users will tend to become owners. Or rather they will tend to become nominal owners, for while they will retain that security of possession and that power of transferring possession that now attaches to ownership, the state, in taking a larger and larger proportion of the value, will in greater and greater degree make the whole people the real owners. But we shall steadily and rapidly approach the point when there will be no landlords in the strict sense—that is to say, no landowners drawing rent from land users for the use of land alone. Landlords we will continue to have in the colloquial sense, and must continue to have them so long as there are people who travel and who wish to stay in hotels for longer or shorter times, so long as there are some people so situated that they prefer to hire rooms by the week or month or houses by the year, or to use buildings or other improvements that they do not care to, or are not able to buy outright. These "landlords," as they are called—though economically they are both landowners and capitalists at the same time—will in their charge for the use of the buildings or other improvements, also collect from these transient land users a rent for the use of valuable land, and this the community will take from them again as "nearly as may be," in the tax on land values. These are the landlords that Mr. Shearman doubtless had in his mind when he spoke of the necessity of landlords to the collection of rent by the state.

Now, when we get within appreciable distance of the point of taking all economic rent, how are we to continue? This, though now purely a theoretical question, will then become a practical question, for if we strive to go to the point of theoretical perfection—that of taking the whole economic rent, the selling value of land would disappear, and we should no longer have the same basis for making the assessment of land that we have had [for such a long time]. Three courses would be open to us:

1. We might simply shift our assessment from the selling value of land to the using value of land, which would remain though the selling value by reason of the single tax should disappear.

2. We might assume on the part of the community the formal ownership of land, and let it out from time to time to the highest bidder.

3. We might stop short of attempting to take the full value, and leave such a small margin to the owner or holder as would give a selling value by which to assess.

Taking everything together and judge as well as one can judge at this distance from conditions that will prevail when this question becomes a practical one, it seems to me that the last course would be the best. It has many advantages, and the only objection that I can see to it is that in this way we could not collect the full amount of economic rent.

But this disadvantage also attaches to other plans. It must, in fact, in greater or less degree attach to any plan that will not be open to the opposite, and, as it seems to me, more serious danger, of taking more than economic rent.

The first plan is by no means impracticable. For it is the estimate of the use value or expected use value of land that always determines its selling value. But to ascertain the use value of land under conditions in which selling value has disappeared and the only letting or transfer of the possession of land is with improvements, would necessitate the fixing on each piece of ground of a judicial assessment of rent with little to guide it but public opinion. We should not only lose that quick appreciation of values which comes with the enlistment of individual interests, but though public opinion might be greatly improved in this respect, it seems to me that the natural disposition to be on the safe side with regard to the individual, and to be slow about increasing rents where there is no tangible change in values, would result in leaving a considerable uncollected margin—probably as much, and possibly more, than it would be necessary to leave under the third plan.

As to the second plan, there are very serious objections in my mind to the formal assumption of ownership of land not needed for community uses, and to the letting out of land by lease. But without entering into those which relate to the increased complexity of administration and dangers of collusion and corruption, this mode of treating land would certainly engender speculation. The shrewd or fortunate bidder would make money by getting land at a rent that during the terms of the lease would be less than the economic rent, and the too sanguine or less fortunate bidder would lose. But on the whole, would not the margin be against the community, and the failure to get the whole of economic rent be likely to be at least as great as though the third plan were adopted?

But this question of how we can come nearest to taking the whole of economic rent is not merely at present only a theoretical question—it is a question on which all of us will have more light as we advance further on our road. That road stretches before us for a long distance clear and plain. Whatever we may deem it best to do when we have carried the single tax to . . . the next step when selling values will vanish, what we have now to do is to get the single tax instituted—to abolish all taxation and save that upon land values. There is enough work with this to call forth all our energies.

And it is also well to remember that the great benefit of shifting taxation onto land values, and appropriating at least all but a small fraction of economic rent, is [beneficial for] the great fund which it will give for public uses without hampering industry or taking from anyone what his labor or his thrift entitles him to have. It is in setting free productive forces and securing equitable distribution, by destroying land speculation and monopoly; [which will open] to labor its natural and necessary field by removing the restrictions now imposed on production and exchange. No little margin that we may have to leave to landholders by reason of the impossibility of attaining theoretical perfection through human laws and agencies can prevent us from securing these advantages.

"George in Australia: The Single Tax in Adelaide"[17]

. . . A question from the audience.
If the single tax in its entirety were to be carried out tomorrow morning before breakfast would you compensate the man who had the day before invested the hard earnings of a lifetime in land?

Mr. George would not. If the single tax were to be carried out tomorrow, that man should certainly have some little inkling today that it was coming. (Applause) If he were fool enough to invest his money in that way they would agree with him he deserved to lose it. That was not a flippant answer; it exemplified a principle. What would be the consequence if they did so? Wherever they proposed to compensate the people land speculation would go on right to the very verge, and speculative land values would be allied right along. If they proposed not to compensate anybody the consequence would be that the prudent would discount it, and instead of there being a steady advance on land values and in speculation there would be a steady decline. Surely in this country and any English-speaking countries the people have sufficient notice as to when it would be adopted.

"Lecture in Birmingham, England"[18]

... Don't be afraid of opposition: opposition is a good thing. (Applause) Oppositions! Why men who oppose a truth do more to forward it than they can who are its advocates. (Applause)

I was in Cardiff the other day, and went into some Turkish baths there as soon as I got into town; and when we were sitting in the bath—you know how it is in those places—the men got talking about this American Henry George, who had come to talk to them—that he preached confiscation and robbery and thievery—and they said they hoped people would not go to hear him. The Americans were all a set of liars. (Laughter) And as I chipped in; and I said "Yes, all excepting the Canadians" (renewed laughter), and then I just went and I stood up for the landholders and said there had been a lot of growling, and one thing and another. Well, in ten minutes they were howling confiscators. (A laugh and applause) I am not going to go over abstruse questions of political economy tonight. (A voice: "Why not?") Because I haven't time (applause); I am only going to talk for an hour, then you may choose to ask me questions. I am willing to argue the question from any standpoint with any individual—as a matter of political economy, as on the historical side or as a matter of expediency or any other way—and I am to speak, I believe, in this town hall of yours before I leave England (applause), and if there are any of those gentlemen who want to come up and argue that question with me I am very willing to meet them. (Applause) It may be argued in a great many different ways, but I prefer the ground that its opponents have taken, the ground of justice. (Hear, hear) I believe that justice is the supreme law of the universe (hear, hear), and if any man will show me in anything I have advocated that which is unjust I will retract it there and then. (Applause) I have received a great many letters and a great deal of personal advice, urging me not to say anything about this matter of compensation. But it is the very heart of the question (hear, hear), and it can not be avoided. [People] say nationalization of the land is impossible, simply because compensation is impossible. They tell you, of course, you cannot think of nationalizing the land, of resuming your birthright without compensating the present owners, and that of course would saddle you with a debt two or three times as great as your public debt. There is a great deal of divergence of opinion upon this matter of compensation, and I attach no importance to this divergence. I am ready to argue with any man, no matter how far he goes.

There are some, like my friend Walker here, who are thoroughgoing compensators. Compensate the landlords, they say, after you have nationalized the land. There are others who say that the landlords ought to be compensated first and the land nationalized afterwards. Then there are others, like Miss Taylor,[19] whom I heard last night lecturing for the Land Nationalization League, that insist upon compensation; and Miss Taylor insisted very earnestly upon compensation—at least upon compensation to the men who could show that they had, by the earnings of their labor, paid somebody for the land. (Applause) What Miss Taylor proposed in the ways of compensation was this: She proposed that the landholders of England should pay up, with interest and compound interest, all the back taxes at 4% on the pound from the time of Charles the Second[20] (laughter and applause); and then she said that part of this money should be used to reimburse the people who had bought land with the fruits of their own labor. (Hear, hear) Then there are other compensators. Why, a clergyman of the Established Church in the West of England the other day was telling me that he met another clergyman of the Established Church in a railroad train, and they got talking about this matter, and the clergyman No. 2 said that he was opposed to George because he did not advocate compensation and they got talking for a while. The clergyman said, compensation is justice; but, come to find out, the men he wanted to compensate were the men who had been deprived all their lives of their rightful share in the land. (Laughter and applause) I am concerned only with the principle, and it is a wide principle. It not only goes to the heart of the land question; it goes further and to other things—can we not abolish the wrong without paying those who have profited by the continuance of the wrong? (Hear)

Now, to give an example—. . . as it goes into the tariff question. They say, here all over the United States "Manufacturing industries have been established under this tariff; they have invested their capital. It would be compensation to suddenly abolish the tariff. You must keep up a tariff. You are in honor bound to keep up a tariff. You are in honor bound to keep up a tariff for a long time—to let them slide quietly out." That I absolutely deny. (Hear, hear) I take my stand on the tariff question. As I have told audiences over there, so far as I am concerned I want it utterly abolished at ten o'clock tomorrow morning. (Laughter and applause) When men will go to Congress and lobby and bribe and logroll to put on a tax upon the consumers of the nation by which they selfishly profit, I will not admit that they have any rights. (Hear, hear) And, further than that, I believe it would be the quickest and the easiest way to read just matters.

This long, lingering dragging out of justice is bad on all sides. If you are going to do a thing do it quickly and be done with it. Now the trouble about compensation is this: I really cannot see any way of compensating for an injustice without to a greater or less degree continuing that injustice. (A Voice: "Prove it to be an injustice.") If you propose to pay to the landholders all that their land is worth, what benefit is it going to be to the nation? We should die and our children would die before we see it. It is substituting one tax for another. (Hear, hear) And if you propose to take anything at all from the landlords why not go to the full extreme (laughter and applause): "It is as well to be hung for stealing a sheep as for stealing a lamb." (Laughter) This thing of compensation has been carried to an absurd length. Here, because Charles the Second or Charles the First[21] or some other of your monarchs dead centuries ago (a laugh) settled a perpetual pension—upon some of his panders (hear, hear) or some of his flunkeys, you have held here that people cannot stop paying that unless they buy 'em off. ("Oh") Why, look at the rotten boroughs. In Ireland when the Irish Parliament was abolished the men who made merchandise out of the law making powers who hold their election year after year were compensated for it. (Hear, hear) You compensated too the West India slave holders when you abolished slavery and instead of doing a good thing it seems it was that you did a bad thing—an evil thing that has strengthened slavery all over the world. (Hisses and applause) A thing that led our people in the United States to believe that slavery would never be abolished without compensation and that kept the price of slaves up to the highest pitch until the war had actually commenced.

I do not believe in compensation because I believe in the sacred rights of property (oh, oh)—because I do believe in the command "Thou shall not steal." (Applause) I believe that the right of property lies at the very foundation of the social order and that no community can be prosperous or any state secure when the right of property is denied, and the heaviest indictment against the present state of things is that it is a denial of the right of property. (Hear, hear) What is the right of property? From what does it spring? Is it not, as Adam Smith says, that the first and most sacred rights of property is the right of a man to himself and to the produce of his own labor (hear, hear); and is not a system which takes from laborers the produce of their labor and puts it in the hands of men who do nothing whatever to earn it—is not that system a denial of the first and most sacred right of property. (Applause)

Why, you have only to look around and see it. Here is this flourishing town of yours. You have a great landlord named Lord Calthorpe (hisses and applause), a man, I believe, who never comes to the town from year to year, yet who draws from it yearly an enormous sum. For what? For land that existed before he was, before any of you were, before our race was—for land that will exist long after he and we are dead and gone. Where does that wealth come from—that money, as we call it? It comes necessarily from the working men of Birmingham. (Applause) Here you have another family, I am told, who owns land in the center of the town, land that has gone up within some years past in some places twelve thousand per cent. What made it go up? It was not something that his family did, who don't live in Birmingham, but what you men of Birmingham did. The rents that men draw are so much taken from your property (applause), so much confiscation that goes on year by year. (Hear, hear) Confiscation! Why, look at your city improvement scheme; where you undertook to improve and beautify your city, and you had not merely to buy out the landlords, if I am correctly informed, but to pay blackmail to the landlords, over and above the value of the property (applause), and today your improvements are stopped and you have awkward corners and narrow streets. Why? Simply because these "dogs-in-the-manger" sit there and say that you can't improve your city without paying toll to them. Confiscation! Why, look at the railroads of this country. According to Samuel Laing, MP, in a recent article—and he ought to be a good authority—the railroad here had to pay to landowners £50,000,000 over and above the market price of their land, for the privilege of constructing railroads that added to the value of the land that was left to the landowners over £150,000,000. (Applause and "shame") Where is the confiscation there! Today here, you men of Birmingham are complaining of your railroad rates. How can you blame the railroads when you suffer them to be robbed in that manner, when to ease off the tax upon the landowners you impose a tax upon the persons who travel. (Hear, hear) Confiscation! Why, I read in a West of England paper the other day of a place where a local railroad had been absolutely abandoned for the time, after a great deal of money had been spent, because two great landowners blocked the road. Confiscation! Why, a gentleman of this town told me that he had arranged to buy a piece of property that was necessary for him, for £1600, and when the landowners found that it was he, and that he was anxious to have it, he stuck another thousand pounds on the price. (Laughter) Confiscation! Why, down in Cardiff they told me a case where a tenant and leaseholder who had twenty years of his lease yet to run wanted to improve the house—to add to it and to put it in better condition—and a term of the lease was that at the expiration that house went to the landlord; but there was a clause in the lease that he could make no changes without the consent of the landlord, and the landlord refused to give this man permission to improve the house unless he would take a new lease, give up the twenty years yet to run and raise the rent from £5 to £50. Bah! To talk of compensation! (Laughter and applause) Well, there was another case a gentleman told me, in a Welsh town not far from there, in which a tenant wanted to make some improvements in the house, to better it and to paint it, and the landlord would not say either yes or no about it, so the tenant got tired and went to work and did it. The landlord came in, and looked over the house. He said "It looks very nice; very fine; I think you can pay a little more rent," and he did put it on and absolutely made him pay it. (Laughter) Confiscation! Why, that in Ireland has been done over and over again. (Applause) Confiscation! Why down here in Newport, near Cardiff, there is a Wesleyan Methodist Chapel, on the land, I believe, of Lord Tenderness—some such name as that. They have a lease that has yet twenty years to run. They pay £8 a year ground rent. The congregation has outgrown the size of the chapel and they wanted to make it larger; and they can't get permission to enlarge this place of worship unless they will give up their present lease and take out a new one at £100 a year. (Sensation) Talk about confiscation! (Applause) Down there in Cardiff there is a company who wanted a little while ago to build a factory on a certain piece of ground. They would have employed hundreds of men and added much to the business of the town. But they could not get a lease where they wanted it; the only way they could get that ground to build on was at a notice of three months. Of course they refused to build. Why, here in the papers the other day, at some place near here, I think, a little manufacturing town, Lord Somebody-or-other absolutely won't allow another cottage to be erected.

And look all over land on and everywhere—in every one of your cities—how this monopoly of land, by the high prices that it compels, prevents the building of houses and forces families of English people to herd together as swine. (Applause) According to Sir James Caird,[22] the increase in the rent of agricultural land—mind you, not the land of the cities and towns and mineral land, where there has been the great increase of rent, but the increase in the rest of the agricultural land—between 1857 and 1875, the increase in the value was £331,000,000, for which he estimated the landlords contributed about £60,000,000. Where did the rest come from? Created by the growth of the community. Created by you, common people of England, you common Englishmen and Englishwomen (laughter and applause), who have not a right to an inch of your own soil. An American or any other foreignor who comes over here and buys land, as one of my countrymen has in the islands of Scotland, cannot clear you out except at a preposterous price.[23]

Is it not about time that in thinking of these questions we came down to first principles? (Applause) Is it not about time that we asked who made the land (renewed applause) and how does any man get a title to it? Why, go there to London—go down to Euston Station. You find the street blocked with a fence, an iron fence—I suppose there may be many people in this audience who have lost a train by having to go around that fence or wait while a great fat fellow comes out at a snail's pace and opens it—put up and maintained by his Grace the Duke of Bedford! Why, go a little further and look at those London squares—Lincoln's Inn Fields and all those squares—squares with grass and trees and sometimes, in the summer time flowers: great high fences, gates locked and barred, and not a living soul in them, while around in the by-streets within a stone's throw you find hundreds of little sickly squalid children playing in the gutter. (Hear, hear) Heavens and earth, men! Is it not time that some missionary should come from somewhere? (Loud and continued applause) Talk about the heathen! Talk about their little brass idols or any other idols (laughter)—where are there heathen so stupid as that? Only one example I know of, and that was down in the South Seas, where there existed the custom of the taboo and where you of England and we of America send missionaries to convert men. (A laugh) These stupid ignorant subjects had such a veneration for their high chiefs that when a high chief tabooed a place not one of them dared to go on it. He might die with thirst or with hunger rather than drink at a tabooed spring or pluck the fruit of a tabooed grove. He would go round for miles rather than set his foot on a tabooed path. It was very stupid; but what have you here—all taboo. (Applause) They have land in abundance, land enough to give every family its house and its garden, while thousands and thousands of families are crowded—men, women and little children, into a squalid room. Thousands of acres you may see, as I saw when I was last in this country, lying vacant, absolutely vacant—rich land—while men all over the country are out of employment, only anxious for employment. (Hear, hear) What might labor have been doing on that land? What is that but the English form of the taboo? The truth is that vested interests ought not to stand and cannot stand before natural rights. (Hear, hear)

It is said that men bought the land. Well that is true, I think, of very little of the English land. (Laughter) Whom did they buy it from? You know as a historical fact how it was that the land of England passed from the ownership of the people into the possession of the owners. Why, it is said that before William the Conqueror brought his gang of thieves and robbers over they sat down and they had got a map of England from somewhere (a laugh), and they just mapped it out between them and not a penny of compensation! (Applause and laughter) But, bad as that was it was not private property in land. Indeed, at that time nobody among our forefathers had thought of such an absurdity. This thing of absolute individual ownership of land is only a modern thing. It only dates fully in England for two centuries back. Then the land of England was merely divided up by William the Conqueror into knights' fees and the men who had the land were the men who had to do the fighting (hear, hear); and in all the wars that the England of our forefathers waged there was not a penny of debt until you came down to the time of William the Third.[24] I won't go over the whole story. You know it—how the Church lands, appropriated for purposes of worship and education, were divided among a crowd of profligate and greedy courtiers; how the Crown lands, that under the old system maintained the Civil List, were given away to profligate courtiers; how the commons were enclosed, (hear, hear), and are—yes, even today—being enclosed. Why, a clergymen told me the other day that he went up to the estate of the Duke of Wellington and a Lord Somebody—I forget his name. He said to the gamekeeper "Why, this is a new park." "Oh, yes," the man said, "this was a piece of land that was going to waste and nobody doing anything to it, and so his Grace took it in." (Applause) They told me at Cardiff that a great part of the most valuable estate of the Marquis of Bute was a moor. There are glassworks on it now and docks, and it yields an immense rental, but it was a moor that a little while ago belonged to the town. Well, the only people who had any of the rights in that town were a body of freemen, just a handful of them, and the Marquis of Bute, the father of this one, used to give an annual dinner to these freemen, and he dined them and wined them (laughter), and finally they came to the conclusion that the land was not much use to anybody and about the best thing they could do with it would be to give it to the hospitable Marquis. And so they did. I don't know whether there was anything implied in a contract, but the understanding among them was that the dinners were to be kept up. (Laughter) My informant tells me the dinners stopped. (Renewed laughter) But the Marquis's son has the land now. Some men did buy their land; unquestionably some men did. I don't think there are many. I am curious to know how many there are who have bought their land. Now the reason you can't make the discrimination between these men who bought his land and the man who did not is simply this—that if you go to do this the men who have not bought their land will simply sell their land to somebody else. (Laughter and applause) What is the difference? The principle is well settled in law, and rightfully settled, that the purchases can get no better title than the man he purchased from has to give. Surely if a man takes a thing that is not rightly his he does not convey a title when he sells it to somebody else.

Why it is a piece of juggling. It reminds me of a story they used to tell when I was a boy about a Dutchman who used to keep a grocery store. A fellow came in to him and said: "I want to buy some crackers." The grocer weighed out the crackers and gave him the crackers. Then he said: "I have changed my mind; I would like to have some cheese. You take back the crackers and give me the cheese." He got it, and started off. The Dutchman said, "You haven't paid me." "Paid you for what?" "Paid me for the cheese." "Yes, but I gave you the crackers for the cheese." "Well, but you haven't paid me for the crackers." "Well, but I didn't take the crackers." (Laughter) Then the Dutchman said: "I know, I am out the cheese anyway; I haven't got anything for it. You will have to pay me." In the same way may the people ask, since they are out the land, what are they going to get. (Laughter) It is said that the present landholders have acquired title to their land, a valid title, by consent of the state. Who is the state in this case. (A voice: "That's the question," and applause.)

In the case of the lands of England is it the people of England or your upper House of Parliament, which is composed of men who sit there because they are landlords—your hereditary legislature? Your lower House of Parliament is largely composed of men of the same class. When since the Conquest have the real people of England had an opportunity to assert their right? (Applause) If they have not done it, why? Because they have been impoverished . . . and kept in ignorance, and because it has been preached to them, day by day, and year by year, that this order of things was the natural order of things and if they wanted to avoid hell hereafter (applause) what they had to do was to obey the powers that be. Why, if in a family to whom an estate was left, the older brothers were to simply seize it, and cut out the tongues, and put out the eyes of the younger ones, would it give them a right because these little ones made no complaint? What complaint can those poor people make from whom comes up that "bitter cry of outcast London?"[25] What can those agricultural laborers, men who must live a life of poverty and die the death of a pauper, what can they do? Why, is it not an absurd thing? Well may we ask with Herbert Spencer[26] "at what rate per annum does wrong become right?" Because a man takes my earnings today, and he had them the day before, does it give him the right to take them tomorrow? (Cheers) Why, the thing is absurd; and observe, it is not proposed to take from the landlords anything save the power they now exercise of taking the fruits of the labor of others, without giving them any recompense. (Cheers) No one I think proposes to deny to the landlords their equal share in the land of England; it is proposed to give them as much as anybody else. (Hear, hear) How can they complain of that? Now it is said that such a thing will injure the poor. Always so! Just as it was in the slavery fight when it was the poor widow that was put to the front, the poor widow who had only three or four slaves upon which she depended for a living—were we going to rob her? —it is the poor widow who is put to the front here. Speaking in St. James Hall the other night I spiked that gun[27] by proposing that the first thing should be to pay all the widows on a good round pension. Haven't heard anything of the widows since then. (Laughter and applause)

But now it is the poor working man; it is the man who has worked and toiled, and bought himself a little home. Well, now, look at that case. Here around your towns is a lot of vacant land, land only used for agricultural purposes. What taxes are paid on it? Why, almost nothing. The moment that land is cut up into little plots and houses are built upon it, then down comes the rate gatherer and [he] wants one-third or one-fourth of the rent. Is that the way to encourage the building of houses? Why, take any man—let him be a freeholder, let him own his land out and out—say nothing of a tenant but let him be a freeholder—you would take taxes off his house, you would take taxes off all he uses and consumes, and make it up with a tax on the value of the bare land; and he will necessarily be a large gainer. (Hear, hear) As a mere matter of taxation it will be money in his pocket, to say nothing of the enormous stimulus that will be given to industry and trade. (Applause) Justice hurts no one. (Hear, hear) Justice, I believe, is the eternal law. What we have to fear, as all history teaches, what we have to avoid, is not justice, but injustice. (Applause) That is the thing that brings the poverty.

I am not starting any paradox—I firmly believe it—when I say that, even considering the interests of the landlord class, the best thing is to destroy their unequal privilege and to do exact justice between man and man, to acknowledge the rights of each. (Applause) It cannot be good for any man to be placed, in wealth or in station, way above his fellows. Look at that child of four years of age who, by the untimely death of his father yesterday, is heir to an estate of millions of pounds a year. Take any boy, and let him grow up knowing that that enormous sum will come to him, and let him be surrounded by flunkeys and panders and only a miracle can make a man of him. (Loud applause) Envy the rich! I have not in any heart the slightest particle of envy for the rich. I fear poverty. I know better what it is than some of these men who talk so idly of the sufferings of poverty. I fear poverty, for it is indeed the deepest hell that man can know. (Loud applause) It is not that you may go cold and may go hungry, but that the finest feelings of man's noblest nature are cut and lacerated and seared day by day. But I don't envy the rich; and I would not be rich.

Once, when I was a young man, it was my ambition to have an income of five million dollars a year and I wanted to go round like Monte Cristo.[28] (Laughter) But bye and bye, when I came alongside of men who were rich, I learned absolutely to pity them. When I saw men coming up from the workshop or the little merchant's counter into positions of enormous wealth, I saw that they were surrounded by flatterers and sycophants, that they had constantly on their minds the care of these great fortunes, that they did not dare to believe when a man came to them and took their hand and said he liked them that he was in earnest, and when a woman smiled on these men thought she had designs. (Laughter and applause) No. The state of equality is the best state and the highest state. Where is it, from what class is it, that have come the men who have made this great English literature? The men of whom we of the English-speaking race are most proud. Have they come from the very rich? Have they come from the ranks of landed aristocracy? No, no more than from those who were ground down by poverty. No, they came from the ranks of the men, who, without having had too much to raise them above their fellows, had enough to give them leisure, and that is the condition all men ought to have. (Cheers)

Not in envy, not in malice, but in justice and in love, even to those people who think we are going to rob them, ought we to reassert, the natural inalienable rights of men, the rights of our forefathers on this island generations ago. But there are other reasons. Turn your eyes to the poor in this England of yours, to that festering mass of poverty, and misery, and vice and crime. (Hear, hear) Read the "Bitter Cry of Outcast London" and similar accounts.[29] What are you going to do with these people? Are they not your own flesh and blood? Those little children, are they not just such children, as was that child whom Christ set among his disciples, and said that it was better that a man had a millstone tied around his neck and he fling himself into the uttermost depths of the sea rather than to offend one of those little ones? (Cheers) What can you do for them? Charity! Charity will only degrade. (Hear, hear) Charity will do nothing, [what is needed is something] higher than charity . . . —it is justice. (Cheers) Charity! Why, men, did you ever think of it? I speak with all reverence but so long as the laws of the universe are what they are, it is not in the power of Almighty God to relieve that suffering, that unseeing, that starvation so long as private property in land continues (Cheers) Our record we have. You remember when the children of Israel crossed the desert, and they cried for water and Moses struck the rock with his staff and the water gushed out? What good would that water have been to the Israelites, if there had stood somebody there to say "That rock is mine"? (Hear, hear) Why, think of it. If manna were to fall from heaven upon these islands of yours what good would it do people? Who would own it? Where would it fall? It would fall on the land, and necessarily it would belong to the people. I will stop here because I have exceeded my hour. (Loud cries of "go on.") Why think of it. I am talking this way because I want to shame you. Supposing you were to get to the kingdom of heaven, and you found this system existing there, and that those who had got there first had preempted it.

What good would be the fruits of Paradise to you? Private property in land. Why it is simply a form of slavery. (Hear, hear) Necessarily and absolutely the man who owns the land or which, and from which, another human being must live is his master, and his master even to life or to death. Under the state of things which we see here, and which exists all over the civilized world, for we are imposing it on the other side of the water, on our own virgin confinement, are there not slaves? Are not the working masses of these civilized countries slaves, just as utterly as were the chattel slaves, only they do not know their particular master. (Hear, hear) When a man, without doing a thing, can draw from the earnings of the community the results of labor, when he can have a palace, and yachts, and horses, and hounds, and all the things that labor produce, is not the laborer necessarily robbed? Are not the fruits of his labor necessarily taken without any return to the man who gave the labor? Why in a paper last week, in which I read a column[-long] denunciation of myself and my proposals for "theft and confiscation," (laughter) I turned over two or three pages and there was an article headed "The White Slaves of England," in which it stated, and stated the truth, that the condition of a large section of the English people was worse than that of any chattel slaves. And so it is; no southern slaveholders would have worked and kept his negroes as white men and women and children are worked and kept in this free England. (Cheers) I will take the annals of any system of chattel slavery, and for every horror that you produce, I will produce a double horror from the files of our papers. Our missionaries do not read those papers to the heathen. (Laughter)

Every word that is now said against the demands for equal rights in land was said in defense of chattel slavery. I could take such letters as that of the Rev. Page Hopps (hisses and applause) and by simply substituting the word "slaveowner" for "landowner" I would show you precisely what just such preachers were preaching over in my country when I was a boy; when the men who dared to assert the inalienable right, the God-given right of man to his own strength and views, were called communists and destroyers; were told they were attacking the sacred rights of property, and that if those wild notions ever carried, nothing would be secure; when they were denounced in the church, ostracized in public, rotten-egged on the stump, and sometimes driven to their death. The men who were helping the negroes of the south to escape from slavery were termed thieves and robbers; not the man stealers, not the men who tore the husband from the wife, the child from the mother, but the men who would put an end to that state of things. (Hear, hear) But the truth grew and grew, and despite possession, and despite denunciation, and the talk of thievery and confiscation, there came a time when the slaveholders determining at any cost to resist, went a little too far. There came a time when the gun flashed from Charleston

Harbor, a bit of bunting flag, and a million men spring to the deathlock—and slavery was dead (cheers); died in blood, and flame and agony, died at the cost of a million of lives and millions of treasure. Why? Because the nation had done an injustice. When our declaration rang out, asserting the equal and inalienable and God-given rights of Man, our fathers did not apply it to the negroes. That was the right of property. They had been bought with money. So careful were they not to interfere with vested interests that they would not even stop the slave trade, but provided that for a term of years it should not be in the power of the Congress of the United States to prevent men, stolen from Africa, who were brought to our shores and sold as merchandise. And at length the time came, and the nation paid for its injustice. (Hear, hear)

And so, as all the history of the word shows, must men pay for injustice. There is no escape from it. I have never concerned myself with results. If I had asked whether this man is with me or against me I should never have stood here tonight. (Cheers) What is coming I do not know; but this I do know, that in the history of the world and in the providence of God, the time has come when this injustice that is eating the heart out of our civilization; when this injustice that condemns little children to a life of misery and vice, that destroys the mind and soul as well as the body, cannot possibly continue. (Cheers) The struggle has begun, and it must go on (cheers); and you men of Birmingham, you leaders of the van of Radical England be true to yourselves, care nothing for denunciation, put aside all those fears and old superstitions; ask only for what is true, only what is right, and go forward. (Loud cheering)

The chairman: Mr. George is willing to answer questions, not to have a debate.

A gentleman in the hall asked whether Mr. George was a direct advocate for plain and simple confiscation, without any compensation whatever: and if not in all cases, where would he draw the line.

Mr. George: I mean to draw no line. (Cheers) I am a believer in the absolute rights of man, I believe that every Englishman on this island has an equal right to the soil of that island. (Cheers) It is the right that adheres to every child as it comes into the world, and I would pay nothing for the resumption of it. (Cheers)

The questioner asked Mr. George whether, if he went into a shop and bought a loaf, which be afterwards found had been stolen, would he consider that loaf his property.

(A voice: It is not land.)

Mr. George: I will answer you in a word.

The questioner: I will speak to land if you like.

Mr. George: If you can understand English—

The questioner (interrupting): I ask you when I have bought and paid for land by the labor of my hand and brain, whether I am entitled to it or not.

Mr. George: Yes, whenever you can show a title from any man who had a right to give you a title (oh, oh, and cheers), from the maker of the land, or any who got the title from the maker of the land—until that time, No. (Cheers)

The questioner: Then let me tell you, Mr. George, you may go back to your Americans in America and tell them to restore the land to the red Indians. I tell you that Englishmen believe in vested rights. (Cries of order.)

The Chairman: The object of the meeting tonight is to give Mr. George an opportunity of expounding his views. Mr. George is willing to answer questions, and I therefore appeal to the audience to listen to the questions with perfect silence and then we shall hear Mr. George's answer and we shall be able to form our opinions.

A second questioner asked whether Mr. George would not approve a plan, whereby the burden of the national debt which had been incurred for the protection of the land of the landlord might not be thrown upon the shoulders of the landowners.

Mr. George: I am not here to advocate plans. Whatever plan you men of England choose to adopt, that is your own affair. One plan may be best for one country, and another for another country, but the eternal principle is the same all the world over. (Cheers) You may, if you choose, compensate your landlords, you may make up a collection for them. (Laughter) Let every man who thinks the landlords ought to be compensated, put his hand in his pocket. (Laughter and hear, hear) What I contend for is this: not one of you, and not all of you together, have a right to say that the humblest English child shall be denied its birthright until it compensated the landlords.

Mr. McClelland asked what Mr. George would do with the land in Ireland, where at the present moment the people were in favor of peasant proprietary

Mr. George: I would give the land to the people (cheers), I would form no peasant proprietary. The principle is the same whether a man holds a quarter of an acre, or a quarter of a million of acres. I care nothing for the tenant farmers of Ireland, the men I care for are the agricultural laborers. (Cheers) Elevate the condition of the whole of society; anything short of that merely divides the people into the rich and poor. Peasant proprietary is impossible. (Hear, hear) This land of England was once cut up into small estates. Only two centuries ago, historians tell us, the great majority of English farmers were owners of their own land. Where have they gone now? What is going on in the United States? The small American farmer is being exterminated; the majority of the American people do not realize that fact, but it is so. I know of farms of 60,000 acres made out of small farms. Concentration is the law of the time, and you cannot avoid it. Peasant proprietary! They have got peasant proprietary in France and there are 150,000 unemployed workmen in Paris. They have peasant proprietary in Belgium and M. de Laveleye,[30] the very highest authority, says the tenants there are rack rented even worse than in Ireland.[31] Do not stand at any of these miserable half way houses, go to the eternal principle.

A third questioner asked whether, if the land was held by the country, it would not be the duty of the government to let every acre of land at the highest rent they could get, and if so, how would the poor man be one bit the better for such a condition?

Mr. George: Unquestionably it would be the duty of the Government to rent land for the very highest price it could get. If ten of us owned a horse, and only one could ride him, would it not be the fair thing, and the only fair thing, for the whole ten of us, that that man, if he is willing to pay the highest price for the horse, should ride him? Certainly. The rent, then, would go back to the people. (Cheers) There is no harm in rent. Rent to my mind is one of the most beautiful adaptations of nature, one of those things in which a man who looks can see an absolute proof of a divine and beneficent intelligence. It is that we have perverted the good gifts of the Creator that the children's bread is tossed to the dogs. Rent rises and increases as society progresses. What does that mean? Simply this, that in the order of nature the progress in civilization should be a progress towards truer and truer quality: that the common interest of all should grow larger and larger as against the individual interest. (Cheers) I would like to ask this audience a question for my own curiosity and information. I have been told that English audiences do not, and would not, agree with me on this point of compensation to the landowners before the resumption by the people of their rights. I would put it to the vote of this audience, I want to ask you, all who stand with me, who hold that vested interests cannot stand in the way of natural rights, and that it is not necessary to buy the land from those who now hold it before the people resume their own—say aye, contrary no. (Loud cries of "aye" and "no.") I believe the ayes have it. (Loud cheers)

Letter, "My Dear Dr."[32]

... Yes; when a man's eyes are surely opened to the absurdity of private property in land he cannot look around anywhere without fresh evidence of its wrongfulness and stupidity. It may be slow at first; but the truth *must* ultimately win. . . .

Notes

1. This item appeared regularly in *The Standard* for a long duration. For the origin of *The Standard* see Barker, *Henry George*, 485–486 and George, Jr., *Henry George*, 484–485.
2. *The Standard*, Mar. 2, 1889, GR. George had at first reluctantly accepted the term "single tax," but this piece contains his endorsement of it. See George, Jr., *Henry George*, 496.
3. A school of French eighteenth-century economic thinkers founded by François Quesnay. They believed that all wealth originated from the land, therefore taxation (impôt unique) was to be on only the land. A laissez-faire approach was essential for a prosperous economy.
4. *The Standard*, May 18, 1889, GR. An outstanding example of George linking the Bible and religion with his political economy.
5. *The Standard*, Sept. 10, 1887, GR. Not only was George known for his philosophizing, but here we see him tackle detailed economics.
6. George William Curtis (1824–1892) was an author, orator, and editor of *Harper's Monthly* and *Harper's Weekly*. He was also a proponent of civil service reform, abolition, and women's rights.
7. "The Land for the People" is a pamphlet issued by the Robert Schalkenbach Foundation and reprinted here with permission. It bears the same name as the speech in the previous chapter, but the contents are different. It was an address delivered in Toomebridge, County Derry in Ireland on July 11, 1889.
8. Irish for lake.
9. Usufruct is the legal right to use and/or enjoy the fruits, property, or profits of someone else.
10. Charles Stewart Parnell (1846–1891) was an Irish nationalist leader elected to Parliament in 1875 whose agitation on the Irish Land Question led to his arrest. Economic problems and demands for autonomy were voiced by Parnell and his Irish party. His political activity with Michael Davitt led to the Land Act (1881) and he worked with Gladstone on the first Home Rule Bill (1886).
11. *The Standard*, Sept. 24,1890, GR. An example of the political application of the single tax.
12. George,"The Single Tax: What It Is and Why We Urge It" is a pamphlet issued by the Robert Schalkenbach Foundation and reprinted here with permission (pages 7–10). First published in *The Christian Advocate* in 1890. For a detailed

analysis of George's economics and their ethical considerations George R. Geiger's *The Philosophy of Henry George* should be consulted.

13. George to Thomas Walker, Sept. 25, 1890, #6, HGP. Walker was a British friend and supporter who differed on points of theory. Another example of George's ability to apply his ideas.

14. George (no date) to Carroll D. Wright; #7, HGP. Carroll D. Wright (1840–1909) was appointed by Chester A. Arthur in 1885 as the first Commissioner of the Bureau of Labor.

15. *The Standard*, Aug. 17, 1889, GR. This piece shows that George was not a doctrinaire and was willing to embrace others into the movement to achieve the ultimate goal of land equity. For his controversy with Shearman see Barker, *Henry George*, 539–541.

16. John de Witt Warner was a limited single-taxer elected to Congress.

17. *The Standard*, July 2, 1890, GR. As transcribed. For George's influence in Australia see Geiger, *Philosophy of Henry George*, 390–398.

18. Speech transcribed in the Lecture Theatre of the Midland Institute on June 23, 1884, #9, HGP. For George's influence in Great Britain see Geiger, *Philosophy of Henry George*, 406–424.

19. Helen Taylor (1831–1907) was an outspoken English advocate of woman's rights.

20. The Stuart Charles II (1630–1685).

21. The Stuart Charles I (1600–1649).

22. Sir James Caird (1816–1892) was an agriculturalist, author, and liberal M.P.

23. Possibly a reference to Andrew Carnegie (1835–1919).

24. William III (1650–1702). Son of William II of Orange (Holland), who ruled England jointly with his wife as Mary II.

25. See note 29.

26. Herbert Spencer (1820–1903) was an English philosopher who attempted to correlate natural sciences with philosophy. He was best known for applying evolution to all phenomena including mankind, a practice known as "social Darwinism." George penned *A Perplexed Philosopher* as a rebuttal to Spencer's recantation of a progressive view of the land, including a single tax, in *Social Statics* (1850).

27. An old expression probably meaning to render something useless.

28. Protoganist in the novel *The Count of Monte Cristo* by Alexander Dumas (père), (1844–45).

29. Refers to a series of articles in the *Pall Mall Gazette*, Oct. 1883.

30. Emile de Laveleye (1822–1892) was a Belgian political economist and publicist.

31. Rack rent has two definitions: Rent equal to or nearly equal to the full annual rent of a property or, in this instance, the practice of exacting the highest possible rent.

32. George to My Dear Dr. [Edward R. Taylor?], July 20, 1883, #3, HGP.

Chapter 4

On Government, Politics, and the World

During different periods of George's life the route of the politician seemed the best means to effect change. He ran and nearly won the mayoralty campaign of New York in 1886 and was less successful for Secretary of State for New York shortly thereafter. These losses made George a stronger man of ideals.

To be in political office means having to be confronted with diverse opinions and interests, which require compromise of principle. A person trying to institute reform would be hampered. But more important, there would be a loss of moral suasion. No longer would George have been seen as a symbol of rectitude, for which he was especially known. Perhaps his own sense of self-worth would have lessened. So in hindsight, his political failures may have been a blessing.

As the extracts in this section illustrate, George's views of political parties shifted. During certain moments, convinced that they awaken conscience and embody the will of the people, he felt that party politics were the proper vehicle for change. At other times, he eschewed them altogether. Even when choosing the path of politics, he varied his tactics, depending on national or state issues or the presidential candidate. Note also his denunciation of party bosses, corruption, the links of protectionism and monopoly with government, and the social and political injustice of a society that fostered the violence at Haymarket in 1886.[1]

His view of government in *Progress and Poverty* was a bit amorphous, but by the time *The Standard* appeared in 1886 it had become clearer. What George envisioned was a purified state with a scaled-down government in the sense we know it, but more akin to a benign regulative administrative body. To this end he advocated some surprising initial reforms, such as the abolition of the presidency for its monarchical power and state senates and the national Senate for their conservativeness.

His underlying world view, he continually averred throughout his life, was grounded in the finest democratic traditions of the founding forefathers, especially those espoused by Thomas Jefferson. Despite all her problems, America was sanctioned with a mission to spread these equitable and just ideals throughout the world. Her future as the beacon of freedom was not doubted.

To carry this message to the rest of the world, George traversed the Atlantic and the Pacific a number of times, and he had a pronounced influence in Australia, Ireland, and Great Britain. His letters to his wife also present a man who hungered not only for her embrace but for universal freedom. To this end, George was actively engaged in the particular problems of foreign lands, exhibiting an intimate knowledge of local affairs.

These selections testify to a man with a determined universal vision. The obliteration of tariffs and customs along with the adoption of the single tax was to be an initial stage in the transformation of mankind. It was to be a prelude for the erasure of all territorial boundaries, first among the English-speaking countries, and then throughout the rest of the world. What he envisioned was no less than a confederation of all peoples united in harmony and justice. Potentates, whether Sultans or Emperors were hindrances to a purified world order—the British Crown was not to be exempt.

Letter, "Dear Sir"[2]

You ask me whether, if the Labor Associations of New York were to nominate me for Mayor, I would accept.

My personal inclinations are to say "no." I have no wish to hold office. My hopes of usefulness have run in another line. But there are considerations which, under certain conditions, would compel me to say "yes."

I have long believed that the labor movement could accomplish little until carried into politics, and that workingmen must make their ballots felt before they can expect any real attention to their needs or any real respect for their rights—before they can hope to alter those general conditions which, despite the fact that labor is the producer of all wealth, make the term working man synonymous with poor man.

Since the question of chattel slavery was finally settled I have acted with the Democratic Party in the hope that, dead issues being buried, the living issue of industrial slavery might come to the front. The time has now arrived when the old party lines have lost their meaning, and old party cries their power, and when men are ready to turn from quarrels of the past to grapple with questions of the present.

The party that shall do for the question of industrial slavery what the Republican Party did for the question of chattel slavery, must by whatever name it shall be known, be a workingman's party—a party that shall reassert the principles of Thomas Jefferson in their application to the questions of the present day, and be democratic in aim as well as in name.

I have seen the promise of the coming of such a party in the growing discontent of Labor with unjust social conditions, and in the increasing disposition to pass beyond the field of trades associations into the larger sphere of political action. With this disposition I am in full sympathy. I see in political action the only way of abolishing that injustice which robs Labor of its natural rewards and makes the very "leave to toil" a boon—that monstrous injustice which crowds families into tenement rooms in our cities and fills even our new states with tramps; that turns human beings into machines, robs childhood of joy, manhood of dignity, and old age of repose; that slaughters infants more ruthlessly than did Herod's swordsmen; that fosters greed, begets consumption, breeds vice and crime, and condemns children yet unborn to the brothel and the penitentiary. Seeing this, I welcome any movement to carry the vital questions of our day into politics, and will do whatever I can to help it on.

It seems to me, moreover, a fitting and hopeful place for such a movement to begin is in our municipalities, where we may address ourselves to what lies nearest at hand, and avoid dissensions that, until the process of economic education has gone further, might divide us on national issues. The foundation of our system is in our local governments.

Nor is there any part of our country in which there is greater need of an earnest effort to make politics mean more than a struggle for office than in the City of New York. In this great city, the metropolis of the Western hemisphere, municipal government has reached a pitch of corruption that, the world over, throws a slue and a doubt upon free institutions. Politics has become a trade, and the management of elections a business. The organizations that call themselves political parties are little better than joint-stock companies for assessing candidates and dividing public plunder, and even judicial positions are virtually bought and sold.

With unsurpassed natural advantages, the gateway of a continental commerce, New York is behind in all else that the citizen might justly be proud of. In spite of the immense sums constantly expended, her highways, her docks, her sanitary arrangements, are far inferior to those of first-class European cities; the great mass of her people must live in tenement houses where human beings are packed together more closely than anywhere else in the world; and though the immense values created by the growth of population might, without imposing any burden upon production, be drawn upon to make New York the most beautiful and healthful of cities of the world, she is dependent upon individual benevolence for such institutions as the Astor Library and the Cooper Institute, and private charity must be called upon for "fresh-air funds" to somewhat lessen the horrible infant mortality of the tenement districts. Such parks as we have are beyond the reach of the great mass of the population, who, living in contracted rooms, have no other place than the drinking saloon for the gratification of social instincts, while hundreds of thousands of children find their only play-ground in crowded streets.

Hitherto all movements for municipal reform in New York have sprung from political "halls," or have originated with wealthy citizens whose sole and futile remedy for civic corruption has been the election of respect-abilities [sic] to office. They have aimed at effects rather than at causes, at outgrowths rather than at the root, and they have accomplished nothing radical or lasting.

It is time for the great body of the citizens of New York to take some step to show that they have a deeper interest in the government of this great city than whether this or that set of politicians shall divide its spoils, and to demonstrate their power in a way to make their influence felt in every branch of administration. And in the American city where monstrous wealth and monstrous want make their most shocking contrast is a fitting place to begin a movement which shall aim at the final assertion of the natural and inalienable rights of men.

(A movement begun by the Labor Associations in this spirit and with these aims would not be a class movement. It would be in reality a move-ment of "the masses against the rule of the classes." It would draw strength from that great body of citizens who, though not workingmen in the narrow sense of the term, feel the bitterness of the struggle for existence as much as the manual laborer, and are as deeply conscious of the corruptions of our politics and the wrongs of our social system.) In its broad political sense the term "workingman" does not refer to particular occupations, but divides those who have to work that others may enjoy, from those who can appro-priate the produce of others' work. There is and there can be an idle class only where there is a disinherited class. Where all men stood on an equality with regard to the use of the earth and the enjoyment of the bounty of their Creator *all* men would belong to the working class. "He that will not work neither shall he eat" is not merely the injunction of the Apostle, it is the mandate of Nature, who yields wealth to labor and to labor alone.

It is both the right and the duty of workingmen to turn to political action for the redress of grievances. Whatever excuse there may be for violence in countries where aristocratic political institutions yet exist and standing armies prevent expression of the popular will, here, where man-hood suffrage prevails and the people are the source of political power, the ballot is the proper means of protest, and the only instrument of reform. And it is only by its intelligent use that social disaster can be avoided.

Feeling on these matters as I have said, my sense of duty would not permit me to refuse any part assigned me by the common consent of earnest men really bent upon carrying into politics the principles I hold dear, yet before I can accept the nomination of which you speak, I wish to have it clearly shown that the workingmen of New York want me to be a candidate and will support me with their votes. I have no dread of finding myself in a minority. But enough so-called labor movements have proven [to be] fail-ures. And then they would hurt the very cause we wish to help.

Such a movement as is now proposed ought not to be lightly entered into. The workingmen of New York have it in their power to elect whom they please, and to open a new era in American politics; but to do this they must be united, must be earnest, and must have faith in themselves. Outside of the ranks of organized labor there are thousands and thousands, heartily sick of the corruption of machine politics, who would join in a movement for a principle [which would give a] fair promise of success. But without this promise of success an independent movement could not command even the votes of those who wished it well. For the majority of men, though they may applaud his nomination, will not vote for a third candidate whose election seems hopeless. Therefore, any political movement such as you propose must manifest strength at the outset if it is to prove formidable at the polls.

For this reason it seems to me that the only condition on which it will be wise in a labor convention to nominate me, or on which I should be justified on accepting such a nomination, would be that at least 30,000 citizens should over the signatures express a wish that I should become a candidate, and pledge themselves to go to the polls to vote for me. This would be a guaranty that there should be no ignominious failure, and a mandate that I could not refuse. On this condition I would accept the nomination if tendered to me.

Such a condition, I know is an unusual one; but something unusual is needed to change the habitual distrust and contempt with which working-men's nominations have come to be regarded, into the confidences that is necessary for success. It may be harder to get 30,000 signatures than with the confidence this inspires, to bring several times that numbers of votes to the polls; but unless there is in the movement earnestness enough to do hard [exertions] it is idle to enter upon the work.

With this frank statement of my views and feelings, I put the matter through you, in the hands of the conference and the Labor nominations.

"People's Politics"[3]

. . . Mr. Curtis in *Harper's Weekly* says truly that parties are not developed by following those who merely express sympathy and propose relief. This is the reason why until now, in spite of widespread and bitter discontent with social conditions, no labor party has been able to form. Mr. Curtis says truly that parties are produced by a common agreement upon an object and upon the means to attain it. If he will read the platform of the United Labor Party, as adopted at Syracuse last week, he will behold for the first time since the Republican Party was formed, a party which has come to a common agreement upon an object of the most vital importance, and upon a means sufficient to attain it. That object is the abolition of poverty—the utter doing away with that bitter strife which fills brothels, and prisons, and almshouses, and graves too short for man or woman; which sets man against man and class against class and nation against nation; which stunts bodies and cramps minds and turns generous impulses into tigerish passions; which today threatens our republic with dangers more dreadful than civil war, and is writing the words of doom upon the glistening façades of the highest civilization the race has yet attained. And the means, it is the doing of simple justice between man and man, the acknowledgment that all men have equal rights in the world into which their Creator brings them, and are equally entitled to share in all the advantages which accrue to society at large by reason of those advances and improvements which result from the general growth of knowledge, the general improvement of the arts, and the general progress of discovery and invention.

It is just because it is bound together by a common agreement upon a great object and upon the means to attain it, that the party which at Syracuse leaped into the arena of state politics is destined to grow and grow, no matter who may slink away from its standard or what powers may resist its advance. While Democrat and Republican have lost all grasp of principle; while they represent a merely selfish struggle over the spoils of office, here is a party which knows definitely what it wants, and knows how to get it; a party which will make no concessions of principle to prevent defections or to allay opposition; a party which arouses the same fervor of enthusiasm that carried men into the face of death to save the union and to free the slave; a party whose principles are an inspiring religion which gives to those who once yield to their potency a vivid realization of the fatherhood of God and a deep consciousness of the brotherhood of man. To such a party the future is given.

To all friends of the cause of the emancipation of labor and the elevation of mankind, throughout the state, the country and the world, the United Labor Party of New York gives greeting through its platform. In the Empire State of the American Union we have brought into political issue this widest, deepest question of our times; we have carried forward by a great step in the standard that can never be forced back. No matter what the old parties do or fail to do, it is around this standard that the political contest of this year must rage. New York is for the time the battle ground of the Union.

"Some Considerations"[4]

The communications received by *The Standard* with reference to the policy of presidential nominations by the United Labor Party shows great interest taken in the subject. Although among them there have been a number which assigned weighty reasons for keeping out of the contest, the majority have favored independent action. But through most of these declarations in favor of entering the national field there seems to me to run two questionable assumptions. First, that to refrain from going into the presidential contest would be to abandon the cause; and, second, that the party is a unit upon the tariff question or could ignore the tariff question.

It is natural for men who have taken an active part in organizing a party for the purpose of advocating a great principle, to begin, perhaps to a large extent unconsciously, to think that success of the party and success of the cause are synonymous. We all feel the impulse of organization, and our contests are apt to develop in us an affection for our own party and an enmity for other parties that may at times warp the judgment of the coolest. It is well, therefore, to remember that parties are but organizations of men, and are of themselves neither good nor bad, further than their policy or their conditions may attract good or bad men to them. No matter how high the supportive principle of a political party may be formed; no matter how pure the motives of the men who cluster under its banners while there is no possibility of using it for personal ends, yet, under existing political conditions, just as it advances toward success, so will corrupting influences enter into it. The Republican Party, noble as was the impulse that led to its formation, and rapid as was its growth, did not reach power without having become as thoroughly corrupt as the Democratic Party, which it displaced. And so would it be with the United Labor Party, or the Prohibition Party, or any other party. "Where the carcass is, there will the eagles be gathered together." This is no reason why we should shrink from political action, for it is only through political action that we can improve conditions which produce corruption; but it is a reason why we should always bear in mind that parties are but means to ends, and that it is not well to let either our affections or our enmities engage themselves to mere names. The men, of whom there have been several, who have written to *The Standard* that they had resolved never again to vote either a Democratic ticket or a Republican ticket are themselves, though they show it reversely, still under the influence of that spell which has been such a potent cause of political corruptions, by leading honest men to blindly follow any ring or gang who could capture the regular organization of *their* party.

What we owe fealty to is not party but principle. And for the advancement of principle we are dependent upon no party—not even upon the party we may have organized for the advancement of that principle. What is needed for the advance of a great truth like that embodied in the platform of the United Labor Party is to arouse thought, to provoke discussion, to familiarize with it the minds of men. This may sometimes best be done by bringing it directly into politics, and gathering around its standards those who are willing to cast their votes for it, no matter how hopeless may be the chance of winning an election. At other times it may best be done by refraining from direct political action, and urging on one or the other of the great political parties, or by leaving those who believe in it free to mingle with the adherents of those parties, and among them sow seeds of the truth. But at no time can the men who are bent on advancing a great truth fail to find opportunities to do so. Whether they be gathered into one party or scattered in several, the truth will compel those who see it to become its missionaries. To think the refusal of the United Labor Party to go into a presidential campaign means the abandonment of the cause of which it is an instrument, is not merely to accept the assumption that this would necessarily destroy it, but it is to assume that the organization is more than the principle, that the life of the soul depends on the life of the body. The United Labor Party might not merely decide not to go into the national field in this election—it might definitely and forever disband, without any one who had really felt the impulse of the cause abandoning the cause. Such men as Dr. McGlynn, Rev. Hugh O. Pentecost, Father [James O. S.] Huntington, Judge [James] Maguire, and hundreds of others whose names are familiar to the readers of *The Standard*, would continue to preach the truth and to find opportunities to preach the truth.[5] The tens of thousands of men and women between the Atlantic and Pacific who are now thoroughly imbued with our principles, and are working day and night as quiet missionaries in our cause, would go on with their work; our tracts would still circulate; the discussion we have started would continue, and the people whom we have already set to thinking would perpetuate the impulse and pass on the torch. We should still have our antipoverty societies and our land and labor clubs, and our friends would still continue to work in other organizations. Abandon the cause! We could not abandon the cause if we tried to. And if we could, and did, that cause would still march on and find new advocates. Every one, man, woman, or child, may do something to help forward a cause such as ours; but it has now so far advanced that all of us together could not more than delay it a little. It has passed our power to stop. . . . .

"Our Opportunity"[6]

. . . Our American system of government is not really a system of popular government in any other sense than that the people are the repositories of ultimate political power, and that as such the governing class, are quick to respond to their will whenever they can discern it. But our methods of getting at the popular will, and especially of submitting questions of national policy, are extremely clumsy and inefficient. Practically the [entire] business of government is in the hands of politicians, and as our elective and representative methods have the effect of discouraging statesmanship, these politicians as a class are men who have little concern for principle, and whose sole desire is to parcel out the offices and share in the profits of the governing business. These politicians are normally divided into two great camps or parties, and the law of conflict, the law which compels the opposition to one party to crystallize around another, make the parties who really contend with each other for the power and emoluments of office, save in rare contingencies, practically two. These parties are, by the necessities imposed by our elective system, great machines, requiring for their maintenance and efficiency, extensive and elaborate organization, much work and large amounts of money. Thus they naturally fall into the hands of politicians—the men who are willing to devote their time and money to working them—the men who make a business of this, and who expect to find their profit in it.

And the magic of the possessive case of the personal pronoun—the same tendency which disposes a man to be proud and boastful of *his* country, even though the poor disinherited creature may not have any right to use a single square inch of his country, or to stretch himself out to sleep on it, without buying the privilege from some of the class who really own what he calls *his* country—binds to parties men whose only part in them is to slavishly vote the ticket their managers present. The majority of Republicans or Democrats are such for no better reason than that by some accident they have once taken that side. They are disposed to follow their party whichever way it may go—to support what it proposes and to oppose what it opposes, because they deem it *their* party.

Now, whoever considers the nature of parties under our system of government, and the laws of their being, will see how childish it is to proclaim irrevocable hostility against the old parties because of their corruption, and to hope to purify government by supplanting them with a party of purity, or, as it is sometimes expressed, to form a new party that shall set politicians aside. Politicians are the inevitable outgrowth of our system of politics and corruption comes from general conditions which act upon all parties. No matter how high-minded and disinterested its founders, no matter how lofty its principles, no party could, under the political conditions which exist in the United States, rise to the point of seriously contesting for control of the national government without attracting or developing the same corrupt elements which exist in the old parties.

Nor yet do these corrupting influences wait for the growth of a party to dimensions which entitle it to be considered a contestant for control. When the two real contestants are closely matched, and the prize they struggle for is a great one, it becomes an object for one or the other of the great parties to control and use little parties; and though comparatively insignificant in their numbers, third parties rapidly develop a class of second rate politicians in no wise more scrupulous than those who act with and manage the old parties.

Now we single tax men—we real free traders—are as yet in a small minority. We have not even a skeleton organization, we are without the sinews of war that in our existing system are required for the necessary expenses of conducting any national campaign; we are without a powerful press, without the prestige of former victories and without support from those prejudices which bind the unthinking to a party because they have acted with it and rejoiced in its victories with the feeling that they themselves had helped to gain them.

No one among our friends is wild enough to imagine that if under existing conditions we were to enter the national campaign as an independent party we could have the shadow of a chance of getting a single electoral vote. The only thing that is urged in favor of such a policy is that by "standing up to be counted" we might get an opportunity to advocate our doctrines, and by showing that there were so many voters in the United States who would accept nothing but full free trade, induce, in succeeding elections, others to come to our standard, or one of the great parties to make a bid for our support.

But the truth is, we could not expect more than a small minority of single tax men "to stand up and be counted." All experience shows that the great majority of men will not vote for a candidate himself, [but only if they] believe he has some chance of election. The real reason why I got 68,000 votes for mayor of New York in 1886 and only 37,000 votes in the very same city in 1887 was that in the one case, owing to the pledge of votes with which I entered the contest, it was believed that I might be elected, and that in the other case not even the most sanguine could pretend that I had the slightest chance.[7] And in that election there was really nothing involved in the struggle between the old parties other than the filling of a few subordinate offices within the shadow of this year's presidential campaign. This year, what is at stake is the presidency itself.[8] And this year this presidential contest will be fought between the two great parties upon an issue that will give it an interest far exceeding an ordinary presidential election and make it one of the most strenuous and bitter contests the country has ever known. In this contest we cannot hope to have our friends, who might ordinarily do so, "stand up and be counted." The interest in the struggle of the great parties will be too intense, the issue too momentous. And whatever votes may be counted for a third party, they will hardly be those of the real free traders, the single tax men who have really seen what freedom means. When the robber trusts rally all the forces of protection, when every stump is echoing with protectionist lies and protectionist sophistries, when ignorance and prejudice and cupidity are appealed in order to "down" Cleveland *because* his election will mean a free trade victory, our real free traders, who of all men realize how false are the claims and how pernicious is the policy of protection, cannot look unconcernedly on and see protection win a victory. If a single tax candidate be placed in the field . . . the result will be, not that we will show our strength, but that our enemies will have, in the small vote cast for him, an opportunity to taunt us with the insignificance they will claim that it shows.

Now, the reason why, even if we had the organization and means to enable us to run an avowed free trade ticket, we could not expect real free traders to vote for it in the face of the contest that will be waged between the two old parties, is the reason why we *ought* not to run a free trade ticket. Mr. Cleveland, it is true, is not a free trader, but he nevertheless will in this election represent the van of the free trade fight in practical politics, just as Mr. Lincoln in 1860, though protesting that he was not an abolitionist, represented the van of the antislavery fight. And for us to refuse to support Mr. Cleveland in the coming struggle because his utterances and his position are not radical enough to express our ultimate desires, would be as impolitic and wrong as for antislavery men in 1860 to refuse to support Mr. Lincoln because he only desired to restrict little, not to destroy, the curse of chattel slavery.

When great armies contend, the immediate object for the possession of which their decisive battles are fought is generally something in itself of no moment, and the fate of nations turns on struggles to gain or hold a hamlet, a knoll, a bridge or a farm house. So the political struggles of opposing principles invariably begin with affairs of outposts, and are decided not on an issue joined to the main question, but on an issue joined to some subordinate or collateral question. It makes no difference how small the immediate point may be, so long as it is sufficient to arouse and engage the opposing forces. A proposition to put on the free list one single article, such as wool or lumber, or even peanuts—or a proposition to make a ten per cent reduction in the least important of the protective duties, would be sufficient to bring on the struggle between protection and free trade, if the protectionists recognized in it an attack on their cherished system and rallied their forces to repel it. . . .

Letter, "My Dear Garrison"[9]

. . . But the Democratic Party is of course disgusting. This, however, must be. Parties cannot be better than the people, and our political conditions must in fact be worse. Yet to improve their conditions, and to elevate the masses, we must use them when we can. . . .

"The Democratic Principle: Address of Henry George Before the Crescent Club Democratic Society of Baltimore"[10]

. . . For what are we single tax men, as in this country we call ourselves, but republicans of republicans, in the original meaning of the word—democrats of democrats! If you would follow the Jeffersonian standard, even, as you may think now, and if you would proclaim the Jeffersonian principles, even but a little, then, as far as you have gone in this direction count us with you first, last and all the time. We are with you and of you. For our belief is that of Thomas Jefferson; our aim is his aim and our hope his hope.

We believe with Thomas Jefferson that all men are created equal; that they are endowed with certain natural, inalienable, and God-given rights; that the only legitimate end of government is to preserve and secure these rights, and that when any government subverts them, then it is the duty of the people to alter or amend it. Our aim, as was his aim, is to make the government of this republic a government that will attain this end. Our hope, as was his hope, is not merely for national peace and prosperity, for national strength and true glory, but that the American Republic shall by her example enlighten the nations and lead the world to freedom and to peace. . . .

I have for years ceased to call myself a Democrat in the party sense. Nor have Democrats in the mere party sense cared to claim such men as me. But I know that in inviting me here tonight you have not expected me to preach the duty of voting the straight ticket, no matter what boss dictated it, what "little yellow dog" is put upon it, what league of corporate interests lies behind it; that you have not expected to hear from me partisan praise of one party and denunciation of the other. I care little for men, little for organization, much for principle. The only usefulness of parties to my mind is if they represent ideas and advance policies. And your adherence to democratic principle may often call on you to scratch Democratic candidates as the best means of advancing principles. If you are really and truly a democrat and have no choice but between two protectionists, vote for the Republican protectionist—you will get the simon-pure article. If you have no choice but between two tools of leagued corporations, vote for the Republican tool—you will quicker break such influence in the party you prefer. . . .

Next year we take the census. It will show in our league of states not less than sixty-five millions of people. A people speaking one language, with hardly a variation, living under the same institutions and possessed of an assimilative power that quickly blends into the fiber and substance of their nationality the great immigration from Europe that continues to pour onto our shores. A people, all things considered, more intelligent, more alert, more enterprising, than any people of equal numbers on earth. A people having, on the whole, the highest standard of comfort. A people who have for their heritage the temperate zone of a vast continent, with practically illimitable natural resources—a territory that even in the present stage of the arts would support easily more than ten times their number.

Cast your eyes over Europe with its kings, its privileged classes, its dynastic jealousies, its smoldering traditions of national hatred, and its huge standing armies facing each other in a peace that is little less exhausting than war. Consider this young giant of the west, with its schools and colleges, its thousands of miles of railway, its mesh of telegraph wire, its vast tracts of fertile land which plow has never turned. Consider its freedom from dangerous neighbors, its superlative strength on its own continent, its wide separation from all the causes of quarrel that make Europe even in peace but a vast camp.

Consider the great fact that among us all law reposes, as its acknowledged source of the popular will; that every male citizen has an equal vote; that any male child born may aspire to be president; and that, in all its forms, our government is a government of the people, by the people, and for the people.

Ought not the heart of every American beat with joy and pride as he thinks of his country? Ought not the eyes of all the world be turned in hope and for example to the great republic beyond the western sea?

Great the American Republic is, greater still she must be—great in numbers, great in wealth, great in arts, in arms, in power of all kinds; so surpassingly great in the century that little more than one decade will now bring us to, that to find a parallel for the promise of her relative importance ere it close we must go back to the time when the Roman eagles marked the boundaries of the civilized world.

But there is another side to the picture. The republic! Ah, that word should suggest more than great cities and large populations, more than material wealth and material power. And while we think of how great in all these things our nation already is, how greater still it must be, it is well that we should soberly ask ourselves how much in all that constitutes a true democratic republic we are in advance of Europe.

It was a belief of the enthusiastic republicans of Thomas Jefferson's day that by this time the example of the American Republic would have proved contagious, and that the effect of the rise on this side of the Atlantic of a great nation which exemplified the strength and the benignity of democratic principles would have shattered every throne in Europe and cast down every aristocracy. This is not the case. And why! Because we have not been true to democratic principles; because to Europe today the American Republic is not an example of the beauties and benefits of democratic government, but is rather a warning.

No American who mixes with our kindred on the other side of the Atlantic must feel this, and feel it bitterly. Let him but venture to sneer at the empty forms and expensive pageantry of royalty, let him but venture to scoff at hereditary legislators and the still existing relics of class rule, and see how quickly he will be reminded of the corruption of American politics, of the bosses who bear sway in our cities, of the rings that rule our states, of the corporation attorneys represented in our Senate, of the simple citizens who in wealth and power are greater than any British duke, of the buying and selling and intimidating of voters at our elections, of the organized lobbies of our legislatures, and judges placed on the bench for their services to powerful interests, of our strikes and paupers and tramps. . . .

What about the distribution of wealth? Fortunes such as the world never saw since the days when "great estates ruined Italy" are growing up in the American Republic. We have four or five men who are worth from one hundred millions to two hundred millions apiece, we have sixty or seventy whose fortunes are estimated at from twenty millions to a hundred millions, while as for simple millionaires, they are far too numerous to be counted. Consider what the possession of a single million means. Consider how long it would take an American mechanic or American laborer . . . after supporting himself and his family, to save a million dollars. How many lifetimes? For though he were to live to the age of Methuselah he could not save a million dollars. If you would get any intelligible idea of what these fortunes of millions, tens of millions, scores of millions and hundreds of millions really mean, figure up how many working men's incomes—deducting of course the necessary subsistence of man and family, for even the slaveowner had to allow that to the slave—it would take to make such incomes as these fortunes represent.

And look again. While these monstrous fortunes are gathering in the hands of a few, one has but to read our daily papers to see how familiar we are becoming with conditions that we once thought possible only in effete monarchies of the Old World, and could not exist in the free air of our democratic republic—with tramps and paupers and beggars; with charities that show the need of charity, with destitution and starvation, with crimes and suicides caused by want, or fear of want; with a struggle for existence on the part of great classes of people that makes life hard, bitter, and ofttimes imbruting—a struggle which grows not less, but more intense as these great fortunes go rolling up.

The gulf stream of European immigration still sets upon our shores, but in large sections of the country our natural increase is slackening. There are more and more men who are afraid to marry—more and more who fear that they cannot support children. The gulf stream of European immigration still flows on, for social discontent is rife in Europe, and the conditions that are increasing social pressure here are being felt all over the civilized world. But what is most significant is the change in feeling toward this immigration. . . . [T]he European immigrant is met when he lands by officials, who, if he brings nothing but the power for labor, send him back again. Chronic paupers, criminals, the weak in mind and body are not desirable elements, but [there was a time] when we boasted that this was the country of countries for any one willing to work, and when we welcomed the man who brought nothing but a pair of willing hands as an addition to national strength, a new recruit for the great army that was to overrun the continent and make the wilderness bloom. But now if the immigrant shows, or, rather if it can be shown, that he has made arrangements to go to work, and has secured employment before coming here, then is he not merely sent back, but the American who made the bargain with him is liable to fine or imprisonment. The trustees of a New York church are even now under sentence of the law for having imported a contract laborer in the shape of an Episcopal minister. It is only one step further to prohibit all immigration of men likely to work for their living. And this is the logical outcome of the system we have adopted. By elaborate laws we strive to keep goods out of the country in order, we have been told, to give Americans more work to do. It is but logical, then, to keep out workmen in order that there shall be fewer to do it. . . .

But what I wish to call attention to is the significance of this changed feeling toward European immigration. It tells, more forcibly than figures could, that with large classes it is becoming harder to make a living. It tells of the pressure of an unnatural competition which is forcing men to bid against each other for employment—a competition in which they are learning to look upon work as desirable in itself—upon employment as a boon doled out from some superior class, if not as an absolute charity. . . .

I cannot fill in all the dark shades, but I have said enough to suggest them. This is certain, that, if present tendencies continue the democratic republic which the men of Jefferson's day thought they had founded cannot be preserved in anything worthy of the name. A king can never come—not, at least, until we have run the cycle; as a king never came in Rome after the Tarquins had been expelled.[11] But just as under the simple name of imperator there came in Rome tyrants to wield a more than kingly power, so in America may the ring and the boss come to rule through democratic forms as no European king of our time has dared to rule.

But the great thing in any country is not the character of the government but the condition of the people. Democratic institutions are but a mockery to the man who must crouch and slave to live, and democrat of democrats though I am, I would rather be the subject of king, emperor or tsar, and be able to make an independent living than as a citizen of a so-called democratic republic to be oppressed with want and harassed with care; to be forced to feel that the fellow creature who gave me the chance of making a poor living by hard work was my benefactor and my master. "The greatest glory of America," said Carlyle,[12] "is that there every peasant can have a turkey in his pot." Alas, that glory is passing away and we are rapidly tending towards conditions in which the lot of the masses will be harder than it is in Europe.

What is the cause of all this—of this political corruption, of this rule of bosses and rings and corporate influences, of the widespread purchase and intimidation of voters, of the decay of our commerce, of the increasing intensity of the struggle for existence, of the growth on the one side of the millionaire, and on the other side of the tramp.

In Europe there are those who point to these things and say, "These are the results of your democracy. Popular government with you is a failure for the reason that it has always been a failure. The masses must work and cannot therefore think. They cannot rule and must always be ruled. Which is better, the rule of the aristocrat or the rule of the demagogues? Which is safer, the king by blood or the king by corruption?" And there are those in our own country who think the same thought, even if they do not utter the words.

It is not true! Thomas Jefferson was not a dreamer of dreams; a mere doctrinaire imbued with the impracticable vagaries of Rousseau and the French Revolution, as some Americans now style him, and many more think him. He is the greatest of philosophic statesmen this country has produced; a man far in advance of his own time and yet in advance of our times. Nothing that the finger of scorn can be pointed to in this country; nothing that we may lament in our conditions, is due to an excess of democracy, but to a want of it. If we would preserve the Republic in anything more than a name, if we would have it fulfill its high promise, we must be, not less democratic, but more.

What shall we do?

Before going to deeper matters let me speak of some things which, for want of a better word at the moment, I will call the mechanics of our institutions.

One of our besetting sins has been a vanity which has led us to think that we have solved all political problems and that our institutions in all respects are the best that can be devised. The government when formed was a great advance over what then existed in Europe. But with that advance we stopped, though changing conditions have made devices which worked well enough in our earlier days, unsuitable for the present time. In essential respects the constitution of Great Britain is today more democratic than is ours. We have retained our copy of King, Lords, and Commons, in President, Senate and House of Representatives, in full force and vitality—not only in the federal but in our state governments, whereas the slow but steady democratic advance in Great Britain has virtually done away with the King by making the occupant of the throne little more than a society leader and political dummy, and has all but done away with the House of Lords. We have a Supreme Court, which, by interpreting a written constitution, can check for a while at least the popular will. In Great Britain one representative body is all that need be secured to change any law or work any reform. Our type is not as quickly responsive to the popular will and does not as readily lend itself to the bringing of important questions before the people as does the type into which the existing British government has been slowly modified. . . .

Nor have we been true to the principle of local self government—the principle that alone makes possible this great league of states—this nation that may cover a continent. I speak not of the reconstruction acts and carpet-bag rule in the south. That is gone. Nor do I speak of our conduct towards the Mormons, where we have really been carrying on a religious persecution. But this fashion of governing cities by commissions and boards, and special laws passed by legislatures is utterly violative of the democratic principle.

But beneath everything of this kind there lies as the vital danger to the republic the increasing inequality in the distribution of wealth. Let the forms and adjustments be what they may, democratic government worthy of the name is only possible where the personal independence of the masses gives root for the civic virtues, and every citizen has an interest in the well-being of the state. But where some are so rich that they need have no care how public affairs go unless in something that immediately concerns them, and when to get more or to defend what they have they can throw thousands and thousands of dollars into politics; and where others are so poor that a few dollars, a petty office, a week's work, even a free lunch and a few drinks are more to them than any public question, then democratic government rots at its very foundations—then democratic government becomes not the best, but the worst of governments.

Look at the misgovernment and corruption of our great cities, at the robbery and jobbery of their administration, at their rings and their bosses. Bad political adjustments, and failure to regard the principle of local self-government, may have hastened this demoralization, but its deepest cause exists in the social condition of the people.

What sort of government would you have expected of Rome when the aedileship and praetorship and tribunate and consulate and the absolute command of provinces, and the license to despoil great kingdoms, were being bought of the Roman voters with feasts and games and gladiatorial shows? I will not speak of Baltimore, for I am not familiar enough with your city, but go to New York and see the Billy Muldoon associations, the Pat Divver clambakes;[13] note the gang of retainers that each ward and precinct leader rallies around him, and see if you cannot find a suggestion of Rome. It is nothing yet as compared to Rome. But the republic is still young.

Make no mistake. Democratic government becomes the worst government when the voting power is in the hands of proletarians, and the patriot may soon sigh for constitutional monarchy, or even an intelligent despotism. Make no mistake. A property qualification of the suffrage is not entirely devoid of reason. Every voter ought to have "a stake in the country."

Is this to condemn democracy? No; it is to say that in a true democratic republic every citizen would have an interest in the state.

Here, at last, we see that the problem of democratic government rests on something that we usually consider beneath our politics; that the social problem underlies all that we think of as political problems.

If mankind must be divided into the very rich and the very poor; if it is in the nature social growth, of material advance, to increase the gulf between the rich and the poor, then indeed Jefferson was a dreamer; then indeed democracy can only exist in new and poor countries; then indeed the poets have been right who have sung of liberty as loving the rocks and the mountains, and as shunning the great city and the crowded mart.

But consider. What is the cause of the growing disparity in the distribution of wealth that we see in this country?

First and foremost, the power of government has been deliberately and continuously prostituted to make the rich richer and the poor poorer.

Government has no purse of Fortunatus.[14] It cannot give to one man without taking away from some other. Look how our "generous government" has made men rich by donations. Look at the subsidies from nations, states, counties, cities and towns. Look at Stanford and Huntington with their hundred millions apiece.[15] Look at the franchises which have built up so many great fortunes, at the surrender of the iron highways that have become the common roads of our time to private interests and corporate greed. Look at the Standard Oil Company, with its private fortunes of a hundred millions each; look at the dressed beef combination, at the rings and monopolies that have their efficient cause in the control of a public function given to private citizens, and the discriminations they have been allowed to make.

Look at our tariff. Here we see the power of the government applied directly, purposely, continuously, and unconstitutionally, to give some citizens an advantage over other citizens—to make the rich richer and the poor poorer. Look at Mr. Carnegie, with his income of millions and his castle in Scotland; look at the men of whom he is the type; and then at their workmen, the poor, deluded creatures, who have been told that it is *they* who are protected; that this precious system of robbery is all for *them*.

No man, if he thinks of it can be a democrat really and truly, and be also a protectionist. I know that Jefferson himself was not quite clear on this point; I know that there are expressions of his which protectionists quote with something like comfort. But the Jeffersonian philosophy is clear; the Declaration of Independence is clear. Jefferson was a great man, but still only a man. He grasped great truths and saw their relations clearly, as far as the conditions of his time called on him to look. But no man probably ever sees all the relations of a fundamental truth. It is in the nature of fundamental truth to grow and grow upon us, and, like all men who build on truth, Jefferson built better than he knew.

In his time protection in the United States had only made its first small insidious advances and his attention had never fairly been called to the question of protection, just as there are today numbers of intelligent men in the United States who have not even yet fairly begun to think of it. But what was the little tender shoot of Jefferson's time has become the giant poisonous tree of ours. Instead of a modest entreaty for a little aid to infant industries, we have not the brazen demand of great rings and monster combinations. The little beggars have become sturdy vagrants.

The protection is utterly inconsistent with the democratic principle, we have but to think a moment to see. Government of the people, for the people, by the people. What does that mean! Not government for manufacturers, nor for farmers, nor for coal miners, nor for factory hands, not for employers nor working men, but government for the whole people without favor or distinction. Now what is the protective system? It is simply an indirect form of the subsidy system. It has for its object the enrichment of certain citizens by compelling other citizens to buy at higher prices. This is the primary end and aim of protection. If a protective duty does not raise prices it has no protective effect. It can only protect, as it is called, by enabling certain sellers to demand of buyers higher prices than the free market would give them.

Can anything be more clearly opposed to the democratic principle than this governmental favoritism—this use of the law making power to enrich the few at the expense of the many? This is the system that has driven American ships off the ocean; that is so handicapping our manufacturers that they cannot export. This is the system that has placed a great nation of 65,000,000 people—a people so intelligent, so active, so inventive, so prompt to use all labor-saving devices, that all they need ask anywhere is a fair field and no favor—in the pitiful attitude of crying for a baby act, and actually believing that if a paternal government did not keep its officers at every port to levy blackmail upon goods brought into the country, the wicked foreigners would swoop down and American industry go to the "bow-wows."

Look at the indirect effects of this system. It has corrupted our politics from the primary to the Senate. It has given to enormous moneyed combinations a selfish interest in our politics. It has been the fruitful cause of extravagance and waste and demoralization. The depreciation of our currency during the war resulting from the repudiation of the greenback by the government which issued it, the gold speculations, the strangling contraction, the whole fiscal system worked as a potent engine for enriching the few at the expense of the many —springs from the protective idea. The monstrous surplus wrung from poor people by the most onerous taxation, to be piled up in treasury vaults, is another of its results. The spectacle of the American people being taxed two millions of dollars per month to dig silver out of certain holes in the ground in Nevada and Arizona in order to plant it in other holes in the ground in New York and Washington, is another of its results. And so in every direction has it brought reckless expenditure and profligate waste. Thanks to the protective system, the difficulty with us in a so-called democratic republic has not been to impose taxes upon the people, but to abolish taxes upon the people. Whenever any motion has been made to abolish or reduce one of these protective taxes, Congress has been surrounded by a clamorous lobby ready to beg, to buy, to cajole, to logroll, to bulldoze, to do anything to prevent the repeal of that tax; and when, as in the last Congress, a Democratic House did succeed in passing a poor little reduction bill, a Republican Senate stood firm against taking off one penny of the taxes of the people. What has been, and is today, the effort of the party in power, aided unfortunately by many so-called democrats, but to keep up expenses and to make profligate appropriations in order to prevent any reduction of this taxation?

The whole system which has, and is costing so dearly, is diametrically opposed to the democratic principle, is diametrically opposed to the Declaration of Independence. The right to life, liberty, and the pursuit of happiness. Does it not clearly include the right of every man to freely exchange his own productions—to sell where he can sell best, to buy where he can buy cheapest?

But it will be said public revenues must be raised, and taxes must be levied. Very well. But the democratic principle requires at least that the public revenue shall be raised without unduly and disproportionately burdening any citizen. Protective duties do unduly and disproportionately burden some citizens and do so for the avowed purpose of enriching others.

And though not so wantonly and not so outrageously, all tariff taxes have this effect. These taxes finally fall on the consumer—they fall on men not in proportion to their means but in proportion to what they use, on the poor far more heavily than on the rich. And being passed from hand to hand, increasing as they go, they cost the ultimate payers far more than they yield to the treasury.

Thanks to that clause in the Constitution which prevents the levying of tariff duties by our states, we do enjoy free trade within the limits of the Union, and it is unquestionably the greatest of the blessings which the Union has given us. But the taxation of our states also tends in the same bad direction. The attempt to tax capital and personal property everywhere results in putting the heaviest burden upon the poor and letting the rich escape.

And all this taxation is in great degree taxation against prosperity—taxation which punishes enterprise and fines industry and thrift. In any of our states let a man improve a farm or build a house or erect a factory or do any other thing that adds to the real wealth of the community, and down comes the tax assessor and fines him for adding to the wealth of the state.

Is that wise? Is it right? Is it in accordance with the equal right of men to pursue happiness?

Now public revenues can be raised without punishing industry, without repressing thrift, without employing hordes of tax gatherers, and without the fraud and corruption and injustice that attends our present system of taxation. There is one tax by means of which all the revenues needed for our federal, state, county, and municipal governments could be raised without any of these disadvantages—a tax that instead of repressing industry and promoting inequality in the distribution of wealth, would foster industry and promote natural equality—a tax that is only a tax in form, and that in essence is not a tax, but a taking by the community of values arising not from individual effort, but from social growth, and therefore belonging to the whole community. That is the tax on land values. A tax not on land, be it remembered, but a tax upon land values, irrespective of improvements.

That is the tax in favor of which we single tax men would abolish all other taxes. . . .

"Reception to Henry George: Monster Mass Meeting at Cooper Union"[16]

. . . No, I am not proud of the American Republic, and no man who loves his country, no man who has ever realized what that banner might represent, no man who has ever felt what was the height of her destiny, how she might lead in all good things in the world, can be proud today of the American Republic. (Applause) But I am as never before hopeful of the American Republic. (Applause) Not yet. Freedom is not here yet, but she will come, aye, she is coming. (Applause) And the men whom you represent, the men who today stand for the principles of Thomas Jefferson, the men who today strive not for the rights of a class, not for the rights of labor, but for the rights of men (applause); the men whose motto is there, "free trade, free land, free men" (applause), are the vanguard of the men who she ought to be; the men who will make her a beacon light to all the world, and carry her to her true place, the leadership of nations. (Applause) Why, if we had done nothing more than to secure, as far as it has yet gone, the triumph of honesty in the adoption of the Australian ballot system,[17] we should have done something that would give us hope for all the future, and I congratulate you, men of New York, I congratulate you especially, upon the victory that has been won in your state; the victory that has been won in forcing by sheer force of appeals to public intelligence and to public spirit and to public virtue that reform into law with the signature of David B. Hill.[18] (Applause) (A voice cried, "It was uphill work," which created much laughter.) More the honor then for its accomplishment, and there is still more uphill work to be done. (Applause) But that work is being done faster than we dared to anticipate, and of that this conference is one of the proofs to me. People constantly tell me that I am over sanguine. I did not think that it would be possible at this time to assemble at one end of the United States a representation of the active single tax men from all parts of the country as has been assembled here today and will assemble here tomorrow. (Voice, "Don't forget Canada.") (Applause) No, I ought not to forget Canada when I speak of the United States. In these respects I include Canada. (Applause) I hope the time may come and come soon when between Canada and the United States there will be nothing more than the line which divides Pennsylvania from New Jersey. (Applause) And as the single tax men would annex Canada, so would I annex the Australian colonies and annex the English-speaking countries on the other side of the water. (Applause)

What is the real thing that divides us today? Different forms of government? Simply the tariff line. Throw down the tariff line; give between Canada and the United States the same freedom of exchange that exists between the states of the American Union, and we would rapidly become in all respects one. Do the same thing between the United States and the Australian colonies, and in spite of the distance, so great would be the commerce, so large the intercourse, that we would essentially become one people. (Applause)

Strike down the tariff between us and our brethren on the other side of the water and you would have to take your choice on every day of the week between an afternoon and a morning boat. (Applause)

Aye, the destiny of this republic ought to be something more than to merely carve into states of her Union the country that lies between Canada and Mexico and the Atlantic and Pacific. It ought to be hers to lead in that greatest of great political movements—the federation of the entire English-speaking race. (Applause) And she could do it were she simply true to the principles of the Declaration of Independence, did she simply not try to restrict liberty under the name of giving protection, but to give freedom, to trust liberty and to hold fast to her. Nor is this mere sentiment. I would have that freedom of intercourse between all the nations of the earth, beginning with the English-speaking nations, provided a beginning was to be made, not merely for the sake of the great league that would be represented, but for the sake of the individuals of whom our nations are composed.

I think the more a man travels the more he sees of the world; the more he realizes that the whole earth and not any little part of it was created for man. (Applause) And his tastes and desires can only be satisfied where he can take the best from every clime; where he can enjoy the instruction that comes from seeing all parts of it. I think the more a man travels the more he sees of this world; the more he sees that it is not a poor world but a rich world; that if there is poverty today all over the world it is not from want of productive force; it is not because the Creator has been a niggard; it is simply because everywhere men's energies are restricted; it is simply because everywhere men are denied the most fundamental of the natural rights of man. (Applause)

Our aim, and it is the same everywhere, is not merely to banish animosities, to still prejudice, to unite the nations; it is to abolish poverty; it is to take away forever that unnatural thing, undeserved poverty. (Applause) And that, too, not by protecting men, not by coddling men, not by condescendingly attempting to do something for any class, but by the simple means of assuring to all men equal rights, by the simple means of opening to all men those opportunities for the employment of their powers that the Creator of this world has given to them. (Applause)

"Campaign Notes"[19]

The truth is that there is no ground for making executive clemency in behalf of the Chicago anarchists as a matter of right.[20] An unlawful and murderous deed *was* committed in Chicago, the penalty of which by the laws of the State of Illinois is death. Seven men were tried on the charge of being accessory to the crime, and after a long trial were convicted. The case was appealed to the Supreme Court of the State of Illinois, and that body, composed of seven judges, removed, both in time and place, from the excitement which may have been supposed to have affected public opinion in Chicago during the first trial, have, after an elaborate examination of the evidence and the law, unanimously confirmed the sentence.

That seven judges of the highest court of Illinois, men accustomed to weigh evidence and to pass upon judicial rulings, should, after a full examination of the testimony and the record, and with the responsibility of life and death resting upon them, unanimously sustain the verdict and the sentence, is inconsistent with the idea that the Chicago anarchists were condemned on insufficient evidence. And the elaborate review of the testimony which is given in the decision of the Supreme Court dissipates the impression that these men were only connected with the bomb throwing by general and vague incitements to and preparations for acts of this kind. Even discarding the testimony (contradicted by other testimony) that [August] Spies handed a bomb to the man who is supposed to have thrown it, there was enough evidence left to connect the seven men with a specific conspiracy to prepare dynamite bombs and to use them against the police on the evening on which the bomb was thrown. It was not indeed proved beyond any reasonable doubt that these men were engaged in a conspiracy, as a result of which the bomb was thrown, and were therefore under the laws of Illinois as guilty as though they themselves had done the act. It may be said that these men had worked themselves up to the belief that it is only by acts of violence and bloodshed that social reform can be attained, but that does not affect the justice of their sentence. No matter how honest or how intense may have been their conviction on this point, organized society is none the less justified in protecting itself against such acts.

There may be countries in which the suppression by an absolute despotism of all freedom of speech and action justifies the use of force, if the use of force ever can be justified. But even in such countries complaint cannot be made when the sword is unsheathed against those who draw the sword. In this country, however, where a freedom of speech which extends almost to license is seldom interfered with, and where all political power rests upon the will of the people, those who counsel to force or to the use of force in the name of political or social reform are enemies of society, and especially are they enemies of the working masses. What in this country holds the masses down and permits the social injustice of which they are becoming so bitterly conscious, is not any superimposed tyranny, but their own ignorance. The workingmen of the United States have in their own hands the power to remedy political abuses and to change social conditions by rewriting the laws as they will. For the intelligent use of this power thought must be aroused and reason invoked. But the effect of force, on the contrary, is always to awaken prejudice and to kindle passion.[21]

There is legitimate ground on which executive clemency may be asked for the Chicago anarchists—that, being imbued with ideas which germinate in countries where the legitimate freedom of speech and action is sternly repressed, they were not fully conscious of the moral criminality of their action, and that the main purpose of their punishment—the prevention of such crimes in future—will be as well served, if not even better served, by a commutation of the sentence of death into a sentence of imprisonment.

This last is a very strong ground for the interposition of executive clemency, and it is sincerely to be hoped that the Governor of Illinois will see its force. A tragic death always tends to condone mistakes and crimes, and a certain amount of sympathy will undoubtedly attach to the Chicago anarchists if they are hanged, which would not be aroused if they were merely imprisoned.

But in whatever expression of opinion associations of workingmen who do not themselves believe in the use of dynamite may see fit to make upon this subject, there should be nothing which tends to put the Chicago anarchists in the light of leaders and martyrs in the cause of American social reform.

There are certain lessons connected with this Chicago tragedy that are well worth the consideration of every thoughtful American. The appearance in this country of a violent phase of anarchism is not to be imputed entirely to the ignorance or viciousness of foreigners unacquainted with our institutions. If they did not find in this country deep and grievous social injustice, they would not retain the idea of violence as a remedy for social evils after coming here; and were it not for this injustice which large bodies of our people keenly feel, the man who should propose violence or plot violence as a means for improving the condition of the people would be laughed into silence. The really dangerous thing in this country is not the presence of foreign-born incendiaries, but the existence of industrial conditions, which, in the midst of plenty, deprive the laborer of what he knows to be the fair earnings of his toil, and condemn men able to work and willing to work to enforced idleness. And the most dangerous men are in reality not the socialists or anarchists, but the comfortable classes who declare that things as they are are just what they ought to be, and who not only do not address themselves to finding any reasonable or peaceful solution for social difficulties, but do their utmost to prevent any such peaceful solution from being generally accepted.

Nor is the talking about force confined to anarchists. The rich and influential are too ready to talk about it, and the condone such applications of it as the employment of Pinkerton's detectives and the clubbing of peaceful assemblages by police. And the readiness with which the idea has spread that the Chicago anarchists have been unjustly and illegally condemned is a grave warning of the loss of faith in our judicial system consequent upon the corruption of our politics. We are yet far from the point at which it can be rationally assumed that seven judges of a highest state court would condemn a number of their fellow creatures to death against law and evidence; but when, as in this state, $60,000.00 is sometimes spent to secure a judicial nomination, and great corporations can make their influence felt in politics to secure friends on the bench, the belief in judicial integrity is surely on the wane.

Letter, "Dear Sir"[22]

... Nevertheless I deem it my duty to join my voice to those who, as a matter of public policy, ask you to mitigate the death sentence. I do so, because I know that there does exist through all parts of the country and among great bodies of men a deep and bitter consciousness of social injustice, and that, rightfully or wrongfully, there also exists, and that in the minds of many men who have no sympathy with acts of violence, a belief that in the excited state of public opinion in Chicago the anarchists did not get a fair trial. Under these circumstances their tragic death upon the scaffold will most powerfully tend to excite sympathy for them and their families, to condone their acts and to throw something of the halo of martyrdom around their teachings. Men who bitterly feel the injustice of social conditions which condemn them to want in the midst of plenty will be told, "These men died in your cause," and the result will at least be to familiarize their minds with the idea of violence. I am [one] of a large number of citizens [who believe that] the redressing of social and political grievances by constitutional means are most keenly alive to the dangers involved in the growth of a spirit of violence. For this reason and because I know that the feeling that these men ought not to suffer death is wide-spaced and deep, I now venture to urge upon you as a matter of wise discretion, based upon considerations of public policy relating not only to the State of Illinois but to the whole country, that you so mitigate the sentences of the Chicago anarchists as to avoid giving to the advocates of violence a most powerful means of appealing to the sympathies of well-intentioned men.

"The Letter Carriers"[23]

Consider the suggestiveness of the celebration. An "army of office holders!" The oldest man among us has heard that phrase from his youngest days. Here, at least, they were, for the first time I think in the history of the republic, a visible form. The long line of men in uniform that moved with measured tread up Broadway and swept around Union Square in military fashion, was a veritable army of office holders, the representatives of a still larger army not bodily present; an army of office holders bound together by common interests and celebrating a common victory—a victory won by their combination and the use of their political influence! Postmaster Pearson, as a civil service reformer, ought not have been absent from such a celebration, or have set his face against it; for it was one of the fruits of civil service reform. When men have a permanent interest in their places, when they are assured of them for life or during good behavior, the incentive and the opportunity to combine to make those places better are much increased. And thus in a certain way the letter carriers' celebration is suggestive of dangers that may come with civil service reform.

        But it is also suggestive of the necessity of civil service reform and of the rapidity with which the functions of government are extending with social development. That a body of office holders so numerous, and charged with functions that are so necessary to the transaction of all business, and to the daily convenience of the great body of the people, should be liable to change with every change in the national administration is not to be thought of. Nor does any one now think of turning over the business of carrying letters, newspapers, and such small packages as are not carried through the mails, to private corporations. But why draw the line at the carrying of letters, newspapers, and small parcels? Is there not quite as much reason that society in its corporate capacity should carry telegraph messages as that it should carry letters? And is there not quite as much reason that it should carry express matter; that it should supply cities with gas and water, and steam and heat; that it should run street cars and transport freight and passengers by railroad, or at least own and control the roads over which freight and passengers are carried? The true reason for carrying of letters by the government is that the business is in its nature a monopoly. But these other businesses are also monopolies in their nature, and as the development and integration of society goes on, still other necessary monopolies are arising. Thus the proper functions of government—national, state, and municipal—are constantly increasing. If we were to attempt to do what clearly could be done better, more cheaply and with greater public convenience by society in its organized capacity than by corporations, what an army of office holders might march down the streets of one of our great cities on any occasion they might select or be called on to celebrate!

But is there really so much to fear from such a great army of office holders of this kind as we are at first blush likely to imagine? Supposing the functions of the post office department were today performed by one great corporation or half a dozen great corporations, controlling, in virtual treaty with each other, the business in various sections of the country. Would there not be in them a greater available power of political dictation and control than exists in the post office department? In other words, cannot the political power of a monopoly be more readily concentrated and used to affect government when outside of government than when made a part of government? Our experience with railroad and other similar companies certainly goes to show that it can.

Consider what our post office department would be if it were managed as our telegraphs or railroads are managed. Instead of being run with public convenience as its primary object, it would be run for private profit, and that not so much for the profit of the stockholders as for the profit of managing rings. It is a great mistake to suppose, as is sometimes contended, that in leaving what are properly public functions to private corporations, we secure even that intelligently selfish management which is prompted by the interest of the owner. Our railways, for instance, are not, never have been, and are never likely to be managed for the interest of their owners. They are managed in the interest of the managers, not the owners, and the stockholder has been plundered as remorselessly as the public. They have made immense fortunes for managers and managing rings, and for the pirates and wreckers who have manipulated the stock exchange, but with all their necessary charges they have as a whole never paid the owners anything like reasonable interest. Their history has been a history of fraud, corruption, and spoliation which has no parallel in our governmental administration, even in the worst days of the Tweed regime in New York.[24] What better could be expected from the management of the postal business of the country if it were in the hands of one or a dozen great joint stock companies? And at every proposition to reduce rates, or [through the interference of] congressional legislation, would not a vast corruption fund be raised and spent? Nay, would not such a corporation, even in self-defense, be compelled to go into politics, as our railroad companies go into politics, and would not its employees be called on at every election to vote for friends of the company? Clearly, when we come to think of it, the vast business of carrying the mails is less of a political factor in the hands of the government than it would be if in the hands of private corporations. And the men who united together to get a reduction in hours could not be got to unite together for a political purpose so long as they did not feel that their retention in place was dependent upon the success of a political party. The acceptance of the idea of permanence in place during good behavior is destructive of that idea of gratitude to party which makes it even more a matter of honor than a matter of compulsion that the office holder who holds [office] by and from a party should support that party. . . .

Strip government of the functions we have improperly devolved upon it—of the attempt to regulate private industries and encourage private enterprises and collect private debts; abolish the whole system of interference down to the licensing of peddlers; substitute for our complex, unjust and corrupt system of raising public revenues, by imposing fines upon production, the simple and just system of taking for public uses those values which the growth and improvement of society creates, and it would be possible for us to put into the hands of government those functions which for the general benefit can be best conducted by organized society, without fear that government would control the people instead of the people controlling the government. . . .

Streamlining the Government[25]

It is much to be wished that at least one of the new states soon to be admitted to the Union would have originality enough to depart from custom to provide for a single legislative body.[26] In our dual legislatures we have followed the English pattern without stopping to inquire whether it was the best or not. In the fear of the smaller states that they might otherwise be overborne there was some reason for the division of the national legislature into two bodies, but there is no such reason for a similar division of state legislatures. The effect of this division of legislative power is simply to lessen the dignity of both houses, to divide and diminish responsibility, to distract the attention of the people and to prevent them from following the discussions and the acts of their representatives. This last reason alone should be sufficient to condemn dual legislatures. It is much more than twice as difficult for the public to follow the deliberations and acts of two bodies than it would be to follow those of one, and the responsibility of a vote where another body must concur is diminished by more than one-half. As a matter of fact, in the United States today, the great mass of the people, save in exceptional matters, know nothing whatever of what their representatives are doing.

An idea has prevailed that two legislative bodies place a check upon over-legislation, but experience does not bear this out, and it is more than probable that the division of responsibility between two houses is far more favorable to hasty and ill-considered legislation than would be the possibility of quick action by one. But it is in the path of true reform, which consists mainly in the repeal of enactments bad in themselves or which have become bad by reason of changed conditions, that the obstructive power of a second house becomes most injurious.

All over the United States the senates have become the bulwarks of corporations and the strongholds of the lobby. As for the Senate of the United States, not only does it already present the monstrous inequality of the representatives of forty thousand people in one state clothed with as much legislative power as the representatives of over six millions in another, but it has become virtually a house of millionaires—a house where sit, not the representatives of sovereign states, so much as the representatives of great corporations and giant trusts. This question of the constitution of legislative bodies has been but little discussed in this country. . . .

On the Presidency[27]

As President Cleveland goes out and President Harrison comes in, it might be worth while for the American people to ask themselves what is the use of a president anyhow. Switzerland gets along without a president, and gets along well. Our presidency was but a substitute for the English Crown, and in England the crown has ceased to be anything at all but a mere expensive legal fiction, while in all the important English colonies the governor, instead of being an actual executive, is little if anything more than an expensive and powerless representative of an expensive and powerless crown. Why should we not abolish our imitation of royalty? Why should not the American Republic also have a responsible government, and get along without the friction of recurring presidential elections, which are at best but a clumsy way of expressing the will of the people on the only questions on which any expression of their will is necessary—matters of legislation?

"The Queen's Jubilee"[28]

The exhibition of sycophancy and fetish worship which has taken place in Great Britain this week is a spectacle for gods and men. It is a doleful commentary upon the advance of civilization and the diffusion of education that in almost the last decade of the nineteenth century the great body of the English people (it would be unfair to suppose that there are not many Englishmen to whom all this is utterly disgusting) should go into a spasm of adulation over a woman of whom the very best that can truthfully be said is that she has never flagrantly outraged any of the obvious proprieties of life.

Victoria Guelph[29] is, as well as her personality can be got at, a greedy, grasping, narrow-minded, commonplace woman, who never did a useful thing in her life unless to serve the purpose of a legal fiction that might just as well have been served by a wax figure from Madame Tussaud's show. Yet a great people hasten to prostrate themselves before her, and to thank her with honors that fall little short of adoration for having permitted them so long to support her and her family; and rejoice over the fiftieth anniversary of her accession to the position of royal figurehead as though it marked some great national deliverance.

The crown in England has ceased to exert any real political power. It is now but a social and political system which divides men into orders almost as distinctly marked as Hindu castes, and crushes the vast mass into poverty and pauperism that a class of idlers may live luxuriously on wealth they do nothing to produce. The slavish adulation of a human being who, without ever having done a stroke of work in her whole life, has become, by virtue of taxes wrung from the hard hands of labor, the richest woman in the world, is in reality an apotheosis of the system which keeps the millions of England on the verge of starvation that a favored ten thousand may enjoy luxurious idleness. This abject prostration of a great nation before a human fetish does not show the survival of ancient superstition so much as the presence of an active living force, which is busy today inculcating the worship of power and wealth, from an instinctive perception that in this way . . . the many can be most easily held in subjection to the few. The English throne is the capstone of a social pyramid of many ranks, each of which is interested in abasing itself before those who are above, in order that it may in return enjoy the abasement of those who are below. And in inculcating this habit of servility, in accustoming the public mind to look upon the useless incumbent of a throne as a gracious benefactor, and in confounding ideas of duty and patriotism with personal devotion to a family, no class is so active and so efficient as the professed ministers of Christ. If this heathenish adoration of a human creature prevails in Great Britain, it is not in despite of what is called Christianity, but because it is a vital part of what is taught to the people as Christianity. Christ, according to the religion that is taught in England for Christianity, is not the friend and deliverer of the poor, but the patron of the rich. He is a guardian of game preserves and mining royalties and city ground

rents; a protector of the smugly respectable, who considers the honor paid
to one's betters as honor paid to Him. Almighty God, the people are virtually
taught, has so ordered this world that while a few roll in luxury the great
mass of its people can only get a poor living by the hardest toil, and large
numbers cannot even get that, but must live, if they live at all, on the crumbs
that fall from rich men's tables; but He has considerately provided another
world, in which things will be ordered more equally and to which such of
the poor will be admitted as have in this life conducted themselves lowly
and reverently toward their betters and not quarreled with the existing
order.

In Windsor Castle is a magnificent marble-lined chamber fitted up at
vast expense as a memorial to Prince Albert. In the center, on a marble altar,
reclines the effigy of Prince Albert clothed in [chain] mail. In the panels of
the altar and around the walls of the chamber are sculptured scenes from
the passion of Christ? It is typical of the degradation of Christianity. The
very life and sufferings of him who came to preach and gospel of equality
and fraternity have been wrested by the same powers that crucified him to
the support of Caesar's tyranny and the justification of Dives' greed.

The official prayer recited before the queen by the $75,000 per annum
Archbishop of Canterbury, in which the Almighty is blasphemously praised
for having "set the crown upon her head," and thanked for "the abundance
of dominion wherewith Thou hast exalted and enlarged her empire," is the
keynote of the prayers and sermons that have been delivered by ministers
of all denominations. Even the pope, utterly ignoring the sufferings of his
Irish coreligionists in this "Victorian Era"—something that he especially
might have been moved to remember, since out of their poverty the faithful
Irish have sent him thousands and thousands of pounds in Peter's pence[30]—
hastened to join in laying the homage of religion at the feet of the established
order, while Cardinal Manning,[31] besides issuing a letter to his clergy, in
which he tells them that Victoria has "shown the heart not only of a queen
but of a mother to all who mourn," and that "her home and her court are
bright and spotless examples for all who reign and a pattern for all her
people," called all the Catholic peers to a special jubilee service, by way,
evidently, of showing that the Catholic Church, although not by law established, is just as good a supporter of "things as they are" as the Established
Church itself can be.

And still more suggestive, and even more disgusting, is the sympathy
and admiration with which a not inconsiderable section of Americans have
watched these proceedings and joined in them as far as they could. So much
does queen worship suit their taste that, not having a queen of their own to
abase themselves before, they eagerly seize the opportunity to do homage
to somebody else's queen. . . .

Letter, "My Dear Sir"[32]

. . . I thank you for your kind invitation, and will seek you as soon as I reach London. I am uncertain how soon that will be, as I find much here to interest me, and, to speak frankly, much that rouses my indignation. Surely the masses of the English people cannot understand the sort of government that they are maintaining here, and how the first principles of human liberty are being trodden under foot by an irresponsible dictatorship wielded in the interests of a panic stricken and maddened class.

But out of this will come good. What is going on here makes it but the more evident that land monopoly has received its death wound. What I regret most are the bitter hatreds that are being amused. . . .

Letter, "My Dear Mr. Ford"[33]

. . . Of course neither you nor I, nor Dr. Nulty,[34] agrees to anything of that sort; but that makes no difference. It is best that Davitt[35] should propose it, for his great work [from] now on is to be rather in England than in Ireland. We'll topple Mr. British Crown before we are done. And I don't care what plan anyone proposes so that he goes on the right line.

"The George Dinner: The Great Banquet at the Metropolitan Hotel"[36]

I am a citizen of the world, as every man must be who really rises to an appreciation of that great truth of which our friend, Dr. [Lyman] Abbott,[37] has so eloquently spoken, who really understands that the blackest atheism lies in the denial of the brotherhood of man (applause); who really appreciates that He who made the earth for man, and put man upon the earth, is no niggard, no blunderer, but has provided enough and to spare for all. And as such I hope that the future may see something grander than this union of states—a league of the nations of English speech that will be the prelude to the parliament of man, the federation of the world. (Great applause) To make us one great people we want but perfect freedom of trade—the rest would follow.[38]

I don't care particularly whether the United States annexes Canada, or Canada annexes the United States (laughter); but I want to see those artificial barriers down, that one may cross the suspension bridge at Niagara Falls without passing a lot of custom house officers on this side, and then another lot of custom house officials on the other side. (Laughter and applause) They are the real separators of peoples. The movement that is beginning here, the movement against this vile protectionist superstition, against this legalized piracy and legimatized thieving, is indeed a movement toward the federation of the world.

Notes

1. See pages 126–129.
2. George to James P. Archibald (Secretary, Conference of Labor Associations), Aug. 28, 1886, #9, HGP. George had lost this election to the Democrat Abram S. Hewitt, however, he garnered more votes than the young Republican candidate Theodore Roosevelt. It is generally accepted that George would have won if it there would not have been ballot improprieties. The final tally was: Hewitt (90,552), George (68,110), and Roosevelt (60, 435). See George, Jr., *Henry George*, 481
3. *The Standard*, Aug. 27, 1887, GR. Here George endorses third party political activity. It was written during his campaign for the secretary of state of New York under the banner of the United Labor party in 1887. For his career in politics Barker's *Henry George* and Henry George, Jr.'s *Henry George* should be consulted.
4. *The Standard*, Jan. 7, 1888, GR. This article was written after his defeat in the New York state election. Here he argues for working within the established two-party system.
5. Friends and supporters of George.
6. *The Standard*, Apr.14, 1888, GR. This piece is similar to the preceding article.
7. See note 3.
8. A reference to the 1888 campaign between Grover Cleveland and the winner Benjamin Harrison.
9. George to William Lloyd Garrison, [Jr.], Sept. 8, 1888, #4, HGP. Although George accepted political parties his true feelings are exposed.
10. *The Standard*, Sept. 14, 1889, GR. One of George's themes throughout his life was the belief that he was carrying on the ideals of Jefferson. See George, Jr., *Henry George*, 599–601 and 604.
11. An Etruscan royal family who ruled early Rome and was driven out in 510 B.C.
12. Thomas Carlyle (1795–1881), eminent British author, critic, historian, and translator.
13. Muldoon and Divver were Tammany bosses. See note 24.
14. Fortunatus was the hero in a collection of late fifteenth-century German tales. He had an inexhaustible purse of gold and a wishing cap, which were the sources of his ultimate ruin.
15. Leland Stanford (1824–1893) and Collis P. Huntington (1821–1900) were well-known railroad barons in the West.
16. *The Standard*, Sept. 10,1890, GR. George's display of internationalism here is quite evident.

17. A ballot, first used in South Australia, which is less apt to be tampered with because it ensures secrecy in voting.

18. David B. Hill (1843–1910), an astute politician from New York, was its Democratic Governor (1885–1892) and U. S. Senator (1892–1897).

19. *The Standard*, Oct. 8, 1887, GR. A sober and interesting commentary on an event that generated America's first Red Scare.

20. A bomb was thrown in Chicago's Haymarket Square during a labor rally in 1886. There were eleven deaths and many wounded. Eight anarchists were tried. One received a jail term, two received commuted death sentences, one committed suicide, and four were hanged in 1887.

21. In another article entitled "The Chicago Tragedy" George wrote that: "Here all power is in the hands of the people—of the working masses, who constitute the great majority of the voters. They can make or unmake politicians; they can give power to this party or to that party; they can rewrite the laws when they will and according to their will. If voters are bought, it is because there are men willing to sell as well as men willing to buy; if legislative bodies are corrupt, it is because voters tolerate corruption and because they tolerate a system which brings corrupt men to the front. It is not any set or sets of bad men who are oppressing and misgoverning the American people, but the American people themselves" (*The Standard*, Nov. 19, 1887, GR).

22. George to R. J. Oglesby (Governor of Illinois), Nov. 5, 1887, #4, HGP.

23. *The Standard*, July 14, 1888, GR. Monopolies were anathema to George for they strangled true competition and the individual laborer.

24. Refers to the group of Tammany Democrats led by William Marcy Tweed (1823–1878) and his associates who were known for their widespread corruption, graft, and patronage.

25. *The Standard*, Feb. 2, 1889, GR. This piece displays George's reformist spirit and desire to make government closer to the people.

26. These states were: North and South Dakota (1889), Montana (1889), Idaho (1890), and Wyoming (1890).

27. *The Standard*, Mar. 2, 1889, GR. Another example of George's hope for democratizing government.

28. *The Standard*, June 25, 1887, GR. George's disdain for the English crown has a special relevancy today with its present fall in stature.

29. Victoria (1819–1901), queen of England. The Guelphs were a European dynasty with traceable roots to the 9th century from Guelph I. Because of the Salic Law (no succession of title through a female), Hanover became separated from the English Crown upon Victoria's accession in 1837.

30. A yearly tax of a penny from each Catholic household in certain countries paid to the Vatican. The Roman Catholics consider the pope the successor of St. Peter.

31. Henry Edward Manning (1808–1892), an English cardinal of the Catholic Church, advocated social reforms and workers' rights.

32. George to Thomas Briggs, Oct. 29, 1881, #2, HGP.

33. George to Patrick Ford, June 8, 1882, #7, HGP. Ford was editor of the *Irish*

World and friend of George, but later they parted company. This letter displays some of the radical elements of George's thinking.

34. Thomas Nulty, the Bishop of Meath in Ireland, irritated the Vatican by his pastoral letter affirming common rights in land.

35. Michael Davitt, an Irish agitator. Although a Fenian and incarcerated from to time to time, he was elected to Parliament in 1880.

36. *The Standard*, Jan. 22, 1890, GR. From a farewell dinner speech on Jan. 20, 1890. Another fine example of George's internationalism.

37. A friend and supporter of George. Abbott presented one of a number of eulogies at George's funeral.

38. Elsewhere in *The Standard*, George made a summons to internationalism by calling for the adoption of an international postage stamp. This, he argued, would streamline relations between countries and destroy national prejudices, followed by the dismantling of armies and the ending of tariffs.

Chapter 5

Georgism versus Socialism

It annoyed Henry George to be called a socialist, as extracts in this section reveal. Karl Marx regarded George with disdain (as with any rival). In a letter to Friedrich Sorge, he describes George's thinking as a "cloven hoof (at the same time ass's hoof)" for it is "theoretically . . . *total arrière* [retrograde]." It is "simply an attempt, trimmed with socialism, *to save capitalist rule* and indeed to *reestablish* it on *an even wider basis* than its present one. . . . [George] has the repulsive presumption and arrogance that distinguish all such panacea-mongers. . . . "[1]

Socialists and Georgists were at times in a shaky relationship, especially during political campaigns, but as events turned out neither side compromised in methods and ideals. Some of the problems of tactics and debate will be made manifest here. Marx looked for his truths in material values, whereas George's were those of the spirit, but both men shared the conviction that if material convictions were bettered with an equality of opportunity, then everything would improve. Marx regarded a proletarian state as the means to a perfected world, whereas George viewed his single tax in the same fashion. The German thinker regarded revolution and war as the motive powers in history. George sought not just a spiritual tranformation, but a revolution in thought and life.

The two opposing sides, in essence, clashed over methods rather than goals. Yet George's system of political economy can be regarded as a clearing house for socialism, capitalism, and even anarchism, which he admired philosophically but scorned any exponents of violence. Socialists would confiscate capital but George would take land rent. The land was to be held in common by the people as a community (George's distinction between private ownership and tenureship in land will be clarified in this section), monopolies were to be run administratively like the post office, and labor was to be private and industrious, but ethical. Whereas George made no distinction between capital and labor, he carried this relationship further by finding no dissimilar interests between the capitalist and the laborer. Marx would find such reasoning anathema. The German would also find George's opening up of free land for agricultural pursuits as a safety valve for the

unemployed laborer reactionary. For George there was no alienation between man and the machine, for the clanging of steel and the shower of
metallic sparks fashioning a useful object were welcomed by him as a
liberating force. George was quite explicit about the fruits of mental and
physical labor and the relationship to their fashioner: for man as man and as
man as creator is repeatedly extolled. Nevertheless, George regarded his
reforms as a transition to a predominately stateless society in which the
government is limited to merely administrative functions. This is also the
goal of his socialist adversaries.

"The New Party"[2]

The cardinal defect of socialism of the German school is its failure to make
a clear distinction between the primary factor of production, land, and the
derivative factor, capital—a confusion largely due to the use of a terminology
singularly lacking in any approach to scientific precision, and to the ignoring
of that power of coordination and adjustment which comes from the free
play of individual interests, and is to the social organism what the uncon-
scious functions are to the human organism. Confusing land with capital,
these socialists imagine that it is as necessary, in order to prevent the robbery of labor, to do away with the private ownership of capital as to do away
with the private ownership of land; and failing to recognize the primary
cause of the helplessness of the mere laborer, where land is monopolized,
and the coordination in production and justice in distribution that would
result from really free competition, they imagine the evil lies in the wage
system, and that competition must be abolished by committing to organized
society—virtually the government—the direction of both production and
distribution, in order to prevent waste and secure to each the fair reward of
his labor. Socialism is not akin to anarchism, as so many who know nothing
of either seem to suppose. It is its antipode. The socialist, as the term is
commonly used to denote German or state socialist, would, to secure the
proper direction of industry and the just distribution of its fruits, commit
its control to government; the philosophic anarchist, seeing the abuses to
which government is liable, would do away with government altogether, and
trust everything to the coordination of individual impulses and needs. Both
make a like mistake in seizing on one side of the truth and ignoring its
correlative.[3]
     There is this truth—and it is a very important one—in socialism, that
as civilization advances the functions which pass into the proper sphere of
governmental control become more and more numerous, as we see in the
case of the railroad, the telegraph, the supplying of gas, water, etc. But this

is all the more reason why we should be careful to guard against governmental interference with what can safely be left to individual action. In some things our existing system is too socialistic and in others too anarchistic. The proper line between governmental control and individualism is that where free competition fails to secure liberty of action and freedom of development. The great thing which we should aim to secure is freedom—that full freedom of each which is bounded by the equal freedom of others.

If it were absolutely necessary to make a choice between full state socialism and anarchism, I for one would be inclined to choose anarchism, preferring no government at all, bad and inconvenient as that might be, to a government which should essay to control and direct everything. And I imagine that this would be the choice of the great majority of the American people, for individualism is strongly rooted in all the habits of thought of the peoples of English speech, and we seem to lack the capacity for governmental direction and administration that has been developed on the continent. This is the reason why socialism of the German school can never make the headway here that it has on the continent of Europe. It is, in fact, the product of a state of society in which people have become largely used to governmental supervision and direction, and are accustomed to look to government as a sort of special providence.

But in the meantime there is no reason why those who entertain such views as I do should not work harmoniously with socialists of the German school as long as we go together, or why we should be perpetually accentuating our differences. The ultimate aims of socialism are high and noble. They seek to obtain for society that abolition of poverty for which we would strive. Any dispute as to means may well be postponed until it is necessary to raise it. I and [the socialist] both wish to reach the Pacific Ocean. I think we shall reach it at San Francisco; he is firmly of the opinion that it will be necessary to keep on until we get to China. So long as we are willing to travel westward in the same car, we can well postpone disputes. . . .

"Socialism and the New Party"[4]

. . . But to permit the simple and obviously just principles of securing equal rights in natural opportunities by taking land values for public uses and of bringing businesses, in their nature monopolies, under the control or management of the state, to be confounded with schemes for abolishing industrial liberty and making the state the sole landholder as well as the sole landowner, the sole capitalist, the sole employer and the sole director of production and exchange, would be to greatly retard the work we have in hand. Such confused theories and wild schemes as those of the doctrinaires of the German socialist school can never stand the test of intelligent discussion or make headway among a people with whom the instinct of individual freedom is so strong as with ours.

German socialism is so confused and confusing in its terminology, so illogical in its methods; it contains such a mixture of important truths with superficial generalizations and unwarranted assumptions, that it is difficult—at least for people of English speech—to readily understand its real meaning and purpose. Let me endeavor to give such a brief account of it as will at least serve to show the differences between it and the theories advanced in *The Standard,* and held by the great bulk of the men who are now united in the formation of a new party.

In the theories of Marxian or German socialism—or socialism as we might as well call it to avoid repetition—the central point is the employer or capitalist. In that form of production which the socialist writers denominate the capitalistic, and which they assume to be that of all production in the grade of civilization to which the most advanced modern nations have already attained, or, at least, to where they are advancing, this employer provides site, building, tools and materials, and buys labor, paying for it wages. He does not, however, pay in wages the whole value which the labor he buys adds to his material, but only a part of it, which the socialist writers put at from one-quarter to one-half. The rest he keeps for himself. He, in short, buys labor as he buys commodities, and the price that he must pay and that labor can demand is, in the socialist theory, fixed by the same law that governs the price of other commodities; that is to say, the minimum on which, in the existing state of society, laborers will consent to maintain themselves and reproduce. The tendency of competition for employment among laborers to reduce wages to this minimum and keep them there is assumed, in the socialist theory, to be the general law, and is styled by them the "iron law of wages." That part of the value created by the laborers, which the employer does not return to them in wages, but keeps for himself, and which is generally assumed by socialist writers to be from three-quarters to one-half of the whole produce, they style "surplus value." Gronlund,[5] however, in his book, *The Cooperative Commonwealth*, which is probably the best popular rendering into English of the socialist theory, gives to this "surplus value" of Marx the much more intelligible name of "fleecings." It is from this "surplus value," or "fleecings," that profits, rent and interest are assumed to come, and from it the employers or capitalists maintain and augment their capital. This, in fact, the socialist writers generally speak of as, and even more commonly assume to be, the source of capital, and from this idea is derived the assertion they frequently make that capital consists of unpaid labor.

Nothing could better show the incoherence of socialism than its failure to give any definite meaning to the term which it most frequently uses and lays the most stress upon. Capital, the socialists tell us, consists of "unpaid labor" or "surplus value," the "fleecings" of what has been produced by labor. Capital, they again tell us, is "that part of wealth employed productively with a view to profit by the sale of the produce." Yet they not only class land as capital (thus confounding the essential distinction between primary and secondary factors of production), but when pressed for an explanation of what they mean when they talk of nationalizing capital they exclude from the definition such articles of wealth as the individual can employ productively with a view to profit, such as the ax of the woodsman, the sewing machine of the seamstress, and the boat of the fisherman. The fact is that it is impossible to get in the socialist literature any clear and consistent definition of capital. What they evidently have in mind in talking of capital is such capital as is used in the factory system, though they do not hesitate to include land with it and to speak of the landlord pure and simple as a capitalist.

The same indefiniteness and confusion of terminology, the same failure to subject to analysis the things and phenomena of which it treats, runs through the whole socialist theory. For instance, in the *Socialistic Catechism* of Dr. J. L. Joynes, which is circulated by the state socialists both in England and this country, the question is asked, "What is wealth?" The answer given is, "Everything that supplies the wants of man and ministers in any way to his comfort and enjoyment." Under this definition land, water, air, and sunshine, to say nothing of intangible things are clearly included as wealth, yet the very next question is, "Whence is wealth derived?" to which the answer is given, "From labor usefully employed upon natural objects." Yet the notion that labor usefully employed upon natural objects produces land is not more unintelligible than the notion that "surplus values" or "fleecings" *produces* capital. As to the latter, it might as well be said that robbing orchards produces apples, and in fact considering that land is by socialists included in capital, it might as well be said that robbing orchards produces apples and apple trees too.

This indisposition or inability to analyze, to trace things to their root, and distinguish between the primary and the secondary, the essential and the accidental, is the vice of the whole socialist theory. The socialist sees that under the conditions that exist today in civilized societies, the laborer does not get the fair reward of his labor, and that the tendency of the competition between laborers is, despite the augmentation of productive power, to force wages to the minimum of a bare livelihood. But, instead of going further and asking the reason for this, he assumes it to be inherent in the "wage system," and the natural result of free competition. As the only remedy for these evils, he would put an end to the "wage system," and abolish competition by having the ownership of all capital (including land) assumed by the state; having all production and exchange directed by the state, and making all employed in production, or, at least, all employed in production for exchange, employees of the state, whose business it will then be to see that they do get a fair return for their labor. In the "cooperative commonwealth," as pictured by the socialist writers, ownership and possession of all means of production, including both land and capital, would be held by the state. The various classes of producers would be organized in associations or guilds in the nature of government departments, whose members would settle their hours of work, the part each should assume, and the relative value of their labor, while the collectivity or general government would, in the words of Gronlund, "only have three functions, of being general manager, general statistician, and general arbitrator. As statistician it will determine how much is to be produced; as manager distribute the work and see to it that it is properly performed; and as arbitrator it will see justice done between association and association and between each association and its members."

Only this ought certainly to be enough even for a collectivity as big as the United States; but in thus minimizing the functions of the collectivity, Mr. Gronlund is evidently thinking merely of its relation with the various producing departments or associations. A still larger job would be that of exchanging things and parts of things after they had been produced by the various associations. To this end the socialist scheme is that all produce for exchange is to be turned over to the general government, which is to give the producers, or rather the producing association, money or orders in the form of labor notes, upon its general stock of wealth, according to the amount of labor which has entered into the productions. The general government, in its capacity of general statistician, or general bureau of statistics, is not only to decide how much of each particular article is to be produced, but at what rates it is to be exchanged and how much of it is to be exported when it is deemed expedient to export. Even newspapers and books are to be produced and circulated in this fashion. If it is possible for anyone seriously to imagine such a scheme in actual operation in a country like the United States, it might be instructive for him to go on and speculate how long it would take it to break up in anarchy or pass into [something] worse than the despotism of ancient Egypt.

The utter impracticability and essential childishness of such a scheme as this is largely disguised to the believers in socialism by a curious pretense of scientific research and generalization, with much reference to the doctrine of evolution. According to the socialist writers all production up to quite recent times was for use, not for exchange, and they even gravely say that capital has only become an agent in production during the last two hundred years or so! Slavery, according to them, was the first method of organizing labor and securing the increased production that comes from it. From chattel slavery, by way of serfdom, the natural evolution has been towards the industrial slavery of the wage system and "capitalist production," in which [we now find] modern civilization. And from this, mankind are to pass by evolution into the socialist organization of production and distribution in which all industry is to be intelligently ordered by the collective will. This evolution, they hold, will be accomplished by virtue of the natural forces, whatever they may be, which produce evolution. The socialists who understand and hold to the Marxian theory hope not so much to assist in hastening its advent as to put men in readiness to take advantage of the new order when it shall come in the fullness of its evolution. Their notion sometimes seems to be that one branch of industry after another will pass under control of the state, until everything has been thus managed and directed. At other times it seems to be that the commercial crises or gluts (which they attribute to a tendency of capitalists to produce as much as possible in order to get the largest profits, while the laborers, not getting their fair share of the produce of their labor, are unable to buy what is thus produced) will finally culminate in a grand breakdown of the present system, when all that socialists will have to do will be to step in and organize industry under governmental direction.

The simple truths which are the grains of wheat in all this mountainous chaff of grotesque exaggeration and assumption are that with the progress of civilization and the integration of society the division of labor becomes more minute and the methods of production require larger amounts of capital. Certain functions are [thus more] developed, such, as the maintenance of highways, the supplying of cities with water, etc., which can then be better performed by the community, than by leaving them to individual enterprise, or (when in their nature competition becomes impossible) to individual or corporate monopoly.

Ignoring the essential distinction between land and capital, regarding land as but one of the means of production, of no more importance than steam engines or power looms, and looking to the direction and employment of labor by the state as the only mode of securing an equitable distribution of wealth, socialists do not appreciate the wide and far-reaching consequences which would flow from the simple reform that would put all men upon an equality with regard to natural opportunities, and which by appropriating its natural revenue for the support of the state would make possible the freeing of production from all the imposts and restrictions that now hamper it. The nationalization of land is included in their program as is the nationalization of machinery, but while they do not attach any more importance to the nationalization of land than they do to that of any other "instrument of production," they also mean by it something essentially different from what is aimed at by the United Labor Party. Frederick Engels, the coadjutor of Marx in founding this German school of socialism, has recently written a tract on the labor movement in America as a preface to a new edition of his *Condition of the Working Classes in England in 1884,* which has been translated from the German by Florence Kelley Wischnewetzky, who is, by the by, a daughter of Congressman Kelley of Philadelphia, and who doubtless comes the more easily to the idea of full governmental regulation and direction of industry from her familiarity with the idea of the direction and regulation of industry by protective tariffs. In this pamphlet Herr Engels thus states the difference between the socialists of the German school and those who think as I do:

> If Henry George declares land monopolization to be the sole cause of poverty and misery, he naturally finds the remedy in the resumption of land by society at large. Now, the socialists of the school of Marx, too, demand the resumption, by society, of the land, and not only of the land but of all other means of production likewise. But even if we leave these out of the question, there is another difference. What is to be done with the land? Modern socialists, as represented by Marx, demand that it should be held and worked in common and for common account, and the same with all other means of social production—mines, railways, factories, etc.; Henry George would confine himself to letting it out to individuals as at present, merely regulating its distribution and applying the rents for public, instead of, as at present, for private purposes. What the socialists demand implies a total revolution of the whole system and social production; what Henry George demands leaves the present mode of social production untouched, and has, in fact, been anticipated by the extreme section of Ricardian bourgeois economists who, too, demanded the confiscation of the rent of land by the state.

The difference is, in fact, even greater than Herr Engels represents it. We do not propose any such violent and radical change as would be involved in the formal resumption of land by society at large, and the letting of it out to individuals. We propose to leave land in individual possession as now, merely taking, in the form of a tax, as nearly as may be, the equivalent of that value which attaches to land by reason of the growth and advance of society—and while thus appropriating for the use of the community a revenue which properly belongs to the community; to do away with the incentive given to the withholding of land from productive use by the individual expectation of profiting by its future increase in value.

The simple yet radical reform would do away with all the injustice which socialists see in the present conditions of society, and would open the way to all the real good that they can picture in their childish scheme of making the state the universal capitalist, employer, merchant, and shopkeeper.

For, if the laborer does not now obtain his fair earnings; if, despite the improvements which increase productive power, wages still tend to a minimum that gives but a bare living, it is not because of any inherent injustice in the "wage system," nor because of any "iron law of wages" which operates because it must. These things are simply the results of the fact that labor, deprived of its right of access to land, the natural and indispensable element of production and existence, and thus rendered helpless, must, as the only means of escaping starvation, sell itself to those who can employ it.

Make land free of access to labor and all else becomes possible. Land is not wealth or capital, but is, on the contrary, that original factor of production from which labor produces wealth and capital. Land is not a means of production, like a tool or a machine. It is the original means of production, without which no other means of production can be used, and from which labor can produce all other means of production. It is not true, as socialists say, that the mere laborer, in the present stage of civilization, could not avail himself of the access to land to get a living. The two essential and primary factors of production—labor and land, even in the absence of secondary factors obtained from their produce, have in their union, today, as they had in the beginning, the potentiality of all that man ever has brought, or ever can bring, into being. Nor is it true, as the socialists seem to assume, that the whole class of producers below that of the employing capitalist are so destitute of capital, so incapable of getting it if they have good opportunity to use it, that they could not find the means to make good use of land if the monopoly that now holds so much eligible land vacant were broken up. Here in New York we see the poorest class of laborers building themselves some sort of shanties wherever they are permitted to use convenient land even on sufferance. And if the valuable land in and around New York that is now held vacant at enormous prices were subject to a tax which destroyed the expectation of profiting by the future increase in land values and compelled its owners either to build, to sell, or to give it away, is there not a great body of wage workers who would hasten to build or to get themselves homes? And with agricultural land, and, in short, all natural opportunities subjected to the same just system, is there not a great body of men now competing with each other in overstocked, unproductive vocations, or selling their labor for wages, who have or could find the needed capital to employ themselves to good advantage? With the glut in the labor market thus relieved, and the increased demand which would come from the relief of production both from the fines of present taxation and the blackmail of land speculation, would not wages rise quickly and high in all branches of industry?

With this liberty of labor to employ itself all the evils of "the wage system" would disappear, and free competition through the interplay of demand and supply would not only fix the returns of the various kinds and qualities of exertion with a justice and celerity to which the best efforts of any administrative bureau would be the clumsiest parody; but would determine the amounts and kinds of the various articles needed to satisfy the wants of society, and the relative values at which they should exchange, with a comprehensiveness, a nicety and a celerity which any general statistician or board of general statisticians, even though he or they possessed all human knowledge and all human virtue, could not hope to approach.

In concentrating effort on the recognition of equal rights to land, the new party is striking at the root of that unjust distribution of wealth which the socialists of the German school blame on the wage system, and of that tyranny which they mistakenly attribute to capital. But we do not propose to stop here. There are other monopolies than that of land, though they are less important, and we propose to break them all up. The kernel of truth in the socialist demand that the state should manage and regulate all industry is that there are many things that already can be better managed or controlled by the community than by private individuals, and with the advance of society these are constantly increasing. While we aim at simplifying government by substituting a simple and efficient plan of raising revenue for the present costly, cumbrous, unjust and demoralizing method, and by cutting off functions for which there is no need, we propose at the same time to push forward in the direction of extending the cooperative functions of the state.

Let the socialists come with us, and they will go faster and further in this direction than they can go alone; and when we stop they can, if they choose, try to keep on.

But if they must persist in bringing to the front their schemes for making the state everything and the individual nothing, let them maintain their Socialist Labor Party[6] and leave us to fight our own way.

The cross of the new crusade has been raised. No matter who may be for it or who may be against it, it will be carried on without faltering and without swerving.

"Single Tax vs. Socialism: The Debate Between Sergius E. Shevitch and Henry George"[7]

Mr. Shevitch's Argument:
Mr. Shevitch then arose and began his address in a calm, deliberative voice. He said:
Mr. Chairman, Ladies and Gentlemen: In coming on this platform tonight I come to you with all due consciousness of the great task which I have undertaken and of my unworthiness to perform it. I ask your indul-

gence from the very beginning. I want only to say that the words I will speak tonight will be that which I consider to be the truth without any reference whatever to personal feeling.

The subject of discussion tonight is the scheme of Mr. George regarding the single land tax, to substitute which for all other forms of taxation will, as he represents, solve the social and the labor questions of our day. I propose to show that this single land tax system is not only insufficient to solve those questions, but if considered alone, if considered as a social panacea, independently of all other social reforms, it will be productive of results which will be more hurtful to labor than beneficial.

I will in the second part of my remarks show how, on account of this false basis on which the labor movement, so far as the United Labor Party is concerned, has been placed, the whole political movement of labor has been sidetracked, has been distorted, and has been put upon a platform on which no true labor movement can stand.

This is what I will attempt to show during my remarks.

Production, as it is organized now, is regulated by two vast instruments of labor; machinery, with all the powers of nature which now produce such tremendous wealth all over the civilized world, and the land, which produces the necessaries of life. Now let us see. If we nationalize one of these instruments of production; if we nationalize what Mr. George calls the natural opportunities given to man by nature—that is to say, the land—will this nationalization of the land by itself solve the social problem? Mr. George does not advocate the nationalization of land. He does not want to disturb anybody in the title to property in land. All he wants is to confiscate the rent, which the present proprietor of the land gets, by a taxation equivalent to the whole rent. But let us study the question broadly. Let us assume that he does want to nationalize the land. What would be the consequence? The consequence would be that a certain lot of land which now belongs to a private citizen, Tom Jones, will belong to the community. The man who builds on that land will have to pay his rent, not to a private proprietor, but to the community. That rent will perhaps in the long run be a little less than the rent he pays now.

Now, suppose a city in which there are ten factories. In each of these factories one hundred men are working for wages. The factories are supplied with all the necessary machinery. These hundred men get $2.00 a day under present circumstances. Now the system of nationalization of land is introduced. The man who owns the factory, the boss, will pay his rent not to the proprietor of the land, but to the community. Will his workingmen in consequence of the simple fact get higher wages? Why should they?

If tomorrow a new machine is made which renders half the men superfluous, the proprietor will throw out half of his hands. Each of these factories will work, instead of with one hundred men, with fifty men. The men thrown out will come to the proprietor and say, "we are ready to work for less wages; give us instead of two dollars a dollar and twenty-five cents." And other men who have no families to support will say, "Give us one dollar a day." The same process of competition between laborer and laborer, ground down by that terrible monster, the machine, will go on whether the land belongs to the community or whether it belongs to Tom Jones. (Applause)

But Mr. George will say: "This is not true. The competition between the laborers will be, if not entirely destroyed, at least greatly relieved by the fact that the land is free, that these men thrown out of employment by the machine may go out somewhere, in the uptown districts of the city, take from the community for a very small rent a lot of land, construct their houses on it and live there in peace." How will they build a house on it? With their hands, with their nails, with their feet? (Applause and hisses) Where is the money to purchase the instruments of labor? Where is that engine of production, capital? They haven't got it. Does land give them capital? Does bare land give them anything except the land? Where are they to get the necessary machinery in order to bring materials so as to be able to subsist from the products of that land? I don't think that any answer can be given to this question. (Laughter) You may laugh, gentlemen, but it is nevertheless a truth. It is not the first truth that has been laughed at in the world. (Applause and hisses)

Somebody will say that the building trades will have a good deal to do. That is true to a certain extent. House rents will certainly grow cheaper. But don't you know that as long as capital, concentrated in private hands, has control of the labor market the rate of wages is regulated by the means of living. If rents grow cheaper wages will have a tendency to fall. With every new machine, and every new invention in industrial production, a greater number of working men and women will be thrown out of employment. The labor market will be crowded precisely as it is now. Where is the difference?

There is one other argument in favor of the land tax. You force those who hold land for speculative purposes to make it productive. This argument we endorse in full; but no single land tax is necessary. What is necessary is simply a land tax especially high on unimproved land, compelling speculators to put their land to profitable use.

The single land tax would be a single tax. All other taxes would be abolished. The tremendous concentrations of capital would be entirely free of any taxes at all. It would mean absolutely free trade. American labor would have to compete with the combined force of capital all over the civilized world. (Applause) If you introduce absolute free trade dozens of branches of industry would droop and die.

A voice: "Name them."

Thousands and thousands of workingmen would be thrown out of employment. A commercial crisis would be the consequence such as we have never seen yet in this country. The labor market would be overcrowded. What would we do with free land then? Sit on it or lie on it or be tramps upon it. (Applause and hisses) Land without the instruments of labor to cultivate it is just as worthless as a boat without sails.

Mr. George takes the example of Robinson Crusoe and Friday. Suppose Robinson Crusoe said to Friday: "You are not only a free citizen of this island, but this land belongs to you just as well as to me. But there is a little hitch in the matter. I expect a vessel tomorrow to bring to me all the necessary engines to cultivate this land and some workingmen, but you are free to do so just as well as I." Where would poor Friday be then, without a penny in his pocket, or without a single instrument to cultivate that land? (Laughter) Would he not be the slave of Robinson Crusoe?

Mr. George does not want the nationalization of land. All he desires can be obtained by the single land tax. What would be the consequence? Take the city of New York. The real estate of this city is held under various conditions at present. Some of it belongs to some men to whom the buildings belong. Some belongs to other men than those to whom the buildings belong. What would be the consequence of the single land tax? First, where the land and the buildings belong to the same men? Now the community gets the full rental value of that land. The man will say: "I will pay that tax and I won't give up the land, or if anybody wants to have that land let him pay for the house, which is worth two million dollars." How are you going to get out of that?

Let us take the instance where the land and houses belong to different parties. The man invites other millionaires to join him. They form a combine and say to those who own the houses: "You will have to pay an equivalent to us for this horrible tax." And the men who own the houses will go to the tenants who rent the offices and say: "Now you will have to pay us so much more in order to compensate for that land tax." The man who rents the office will take it from the one he sells his goods to. Who is that? Who? It is always the same poor wretched beggar, the proletarian, the workingman. (Applause) The whole theory of the single land tax is founded on the sophistry that the present robbery of labor centers in the one fact of private ownership of land, which is not true. If the means of production remained in private hands labor would be robbed just as it is now. The great landowners will immediately form a combine to resist the land tax. In a few years the condition of the laborer would be the same as it is now.

But what will not be the same is this—by that single land tax you will give to the government a tremendous power which it does not possess now.

Mr. George likes to accuse the socialists of desiring a paternal government. I tell you Mr. George's scheme is a much more horrible paternal government than the socialists ever proposed. (Applause and cheers, mingled with hisses) To the government will belong a vast amount of land, and the government will have the possibility of determining the height of the rent for that land. It will furthermore—and that is perfectly right—have the railroads, the telegraphs, and all the means of communication. Think of all the power that government will have. The great industrial corporations, and the machinery of industrial production, would remain just as it is now. Capitalists will have the same powers over the government officials into the hands of the monopolists of industry just as it does now into the hands of the monopolists of industry and land combined.

The single tax does not touch the labor question. That question centers in the robbery committed on labor by those who hold possession of the instruments of labor. And it is not the socialists who say so, it is the men of organized labor. (Applause) Mr. George thinks that rent is the robbery committed on the workingmen. He forgets that at the bottom of that robbery is simply the competition between labor and labor, and that competition will not be destroyed by any amount of single land tax.

The land tax scheme, whether it be wrong or right, is a utopian theory born in one mind, uncorroborated by the actual state of facts. It is a theory of one man, and that theory has been forced upon the large labor movement while that movement was not in any way prepared, not only to understand, but even to critically examine that idea! Mr. George may ask why did all the trades of New York as one man support him in the last campaign? "Where is the difference? I was the same man and my theory was the same." We can answer that. The great majority of the working population of this city supported Mr. George last year, not because of his land theory, but notwithstanding his land theory (applause), as a sincere and honest man—which he is now (tremendous applause)—because he had written in his book, *Progress and Poverty*, one of the most tremendous indictments against the present order of society which has ever been published. (Applause) The critical part of his work is grand. Every man who is dissatisfied with the existing order will shake hands with Mr. George even now. The laboring population accepted him as a standard bearer, thinking he was broad-minded enough to sink part of his petty theories in the one vast, grand labor movement, which is not one-sided, but which has many sides and is as broad as the civilized world itself is broad. (Applause) The man who can force one idea upon millions of people can be the originator of a sect, or, if he is a politician, can be the originator of a political machine; but he will never be the originator of a great political party of labor. (Applause and hisses) When Mr. George attempted to do so he smashed the party of United Labor. (Hisses and applause) As I told him on the Syracuse platform[8] under the ban of expulsion—"If you attempt to force this one idea upon the labor movement, you will smash the party to pieces," and they have done it. (Cries of "No! no! hisses, applause and cries of "Order!" Mr. Gompers[9] and Mr. George both rising and motioning the audience to keep quiet.)

From the very beginning, after the close of the campaign last year, the whole system of Mr. George and his friends has been to substitute for the large party of labor something on the one hand like a church, and on the other hand like an ordinary political machine. (Great disorder, hisses, and cheers) Instead of leaving the movement in the hands of the labor organizations they called a bogus mass meeting in Cooper Union and elected, or rather nominated, their central committee without any other powers than those which Mr. George himself conferred on them. This same line of policy was continued throughout the year; (A voice, "Stick to your subject!") land and labor clubs were formed throughout the state without any constituency behind them—(Cries of "Question! question!" Mr. Gompers rising and requesting the speaker to confine himself to the subject of the debate.)

My reasoning is that a false basis implies a false policy. A certain theory propounded by one man may, as I have said, form a church, but it will not form a great party. The movement of labor has been sidetracked into these land and labor clubs, practically under no control of organized labor whatever, composed of men not belonging to the laboring classes. Mr. George has succeeded in founding what I might call the Church of Progress and Poverty, but he has not founded the great American labor party. (Applause and cheers)

Henry George's Reply:

Mr. Gompers then introduced Mr. George, who was received with intense enthusiasm. He said:

I am about to speak on the time limit, and therefore your applause will simply take away so much of my time. What Mr. George has founded or what he has not founded I do not propose here to discuss. We are here tonight for a more important object. We all agree that labor today does not get its fair earnings. I come to defend what I believe to be not merely the best but the only possible way to emancipate labor. I do not claim for this measure—the taking for the use of the community of the rental value of land—that it would do everything. It is the beginning. After it is done all other things will be made easier, and until we have done that we shall be rowing against the tide in all other reforms. (Applause and hisses)

Now, the great difference between the opinions that I represent and the opinions that Mr. Shevitch represents may be seen in Lassalle's open letter to the workingmen of Germany.[10] He accepted the law laid down by the orthodox political economists—the law that wages must always tend to the minimum which will enable the laborer to live and to reproduce. That he calls the "iron law of wages." There I and those who think with me take issue. We do not believe that there is in nature any such thing as the "iron law of wages." We hold that it is merely the law of wages where natural opportunities are monopolized.

This competition is one-sided competition of men debarred of their natural opportunities for employment. The means of production, what do they consist of today? The answer will probably be land, machinery, and various other things. There was in the beginning nothing but man and the earth. Human labor exerted upon the land brings out, produces, all other means of production. Therefore, it is land that is more important than anything else. Given men and given land all other things can be produced. Give a man everything else and deprive him of land and it avails him nothing. (Applause and cheers)

To recur to that illustration of Robinson Crusoe and Friday. Mr. Shevitch says that if Robinson Crusoe [would] save machinery and tools, Friday would have been perfectly helpless. Well, that I deny. Friday without any machinery, could certainly have gone fishing. (Laughter, applause, cheers, and hisses) If the island had belonged to Robinson Crusoe he could not have done that. Friday could have done without machinery or tools just as Robinson Crusoe did. Friday could have made himself a hut out of the limbs of a tree. Friday could have lived and produced as a naked man, applying his labor to the natural opportunities offered by that island. If three or four others came there, they could have lived and lived well. But the moment Robinson Crusoe owned the land, that moment he could say to Friday: "Unless you do so you [must] walk off." (Laughter) Friday would have been his absolute slave.

Wages in all branches of industry are not what they ought to be. That increase in productive power that comes from discovery and invention does not raise wages as it ought to do. But what is the reason for that? It is perfectly clear that wages in all occupations must tend to a general level. Now, the broadest of all occupations in the United States is—what? (A voice: "Farming.") Those occupations which apply directly to nature, which extract wealth from the soil. Now, in the State of New York, can the man who comes here not merely with his natural powers, but with something more, with a little capital—can he go to work and cultivate the soil? The ordinary renting rate in the State of New York today is one-half the produce. The man who does the labor gets only half of what his labor produces. The rest goes to the owner of the farm. There, in that primary occupation, labor is divested of one-half of its earnings. When, in that primary industry, labor is shorn of one-half of its earnings, what do you expect in those industries that rise above it? To put a tax on the value of land, removing all other taxes that now bear upon labor and to take for the use of the community the value that attaches to land by reason of the growth of the community, would have in the first place the operation that Mr. Shevitch concedes. It would make the holding of land on speculation unprofitable. That of itself would tend to destroy that competition which everywhere tends to press wages down. I don't mean to say that every one would want to be a farmer. That is the one thing all men could be. And enough could and would become farmers to relieve the glut in the labor market. (Applause)

Mr. Shevitch asks what could a man do with his mere hands with the land. We have in this city illustrations of what the very poorest class can do when they have the land. Did you ever see Squattertown? (Applause) There are men who by going on vacant land put up some sort of a rude home. And so everywhere let man have access to land and he can in some way use it.

Take this city of New York. Mr. Shevitch divided the people into two classes—owners of land and houses and owners of land where other parties were the owners of the houses. He spoke of these two classes, and I think, forgot another class—those who own land where there are no houses. (Applause) The effect of the tax on the first class would be to simply make them pay the value of the land to the community and relieve them of all taxes whatever upon the houses. The mere ownership of land would become utterly worthless. Mr. Shevitch paints a picture of the real estate owners making a grand combine and putting up rents, so as to recompense themselves for the additional tax imposed upon land values. If they can do it by making a combine, why don't they do it now? Let us suppose that the owners of used land were to make such a combine, what would they do with the owners of vacant land? Would they take them into the combine also? (Laughter, applause, and hisses)

Here is the principle of taxation: A tax which is levied upon the production of a thing that must constantly be produced by human labor will, by making supply more difficult, raise prices, and the man who pays the tax is thus enabled to push the tax upon the consumer. But a tax upon the value of land has no such effect. Land does not have to be constantly supplied in order to meet the demand. Its price is always a monopoly value, and a tax which falls upon land values does not fall upon all land, but only upon valuable land, and that in proportion to its value.

It is perfectly true that were we to raise all our revenues in this way we could get along without the custom house and have absolute free trade. But I for one can see no horrors in absolute free trade. On the contrary, what labor wants is freedom, not protection. (Applause) Absolute free trade in any sense worthy of the name means free production. Once make production free, then labor can take care of itself. (Applause)

In what consists the value of land? It is a premium, an advantage, which the use of any particular piece of land will give over what the same application of labor and capital can get from the poorest land in use. Therefore, if we take that premium for the use of the whole community we put all land upon a substantial plane of equality. We can abolish all other taxes and enormously simplify government. Opening opportunities for labor, we get rid of that bitter competition that everywhere today tends to force wages down. Then we could go on, not to a paternal government that attempts to regulate everything, but to a government that can control businesses in their nature monopolies. (Applause) Once put the social foundation on a firm and equal basis and then we can march forward in that direction as far as may be necessary. We do not hold that everything is done when this one single measure is carried out, but we do hold that a firm and true beginning is made. Men have lived and can live without the railroad and without the telegraph, but no man ever has lived or ever can live without land. (Great applause)

Here Mr. George hesitated, while the audience remained in silent suspense. Finally he said: "I was stopping, trying to think of some points I have not covered, but I have forgotten them."

A voice: "The ownership of machinery."

Oh, yes; about that factory. (Laughter) Mr. Shevitch says that the owners of those factories may get a new invention which will enable them to produce the same result with only one-half the labor, and then those who are discharged will beg for employment at reduced rates. That would not be so if the men had opportunity to employ themselves. No man will work for an employer for less than he can get by employing himself. The natural result of increasing productive power is to increase the earnings of labor. Employment being free with natural opportunities open, there could be no such thing as dispensing with labor. But the shutting up of natural opportunities drives men back and forces them to seek for employment from those who can employ them.

Consider land and the use that is made of it. The extractive operations on land are not merely farming, not merely building houses. There are a hundred and one operations—fishing and cutting of timber, mining, and so on.

A voice: "Fishing on land?"

Yes; fishing on land. (Laughter) You have either got to sit on a piece of land or stand on it and fish (laughter, cheers, and applause), or if you go upon the water you must use material drawn from the land to prevent you from sinking. There is no productive occupation that is not in the last analysis the union of human labor with land. Until land is free to labor there cannot possibly be anything that will fully emancipate labor. (Applause)

Mr. Shevitch's Rejoinder:

"Mr. Shevitch now has his second inning," said Mr. Gompers, as Mr. George sat down.

Mr. Shevitch at once arose, and was received with applause from the reds. "I would prefer," he said, with a smile, "to get the applause from the other side of the house," pointing to the blues. The latter cheered him heartily at this pleasant sally, and he continued:

Mr. George paused for some moments to recollect some points he had forgotten to answer. It is my impression that he has forgotten to answer nearly every point of my discourse. He has not shown that land taxation is equivalent to land confiscation. He has not shown that under his land tax system a combine of large land holders is impossible. He has evaded that question and he has asked me what would that combine do with the men who had vacant lots? They would leave them alone or take them in just precisely as the wheat merchants do now in cornering the wheat in the West. They take them into the combine and raise the price. That is what the members of the combine in lands would do and who could prevent them?

Mr. George did not show that the competition of labor would be destroyed by that land tax system. He did not show, he simply made an assertion, that natural opportunities would be open to labor. He said that laborers might go fishing, and he very graciously said that he did not expect a man to go naked in the City of New York. But that man would be practically naked and the ideal of George's free land would be Shantytown. When I hear such things on a platform in New York City in the nineteenth century I begin to believe that Mr. George is a Rip Van Winkle of social economy. (Applause from the extreme left) He actually has been born in antediluvian times and has all at once waked-up in time for the Syracuse convention.

At this there was a storm of hisses from [those of] the right and cries of "Question! Question! Question!"

"It is the question," continued Mr. Shevitch amid hisses. "It is the question (hisses), and you can't choke me down. (Hisses and hootings) It is precisely the question, and you shall not choke me down."

The left broke out in applause, and the right went wild with yelling and hooting [mingled with] "Order! Order!" Mr. Gompers had to get up and speak for several minutes before he could quiet the trouble. Then Mr. Shevitch continued:

You surely do not expect me to compliment Mr. George. Mr. George seems utterly to forget that we are living in the grand century of machinery, in a great age of production on a large scale, where the mere laborer is absolutely the slave of those who possess the instruments of labor. This simple land tax does not free the laborer from the competition with his fellow laborer. The laborer with his free land must have capital to construct his house, and capital to begin farming even on a small scale. And there will be a big man with a big boodle, who will come beside the laborer with his lot, and take not one but ten, twelve, twenty or two hundred lots and will begin the cultivation of the soil on a grand scale with all the necessary machinery, and will crush down that freeborn citizen on the lot by his side. (Applause from the reds.) There is no such thing as free competition as long as the instruments of labor are in private hands. The labor question, the social question of the day, is not a fiscal question. The social question of today is the abolition of wage slavery, and that is impossible as long as the instruments of labor do not belong to those who create wealth. And if there is a man belonging to organized labor [who agrees with this,] he deserves to enjoy the paradise of Mr. George in Shantytown, and it is good enough for him. (Hisses and applause)

Henry George Concludes the Debate:
    Then Mr. George arose to conclude the debate. He said:
    The object of the labor movement is the abolition of wage slavery. How do you propose to abolish it? That is the question. (Applause) If any man has any better plan than what I propose let him come and state it. Mr. Shevitch's plan, as I understand it, is that of forming a number of cooperative societies, embracing all the working classes, who are to be furnished by government with capital.
    (Cries of "No, no! no, sir!" from the reds.)
    Well, with machinery, then. That plan, I say, is utterly impossible. There attaches to it the same disadvantages that attach to all dreams of the elevation of the workingman by the formation of cooperative societies. You must raise [the worker] from the very foundation. You must make labor free. Now, such catch phrases as my picture of Shantytown as an ideal city can avail nothing with any thoughtful man. (Great applause) What I say is this: That even the poorest man, if he has free access to land, can make some use of it, and the condition of those Shantytown people, poor as it was, was very much better than that of many who are herded in tenement houses, liable to be turned out at the end of the week or the month. (Applause) This tax that will take the value of land for the community will in the first place put all men upon an equality with regard to land. It will put in the treasury of the community a vast fund for public expenses. It will abolish all the taxes that now rest upon men by the increased prices in the things that they produce. Take the case of the renting farmers, who have to pay one-half of their produce for the use of land; out of the other half they now pay all their taxes. Under the other system these taxes would be taken out of the landlords' hands. (Applause) The tax would do away with all temptation to monopolize land. Mr. Shevitch is mistaken in saying that the laborer would

have to pay for land. There would be no tax upon land, only a tax upon the value of land.

A voice: "What is the difference?"

Here is the difference: that land of itself has no value. Land never has any value until two men want to use it. The prices that are charged for land on the outskirts of a city are a speculative value due to the anticipation of what it will be worth when the population crowds out. Under our system the employment of labor would be facilitated in every direction. Laborers would not be merely saved from paying rent, but would get employment during times when they were not engaged in their trades. Every man who goes to work extracting wealth from nature not only does something to lessen the glut of labor in other occupations, but by producing wealth for which he demands other wealth in exchange creates a demand for labor of other kinds. Take the coal miners who are standing idle in Pennsylvania. Apply this system and it would be impossible for corporations to keep those vast coal fields idle. (Applause) Those men, given the opportunity, could go to work for themselves, and then they could readily get capital enough.

A voice: "Do you see it now?" (Laughter)

Mr. Shevitch says that out in the West men can get all the land they want. If that were true there would be no such thing as tramps in the United States. Not only is that not true, but even on the Pacific, in Washington Territory on the one side, and in southern California on the other, men are paying one-third and one-half the produce of their labor for the privilege of tilling virgin soil. (Applause) It is our system which permits these great values that attach to land by reason of the growth of the community to go into private hands, that gives the speculators a premium for getting in just in advance of the settler; and wherever the settler goes there will he find the speculator just ahead of him.

Now, as to capital. When the farmer has to give up one-half of his produce for the privilege of applying his labor to land; when all through the other occupations the same law holds; when men have to pay to an individual for the use of what they call their country one-quarter, one-third, one-half of the produce of their labor, is it any wonder that the working classes find it very hard to get capital! Capital is produced by labor exerted upon land. Here [due to] the fact that we make the land private property for some [there is created] a constant drain of capital from those who [work on it, which goes] into the hands of those who are merely proprietors and monopolizers. "The destruction of the poor is their poverty." Take from men one-half of their earnings and you reduce their power of treating with others, you reduce their power of employing their labor upon the best terms. You create a fundamental difference, from the foundation, a tendency which on the one hand tends to make one class richer than they ought to be and on the other hand to make the other class poorer than they ought to be. (Applause) Labor is the producer of all wealth (applause), but labor without land is helpless, and that is the reason why any attempt to bring about more healthy social conditions must begin with the land. (Applause) . . .

"Socialism versus the Single Tax"[11]

. . . To the socialist mind capital seems the prime factor in protection—the great robber of labor. Nothing will avail to improve the condition of laborers and stop the tendency of wages to the lowest possible level unless laborers are in some way provided with capital. The charge which socialists bring against the single tax theory is that it does not sufficiently take capital into account. This charge Professor Ely,[12] after lauding state socialism as suggesting "a cause adequate to produce the desired end," thus goes on to make:

> Now, what does Henry George have to offer the laborer in the way of guarantees of permanent and remunerative opportunities for toil? It is when we attempt to answer this question that we come upon the weakest point of his scheme of social reform. His promises are abundant, but I so far fail to see any adequate cause for the effects desired to be produced, that, in spite of myself, I am reminded of the admirable fantasies of a Fourier[13] when I contemplate his bright picture of the future. . . . It is inconceivable to me that any Christian man could fail to endorse the reform proposed by Henry George if it, and it alone would accomplish all that he claims for it. But where is the sufficient cause? It is easy to say if you do so and so, this or that will follow; but rational men want to be shown such a connection between the proposed course of action and predicted consequence that the one necessarily implies the other.
>
> Capital is to remain private property, and employers and employed are still to confront one another in their present relations in the society of the future as conceived by Henry George. Capital and labor, he tells us, are friends, not enemies; naturally there is no antagonism between the two. Right here I take issue with him. What he says is a cheap platitude, but like many another smooth saying it fails to portray facts as they are. Capital and labor, of course, in themselves, can have no antagonism, but there is a necessary divergence of interest between capitalist and laborer in their roles of employer and employed, and the sooner this is recognized the better. It may be an unpleasant fact, but as it is a fact, it is well that it should be known. They are both interested in a large and good product, as a result of their joint efforts; but when it comes to the divisions of their products it is manifest that their interests are antagonistic. If the product is represented by a value like

$1,000.00 it is evident that if A, the employer, takes $400.00 only $600.00 is left for B, the employed, and he cannot give them more without diminishing his own share. A plain recognition of the facts . . . [that] good will, good sense, good feeling, a Christian endeavor, [and other forces] to base the division of the product on some equitable principle . . . may and generally do prevent an outbreak of antagonism, not infrequently, indeed, even prevent its being recognized. But there it is all the same; it lies latent in the nature of things, and may at any moment bring about open conflict, hate, bitterness, and violence.

The controversy about the division of the product is one of the most marked features of our industrial situation throughout the entire civilized world. Why close our eyes to it? Now, Henry George does not propose to alter this fundamental relation of antagonism. He does not propose to unite capitalist and laborer in the bonds of partnership. He does not point the way to such changes in industrial organization to bring about a union of economic interests. This the socialists, going deeper, do.

Now, instead of socialists going deeper, the trouble with socialism is its superficiality. The socialist views industrial relations as they appear on the surface in those centers where they have assumed their most complex and most highly-developed form—where, as pavements obscure the ground and tall houses obscure the stars, the prominence into which the finishing processes of industry are brought obscures the absolute dependence of man and all his works upon mother earth. Socialism could not develop in western Ireland, in the Hebrides, or in any new settlement where industry is in its primitive conditions. But to the factory operative in a great city, whose work is but the tending of costly machinery, who sees his employer growing rich while his own poor wages can only be maintained by labor organizations and their restrictions, and by industrial wars in which labor is pitted against capital in a struggle for who can suffer longest without giving in, the natural surface view is that capital is the oppressor of labor, and that the labor question is, as it is so often called, a struggle between capital and labor. And so to professional thinkers and teachers, who in their studies take the same standpoint, this superficial view may seem the real and the "practical" view. . . . Such a view of industrial relations is similar to that of the Chinaman, who observing that a steamboat went ahead when her wheels turned around, endeavored to construct a steamboat whose wheels should be turned around by the tide.

Professor Ely is a good example—perhaps not the best, but the ablest—of those men spoken of by Judge Maguire, who see the ears of the cat, and the eyes of the cat, and the mouth and the tail and the feet of the cat, but who yet do not see the cat. It is because he does not see the relations of things, which by themselves he clearly perceives, that he does not see in our simple proposition to take economic rent by taxation "any adequate cause for the effects desired to be produced," while he does see an adequate cause in an impossible state socialism.

The connection between the appropriation of land values by taxation and the opening to all of opportunities for labor is that such taxation of land values would bring land speculation to an end and make impossible its withholding from use by those who will not use it themselves.

Henry George has nothing "to offer the laborer in the way of guarantees of permanent and remunerative opportunities for toil." Professor Ely is right enough in that. For Henry George and those who think as he does on such matters do not believe it to be the business of either individuals or governments to guarantee to laborers opportunities for toil, any more than it is their business to guarantee that the sun shall shine, and the rain shall fall and the earth shall circle in her orbit. The Almighty has done all that. He who, by whatever process, brought man into this world, and made the maintenance of his life and the satisfaction of his wants dependent upon his labor, has provided abundant opportunities for the exertion of that labor. As the human eye is constructed to see things, so is the human hand constructed to mold things. And there is in this world, no more lack of things that human hands may mold to the satisfaction of human wants than there is of things for human eyes to see. There is today in the civilized world no country in which there are not natural opportunities of work for every willing hand. While just as advancing civilization, by the microscope and the telescope, and in the closer observation of difference and relations, opens new and illimitable fields to the eyes of man, so does it, by developing new wants and arousing new desires, open new and illimitable fields for man's constructive powers.

Professor Ely and the socialists generally are like those who would teach a blindfolded man to read by raised alphabets, and provide for him a staff with which to painfully grope his way. We, on the contrary, would simply remove the bandage and let him see.

The connection which Professor Ely fails to perceive between what we propose and what we claim that it would accomplish, lies in our belief in the harmony of God's laws; in our belief that right and wrong, mine and thine, are anterior to and superior to all human enactments: that social laws are coincident with moral laws, and that these have the same ever-pressing sanction as have the physical laws. What we propose is not a mere fiscal change; not a mere clever scheme of equalization—it is in conformance to the most important and most fundamental of all human adjustments to the supreme law of justice; a recognition of that natural right of property which exists irrespective of what kings or emperors or parliaments or legislatures may enact, and which is attested by the clear perceptions through moral sense. What we seek by a simple change in taxation is to put all men on the plane of equal opportunity. We would not take from one to give to another;

we would not beg one class to relieve by their alms another class. But by abolishing all taxation upon labor or the products of labor we would leave to the individual the full rewards of individual industry, skill, and thrift. By taking for the community those values which attach to land by reason of the growth and improvement of the community we would take for the benefit of all that which is brought forth by the presence and effort of all. In all things we would follow freedom. Where freedom of competition is possible, there we would leave everything to individual action; where freedom of competition becomes impossible, there we would have the state step in [only far enough] as may be necessary to secure individual freedom.

If there is any Christian man who fails to see in the simple reform that we propose a cause sufficient to abolish all poverty, save such as may result from individual misconduct, then it can only be because he has failed to understand it, or does not in reality believe in the sort of God his religion proclaims.

When I declare that there is no natural and necessary antagonism between capital and labor; when I refuse to join the socialists in their denunciations of capital and capitalists; when I tell workingmen that the real fight for the emancipation of labor is not with capital, but with monopoly, I am not giving utterance to cheap platitudes, but to a profound truth, which every man who loves peace, who values social order, and who would avert a fight in the dark in which blood may flow and cities burn, ought to do his utmost to make clear. I have not failed to note, as Professor Ely will readily see by reference to the books in which I have treated this matter, the obvious fact that there exists between the individual capitalist and the individual laborers, "in their roles of employer and employed," that divergence of interest which must always exist between the correlative parties to any exchange. But does Professor Ely soberly think that this turns my assertion that there is really no antagonism between capital and labor into a cheap platitude, and justifies the socialist doctrine that capital or capitalism is the thing workingmen must fight; and that the only way to secure fair wages is for the state to become the sole capitalist or for laborers to be furnished with capital either by the exertion of governmental power or by the benevolence of individuals?

The "divergence of interest between capitalist and laborer in their roles of employer and employed" is simply that divergence of special interest which exists between every buyer and seller. When one banker buys of another banker a bill of exchange, when the housewife buys from the milkman a quart of milk, or when a newsboy exchanges a nickel for peanuts, this divergence of interest exists just as truly as it exists between the buyer and the seller of labor. But is this divergence of interest an antagonism? Does it justify the one party in regarding the other party to a transaction, in which neither would engage if it were not to his interest, as his natural enemy? Does it justify a demand that the state shall step in to draw exchange, serve milk or sell peanuts? Or does it even justify us in calling on Christian bankers, milkmen or peanut vendors to charge less for their exchange, their milk or their peanuts?

And while there is this divergence of immediate and special interest between the buyer and seller in every particular transaction, is it not also true that there is a consensus of larger and more permanent interests? Is there not a point—constantly varying, though it may be, but still a point—to which it is [in the] best . . . interest of the buyers as a class and the sellers as a class that the price of things, whether bills of exchange or peanuts, should conform? If prices were arbitrarily forced below this point, exchange will cease to be drawn or peanut stands to be maintained. If prices were arbitrarily forced above this point, demand will diminish and supply will increase, and a reaction in the other direction would be produced. And, further than this, is not the point at which exchange can be drawn or peanuts sold to the best interests of both buyers as a class and sellers as a class fixed by conditions outside of each special transaction—by general conditions [relating] to the mutual interests of both, which are not antagonistic?

Professor Ely's illustration involves the socialist mistake of looking on capital and labor as the two factors of production and as the two parties to the division of the produce. As a matter of fact, there are in our highly-developed industrial system three parties of production, and always a fourth and generally a fifth relating to distribution. In addition to A, the employing capitalist, and B, the employed laborer, there are C, the landowner, D, the tax collector, and generally E, the representative of monopolies other than that of land. What A and B can divide between them is not the product of their joint efforts, but the product which C, D, and E leaves to them.

Now, what we propose is to choke off E, the minor monopolist, to abolish D, the tax collector, and to appropriate what now goes to C, the landowner, a mere blackmail which he levies on the produce of capital and labor, for the purpose of making up so far as is necessary what D now collects and for such other purposes as may be useful to A and B. Is it not clear that the common interest of A, the capitalist, and B, the laborer, in doing this is far more important than any divergence of interest as to the division between them?

Consider what this divergence of interest really amounts to. Either A or B may give or take a little more or a little less; but these variations are comparatively slight. What the capitalist (monopoly, of course, eliminated) can take and what the laborer can get, depends upon those general conditions which determine a certain normal rate of return to capital and a certain general rate of wages, toward which the competition of capital with capital and of laborer with laborer tend constantly to bring about the earnings of

both. It is only workingmen in any particular trade who can shelter themselves from this competition by means of trades unions, etc., that they can
force their wages up, and it is only by making a general advance in the trade,
that the employer himself is also sheltered, and he can afford to help them.
Yet the more wages are raised in this way the stronger the pressure comes
from outside competition, and there is a greater tendency towards a break.
And as experience shows, it is only in some occupations and to a comparatively small extent that wages can be raised in this way.

Now, on what depends the intensity of the competition for employment? Evidently upon the opportunities to find employment, and ultimately upon the opportunities which are open to labor to employ itself.
When "thousands upon thousands of men seek work in vain" we must
expect to find wages in the occupations most easily entered forced down to
the level of a bare living, and in other occupations only kept above that rate
by the difficulties of entering them. These thousands upon thousands of
unemployed men constantly tend to force down wages—both by increasing
the market supply of labor and by diminishing the market demand for labor;
since, as they are earning nothing, they have nothing to offer for the
commodities which other laborers produce.

Without entering upon the reasoning which shows that the relations
between the return to capital (as capital) and the earnings of labor are sym-
pathetic, not antagonistic, is it not clear that the way for workmen to raise
wages generally, largely and permanently, is not by fighting employers, but by
massing their forces for the removal of the conditions which cause "thousands upon thousands of men to seek work in vain"? And is it not evident
that in doing this both employers and employed have similar interests?

Professor Ely objects that I do not propose to alter the fundamental
relation of antagonism between capital and labor. This he says, "the socialists, going deeper, do, and the cooperators likewise do." Rejecting the
socialist remedy, he declares the cooperative remedy hopeful.

> They propose to remove the antagonism between capitalists and labor-
> ers by removing the distinction between them, by making all laborers
> capitalists, managing their own affairs in their own way. Both likewise
> propose a cooperative commonwealth, but the cooperators, unlike the
> socialists, wish it to be a gradual and voluntary growth. Thus they hope
> to bring about the longed-for era of industrial democracy.

Professor Ely is indeed a hopeful man. In the face of the condition
of things in which thousands upon thousands of men vainly seek work at
any price that will enable them to live; in which great masses of men who
do find work live only from hand to mouth, and in which great fortunes

are rolling up more rapidly than they ever did in the world before; in the face of an antagonism between labor and capital which he tells us is natural and inevitable, and which is every day becoming fiercer, Professor Ely is hopeful of "making all laborers capitalists, managing their own affairs in their own way"— by the establishment of cooperative societies and profit sharing!

How long does he expect it is going to thus make all laborers capitalists? And what is to become of the unemployed men in the meanwhile, and what of the "antagonism between capital and labor." The utter failure of "the cooperators" to get people to cooperate is notorious. The *Sun* . . . has for some time been amusing itself by advocating the panacea of cooperative enterprises. It says:

> The experiments were followed over a long series of years, and the lesson taught seemed to be uniform and conclusive. The attempts had failed in every instance where the experiment had continued long enough; and in the few instances of alleged success, the report, it is to be presumed, was derived from the new managers, who found it for their interest to give a rose-colored representation of their yet incomplete adventures.

The truth is, that to entertain the slightest hope in cooperation one must shut his eyes not only to all experience, but to all economic principles. A general system of cooperation or profit sharing, if in the nature of things that was possible, would simply amount to a change in the form of wages from a sum certain, as now, to an uncertain "lay" as whalemen call it; and the same causes which now operate to cut down wages to the living point would then operate. Passing such questions as: How in this hopeful scheme could it be proposed to induce laborers to give up wages certain for wages uncertain? How could it be proposed to get the thousands on thousands who can find no employment to cooperate with their employers? And how could it be proposed to make employers who have no profits to share their profits with their employees? I would like to ask Professor Ely what, when the antagonism between capitalists and laborers is removed by making all laborers capitalists, is to become of the landowners? Surely, the united capitalists and laborers are not going to try to get along without land?

To give permanent and remunerative employment to every one of the "thousands upon thousands of men who now seek work in vain" it is not necessary for society to give any guarantees; it is not necessary to nationalize capital, as the socialists would have us do, nor yet to coax employers to benevolently give a larger share of their earnings to their workmen. It is not necessary to call on Christian endeavor to base a division of the product upon some equitable principle. That equitable principle already exists in natural laws, which, if left unobstructed, will with a certainty that no human adjustment could rival, give to each who takes part in the work of production that which is justly his due, and leave to the community and applied to purposes of general benefit, and to the assurance of all against the accidents of life, that "unearned increment," which can be justly claimed by no individual, but is due to the growth and improvement of the community as a whole. By simply abolishing all the taxes that now hamper enterprise, discourage investment, fine industry and punish thrift, and thus leaving to the individual what properly belongs to the individual, while taking for the community in lieu of such taxes what properly belongs to the community, we shall make the monopoly of land impossible. No one under such circumstances will want land except to use it, and when land is wanted only by those who wish to use it, labor will find access to the abundant opportunities for employment that the Creator has actually given to man.

It is a mistake to think that it is necessary either for the state or for individuals to furnish labor with capital before the thousands now unemployed can find work and the cutthroat competition that now tends to force down wages can be stopped. There is no need of our bothering ourselves about capital, as the socialists do. Professor Ely is wrong when he says that the requisites of production are land, labor, and capital. The requisites of production are simply land and labor. These are the two primary factors in all production. Capital is but a derivative factor, formed from their combination. And even if we grant that in the present stage of the industrial arts some capital is necessary for any form of production, this would not prevent very many, probably the large majority of the men now unemployed, from employing themselves if land were open to them. If not among the tramps and paupers, there are certainly in the ranks of the unemployed—for the unemployed run through all gradations of industry—many who have or could command, if they could see profitable use for it, considerable amounts of capital, and many more could command at least some capital. Could such men go to work for themselves they would not only lessen the pressure upon the labor market, but, by producing wealth which they would seek to exchange for other forms of wealth, increase the demand for wage workers. Nor is it necessary that we should confine our idea for the relief of the labor market which would result from making the holding of unused land unprofitable, to the opportunities which would be opened for men to employ themselves. Such a change would give an enormous stimulus to the investment of capital in productive enterprises requiring the employment of labor.

If Professor Ely will come to New York, I will show him a piece of land that nobody is using, nor has it ever been used; that although within the City of New York, is today in the same condition as it was when the first white man put his foot on our shores. If that land can be had without the payment of a blackmail price to the "dog-in-the-manger" who now holds it, I will within fifteen days furnish a capitalist who will agree to put upon it a quarter of a million of dollars's worth of improvements and establish a factory that will give employment to several hundreds of the willing hands that are now looking for work in vain. And not only in this city, but in every city, in every town and every village throughout the United States similar cases may be seen. Why should a man, much less a professor of political economy shut his eyes to such facts, which everywhere stare him in the face, and go meandering around an impossible state socialism or the still more impossible establishment of "the cooperative republic" by means of cooperative societies and profit sharing? The cooperative republic will, I trust, someday come. But its foundations must be laid on justice. To try to build it on any plan that ignores the right of any child of God to the use of the natural opportunities his Creator has provided is to build upon the sand and to invoke the storm.

I have spoken at such length of Professor Ely's article, because it is really instructive. If we trace socialism to its roots we will find one of the strongest of them among the very class that most hate and fear it. Professor Ely is a representative of a large number of "men of light and leading," who, turning away from the simple plan of doing justice, preach a sort of rosewater socialism which "good society" listens to as contentedly as to a charity sermon. But innocuous as "good society" may think it, this starting out with an inevitable conflict and winding up with an injunction to "profit sharing" is a dangerous diversion. Its effect is not merely to turn men away from the true path, but to urge them on a false one.

When Professor Ely calls the statement that there is no real antagonism between capital and labor a cheap platitude, does he expect men who feel the bitterness of low wages and want of employment to wait patiently until capitalists shall be converted to the beauties of cooperation? When he lauds state socialism in its most thorough-going form as adequate to furnish all men employment and give to all fair remuneration, does he expect men who feel the grinding weight of social injustice to turn away from it because "it does not offer guarantees for freedom of action and individual initiative on the part of the gifted"? In this Professor Ely, though of course unconsciously, suggests the English demagogue, who, after lashing his audience into a frenzy of fury against an opponent, advised them not to duck him in the horse pond.

"Awakening Thought"[14]

The title of Monsignor Preston's[15] article ["Socialism and the Catholic Church"] is a misnomer. He discusses the relations of the Catholic Church, not to what is generally understood by socialism, but to the doctrines with which my name has been associated. These doctrines, in his title and throughout his article, he endeavors to confound with socialism in its commonly understood sense, although he must know, if only by the attitude of the socialists themselves, that in vital points they are diametrically opposed to socialism.

Says Monsignor Preston:

> Communism and socialism, in the general acceptation of these terms, are related to each other, and differ only in degree, while they are one in principle. Socialism denies the right of private ownership in capital or in land, or in both. Communism denies every kind of ownership, and asserts the individual equality of all men as to all things. . . . The socialism which has been advanced in this country of late, as a panacea for human ills, denies that there is, or can be, any private property in land. We quote the exact words of Mr. Henry George: "We must make land common property." "If private property in land is just, then the remedy I propose is a false one; if, on the contrary, private property in land be unjust, then is the remedy the true one."

This is the statement of the doctrine that the rights of men to the use of land are equal and inalienable that Monsignor Preston chooses for his attack. Of it he says: 1) "It is contrary to the constitution of all civilized nations and would destroy the present order of society," and 2) "It is contrary to the law of God and the teaching of the Catholic Church."

As to the first contentions of Monsignor Preston I am quite willing to admit them. The great reform I contend for *is* contrary to the constitution of all civilized nations, if by their constitutions is meant existing laws and prevailing customs. But, as had been decided by the Supreme Court of the United States and by the Supreme Court of the State of New York, it is not, as Monsignor Preston says it is, inconsistent with the Constitution of the United States and with the Constitution of the State of New York. It is contrary to the constitution of all civilized nations [in the same way] the denial of the right of property in human flesh and blood was contrary to the constitutions of all civilized nations, a little while ago—[and in the same way] the denial of the divine right of kings or the denial of the right of the state to establish a religion and to hang or burn all who did not conform to it, was contrary to the constitutions of all civilized nations. And it *would* destroy the present order of society, in the sense of destroying that order which everywhere makes the laboring class the poor class and gives command of the products of labor to those who scorn labor [while bringing about a] deepening want with increasing wealth; that builds brothel and almshouse and penitentiary while it erects the church—sets class against class and nation against nation; that makes our Christianity a mockery; and that with every advance of civilization is intensifying forces that must disintegrate and destroy. In this sense I plead guilty to the charge of desiring to overthrow the constitution of every civilized state and to destroy the present order of society. But it might be worth Monsignor Preston's while to observe that this is precisely what the early Christians wanted to do.

Whether "this kind of socialism," as Monsignor Preston persists in calling it, which holds that every child of God is equally entitled to the use of natural opportunities, is contrary to the law of God, is an all-important question; but whether it is contrary to the teaching of the Catholic Church or not is a matter of comparatively little importance. For if a thing be contrary to the law of God, then it must be evil, whether the Catholic Church teaches against it or not. But if it be in accordance with the law of God, then if the Catholic Church teaches against it, so much the worse for the Catholic Church. . . .

"The Right to Land and the Right to the Products of Labor"[16]

The Rev. Howard MacQueary, Rector of the Episcopal Church of Canton, Ohio, sent a communication to *The Standard* a few weeks ago asking whether the single tax doctrine did not lead to communism, because as it seemed to him the equal right to land involved the equal right to things whose materials are drawn from land, such as houses, or in fact any article of human production. His communication was published in *The Standard* of September 12, under the signature of "Truth Seeker," and answered briefly by pointing out the difference between land (the natural reservoir from which the things produced by man must be drawn), and those things themselves, of which while the substance is drawn from land, the essential character is modified by labor. The suggestions do not seem to have removed Mr. MacQueary's difficulty, who again writes:

> . . . You grant that I have a right to a bucket of water which I may bring from the spring, but not to the spring itself; to a log cabin which I may build, but not to the woods from which I cut the logs. In short I may by labor earn a part of the earth, in the shape of water, wood, etc., but not to the whole of the earth. But supposing our nation were to set to work building themselves houses from the common forest, until all the forests were cut down and made into houses, and suppose there should then come into the country by birth or immigration other human beings, would they not have a right to demand of us materials for their

houses? Would we not have to share our houses with them, or allow them to tear them down and build others for themselves? I cannot understand why if labor expended in the formation of a house out of material things should give me a title to the exclusive use of those materials, it should not also give me the same title to land on which I had spent labor. If labor spent in fetching a pail of water entitles me to its possession, why should not labor spent in cleaning out the spring, walling it up, etc., entitle me to its exclusive possession? Why should labor spent in building castles out of the air give me a title to so much air, and not to the air which I may have purified? The only conceivable answer seems to be that by so monopolizing the air itself I might deprive others of their castles. But, this, given time enough, will happen any way, unless, indeed, air were inexhaustible. And however true this may be of air, it is not true of land, wood, etc. The day must come when there will be no woods left, and then those who possess houses must, on your principles, share their houses with the new comers. My simple difficulty is this, if labor spent on one part of the earth gives a title to its possession, why does it not do so when spent on another part of it?

Mr. MacQueary is confusing himself by confounding the natural reservoir, the earth, with things temporarily drawn from it by labor, and using the words possession and ownership as though they meant the same thing. To admit the right of ownership in things which labor produces, or brings forth, from land, and to admit, as we do, such right of possession to land itself as may be necessary to give secure ownership of the products of labor, is quite a different thing from admitting the right of ownership in the natural reservoir itself. The one is necessary to the utilization of man's powers, to the secure possession and enjoyment by the laborer of the fruits of his labor. The other prevents the utilization of those powers and involves a practical denial to the laborer of the fruits of his labor. It enables some men to say to other men that they shall not work; it enables the idler to demand of the worker a portion of the results of his toil.

If Mr. MacQueary had held to the illustration of the bucketful of water drawn from the ocean, instead of substituting for the ocean a spring—in which he evidently confuses the idea of the bounty of nature with that of the exertion of labor by clearing, walling, etc.—he would more readily, perhaps, have seen the essential distinction. The right to the bucketful of water is but the right of labor to its result, and in no wise interferes with the equal rights of others. But the ownership of the ocean itself can in no way be based on any individual right, and would involve a denial of the rights of others. The water which is within the bucket is in itself a natural substance not produced by labor, but the bucketful of water, i.e., the position of the water in the bucket and where it may be carried, is a condition produced by labor. It is to this condition, and not to the substance of the water, that ownership attaches. This can be clearly seen if it be observed that the ownership of a bucketful of water can continue only so long as the change in its conditions produced by labor continues. To spill it or use it is to release those conditions, and to let the freed water return to its natural reservoir. Even, indeed, from the very moment in which labor takes it from the ocean it begins by the operation of natural forces, such as evaporation, to go back to the ocean again. The ownership of a bucketful of water, how long could that last and how could it impair the right of anyone else to draw similar bucketfuls from the ocean? But the ownership of the ocean itself, that could be passed on from generation to generation, so long as mankind existed and were so stupid as to recognize it, and would give to the man or men who from time to time owned it the right to prohibit all others of their fellows from drawing water or in any way using the ocean.

These principles apply as well to the spring. The clearing, walling, etc., of a spring give an exclusive right to the benefits of such exertions of labor, and to such possession of the spring itself as may be necessary to utilize these benefits. And insofar as such exertions of labor may be said to produce the spring, as in the case where springs are brought to the surface of the earth by boring or digging, they give an exclusive right to the use of the water of the spring, to the extent that this exclusive right does not infringe the equal right of others to obtain water from its natural reservoirs.

So the exclusive right to a house, like the right to the bucketful of water, does not attach to the matter of the universe of which the house is composed, but to the position and combination into which the matter has been brought by labor, and to the use of the matter only so long as it retains the impress of this labor. For just as water evaporates, so does the house decay, the matter of which it is composed constantly tending to pass from the position into which it has been brought by labor back into the natural reservoirs again.

Mr. MacQueary is correct in assuming that the equal right to the use of the bounties of nature must limit all exclusive rights. If the natural materials out of which houses are built were limited in quantity as he supposes, and people born into the world were to find all this material in use, so that they could get nothing out of which to build houses, then they might justly claim a share in the material, even though it were already in the form of existing houses. But in supposing this he is supposing a different kind of a world from that in which we live or any other that we can readily imagine. Wood, for instance, is not a fixed quantity which can be exhausted. Even supposing that natural forests can be exhausted, wood is no more a spontaneous offering of nature than are wild cattle or wild grains. It is also a product of labor and there is no practical limit to the ability of labor to produce it.

So it is with other substances which man uses in production. All man's power over the material universe consists simply in changing things in place. We cannot expand the superficies of the globe, nor add one atom to its mass. But neither can we diminish [it]. Our destruction is of the same nature as our construction. We combine and we separate, that is all. But what we combine tends at once to separate again, and what we separate tends at once to new combinations. We may conceive of human beings becoming so numerous on the earth that they could not find space enough, but, if we consider what our production and consumption is, we cannot conceive of human beings using up the materials from which to build houses, to make clothes or to obtain food. Therefore, the exclusive right of those whose labor has produced them to such things as houses, clothes or food can never impair the equal right of others to produce such things from the reservoirs of nature. An acknowledgment of the right of ownership in those reservoirs themselves would, however, impair this right.

But it may be said there are differences in the productive power of labor in different localities, and that to allow those whose labor is exerted at the more favorable localities full ownership in their products, would be to give them an advantage over those whose labor was exerted at the poorer localities, and thus to impair the equal right of all to the use of nature. A little consideration will, however, show that this would not result from full recognition of individual ownership in the products of labor, but only from the recognition of individual ownership in land.

When to produce the needed supply of anything, say lumber, it must be drawn from places where the return to labor is different, the value of lumber, by a well-recognized law, will be determined by the labor necessary to produce lumber at the poorest place for the production of lumber for which the existing demand requires the use. And to all better localities there will attach a value of locality, or ground value, which, speculation and restriction aside, will measure the value of the superior advantage that the use of the locality gives to labor upon it. If we permit individual ownership of land this advantage will go to the owners of the superior localities, and will enable them to obtain a return over and above the earnings of labor, which will give them an unjust advantage and put those who are relegated to the use of inferior localities to an unjust disadvantage. But if we give merely the possession of land subject to a payment to the community which will represent the value of locality—or to put it in practical form, if we impose a tax which will take the value of ground without touching the value of improvements—we put all members of the community on an equality with regard to the bounty of nature, and reconcile completely the individual and exclusive right to the products of labor with the common and equal right to the use of natural opportunities.

This great natural fact of the different productiveness of labor in different localities, will, in the mind of whoever considers it, dispose of all idea that the prosperity of nations can be promoted by restricting trade under the name of protection. It will dispose at once of the anarchistic notion that civilized societies can abolish government and dispense with public revenues. And it shows the shortsightedness of those who say that equality with regard to the bounties of nature can be secured by dividing up land, by limiting the ownership of land, or by abolishing ownership in vacant land.

The root of our social troubles is not in the ownership of vacant land, but in the ownership of land, of which the ownership of vacant land is but an incident and outgrowth. If the ownership of vacant land could be abolished, as Mr. Pentecost[17] seems now to suppose, by simply howling "Thief! thief!"—if the owners of vacant land could thus be induced to pretend to make some use of their land, or even to give up all the land they could not use themselves, or hire out to someone else to use—gross inequality would still remain, and would continually increase.

Nor is it possible in any way to abolish rent without abolishing every vestige of civilization and taking mankind back to nomadic savagery. Rent—economic rent I am of course speaking of—is not the result of human adjustments. It springs from natural laws as fixed and as certain as the law of gravitation. It comes not merely from the differences in composition, in configuration and in climate, of different parts of the surface of the globe, but from the physical constitution of man and his relations to space. Even in a country where there was an absolutely uniform climate and in all respects an absolutely uniform surface, the process of settlement and the progress of social growth would still cause rent to arise. In [its] centers of population, of business and of social life, land would have greater value than in other places, and would yield rent to somebody or other. Whether any of us, if we had been consulted, could have made a different kind of world, is beyond the question. This world in which we live is the kind of a world in which rent must arise with the progress of civilization. The only question with us is what shall we do with it—how shall we conform our social adjustments to this law. If we leave rent in private hands, the most monstrous inequalities must arise between men. A desire to monopolize is aroused, a spirit of speculation engendered, which make it seem today that countries overflowing with natural resources contain more people than they could support. If we take rent for public uses, we put all men on an equality with regard to natural opportunities, we can remove all taxes from labor, give free play to all productive forces and secure to industry, energy, forethought, and thrift their natural opportunities and their natural rewards. And whoever will consider what enormous beneficial changes this simple reform would work in the constitution of society and what great possibilities of advance it would open, will not merely see in rent a natural fact with which it is idle to quarrel, but a most striking evidence of the intelligence and benignity of that power which is behind what we call Nature.

If Rev. Mr. MacQueary will look out on the world and consider man's relations with it, he will lose all fear that production can ever lessen the power to produce: all thought that the moral truth that the laborer is entitled to the produce of his labor can never jostle with the moral truth that we are all equally entitled to the enjoyment of the bounties of Nature. Let him consider this globe circling in endless orbit round the sun—so infinitely small as compared with the outlying universe; so enormously large as compared with the needs of the intelligent beings to whom it is given . . . to dwell upon it [generation after] generation. Let him consider what is involved in the indestructibility of matter and the persistence of energy—how in all their production men cannot diminish the sources of production; how all their consumption is but the breaking up of some combination to form new ones—and he will see that it is impossible to place any limit on the wealth that men might enjoy; and that poverty and all the evils that flow from it do not result from the nature of external things, but simply from the violation by our social adjustments of the moral law which teaches us that we should act toward each other as if we were really the children of the same Great Father, equally entitled to the use of all He had provided.

Letter, "My Dear Hyndman"[18]

I intended to read your *Historical Basis* at sea, but unfortunately left the trunk containing it behind. I, however, got the copy you sent me and have just finished a careful reading. I have read it with great interest, and (except as to certain points) with great admiration. You have put facts together in the most telling way, and have produced such a useful book that I cannot but suggest what seems to me its weakness. This weakness attaches to the economic themes which you have accepted from Marx. I feel it this way because it seems to me that you must have accepted them without any really critical examination. I know, even if it did not stand out here, your profound admiration for Marx. Your book has convinced me of what I thought before, that however great he may have been in other aspects he lacked analytical power and logical habits of thought. Whatever he may have been he most certainly was not the scientific man you evidently regard him.

To demonstrate this as fully as I might from your book would take more time than I could spare for a letter. Nor do I wish to do this so much as to put you upon inquiry. For it seems to me impossible that you can have carefully tested in your own mind the doctrines you have accepted.

Take as a first instance on page 101. From the part that our desires are called out and modified, especially as to relative strength by several conditions there is a tremendous jump to the sweeping generalization that "utility is but a function of society." Can anything be more unwarranted? I think you might better say that "beauty is but a function of society," yet I do not think you would say that (or whether I think from the note, Marx's). Consider your own supporting instances: [sic] I think it would puzzle you to find [that for] the purely savage community [it] would be of no use, or the black fellow who would disdain to accept a tail coat, even if he chose to alleviate the tails. Are not potatoes useful even to fine ladies; and would not the poorest Irish peasant girl consider lace of an ostrich as utility, though (as would the fine lady) if it was a question between food and lace she would prefer potatoes. Or again: How can you inquire in such a sweeping generalization as that "It is not the individual even who forms the judgment as to the utility; but the class or social position in which he is placed forms it for him." How consistently with this can you explain the difference of judgment between yourself and Saunders as to wine; between me and Durant[19] as to tobacco; or such differences not only between members of the same society and class, but the same family. And how does the statement that " . . . things in themselves are useful which may have no exchange value such as air, water, and virgin soil" tally with the statement that "utility is but a function of society?" What does "absolute utility" and intrinsic utility," (elsewhere used) mean?

The serious fatal weakness here shown seems to me to run all through what you have taken from Marx. Whatever may be the value of his historical researches he certainly seems to me from such light as I can gather from your and [other] writings a most superficial thinker, entangled in an inexact and vicious terminology.

It was a long time before I could understand what you meant by the "thing of surplus values." I now discover it simply means that workmen do not get their due share of the wealth they produce. Is this a theory? And I am unable to discover any real light which Marx has thrown on this pertinent fact. To give a thing a sounding and to many a misleading name is not to explain it.

The real explanation I think you already show in the historical part of your book to be the monopolization of land. All the evil effects of machinery or changed methods are due to this closing to the masses of the natural means of production. Instead of the landlord having the men [go] hungry or of the capitalist, it is the monopolization of land which makes possible the "exploitation" of labor by capital.

Here as I conceive it is the real difference between us:

We both see the evils produced by the competition for employment of men deprived of the natural means of employing themselves. . . .

Letter, "Mr. Dear Walker"[20]

... I have been reading Hyndman's *Historical Basis*. It is a pity to see a man of such force following so blindly such a superficial thinker as Karl Marx. Marx's economics, as stated by Hyndman and all his other followers I have read will not stand any critical examination. Whatever he may have been he seems deficient in analytical power. I think I will have to write something about these socialist doctrines. I mean, as to those points in which they differ from us. They can be easily torn to pieces, yet are doing harm by confusing [opinion].

Notes

1. Karl Marx to Friederich Sorge, June 20, 1881, in Karl Marx and Friedrich Engels, *Letters to Americans: 1848–1895* (New York: International Publishers, 1969), 127 and 129. In two letters on pages 175–177 George expresses similar feelings towards Marx.
2. *The Standard*, July 30, 1887, GR. For the differences between the socialists and George see Geiger, *Philosophy of Henry George*, 227–284.
3. Marxism is a form of authoritarian socialism since it relies on the state. Libertarian socialism embraces the different varieties of anarchism.
4. *The Standard*, Aug. 6, 1887, GR. For George's political problems with the socialists see Barker, *Henry George*, 496–498
5. Laurence Gronlund (1846–1899) was as an influential socialist of the German school who emigrated from Denmark. George at first admired the author of the *Cooperative Commonwealth*, but their ways parted, especially with the publication of the pamphlet "The Insufficiency of Henry George's Theory."
6. The Socialist Labor Party was formed in the 1870s and led by Daniel DeLeon in the 1890s.
7. *The Standard*, Oct. 29, 1887, GR. This debate took place on October 23, 1887 at the Miner's Theatre in New York. The byline for its reprint was the following: "The building was packed as it had never been before fully three thousand people being jammed within its walls and over a thousand other clammering in vain for admittance." Sergius E. Shevitch was a socialist who was denied a seat at the United Labor Party convention at Syracuse in 1887.
8. See pages 108–109.
9. Samuel F. Gompers(1850–1924), labor leader and founder of the AFL, was an early suporter of George's politics, but later withdrew.
10. Ferdinand Lassalle (1825–1864) was a founder of the German labor movement, a leading socialist, and an active journalist.
11. *The Standard*, Dec., 31, 1887, GR. An example of George lambasting the socialists.
12. Richard Theodore Ely (1854–1943), an eminent economist and author, in-

itially attacked George for not being radical enough, but later criticized him as too radical. See Mason Gaffney and Fred Harrison, *The Corruption of Economics* (London: Shephead-Walwyn, 1994), 82–103.

13. Charles Fourier (1772–1837) was a French utopian thinker who advocated a society based on small economic units called phalanxes.

14. *The Standard*, Apr. 7, 1888, GR. Here George responds to the charge of being a socialist.

15. Thomas S. Preston, Vicar-General of the New York Diocese, had condemned George's ideas.

16. *The Standard*, Oct. 5, 1889, GR. The dignity of labor and its rewards are here set out in detail. The just returns of labor was one of the similarities between George's political economy and socialism but they differ in conceptualization. The former is based on individual morality and accepts private possession as a product of labor whereas the latter seeks a communal/class morality with labor as an end in itself.

17. Hugh Pentecost was a supporter of social reform and shared some views with George, but differed on others.

18. George to Henry Mayers Hyndman, June 22, 1884, #3, HGP. Hyndman (1842–1921) was the first influential British socialist and although he differed with George the two nevertheless associated with each other. For more on Hyndman see Geiger, *Philosophy of Henry George*, 236–240.

19. William Saunders and James Durant were English supporters of George.

20. George to Thomas F. Walker, June 26, 1884, #3, HGP.

Chapter 6

On Sundry
Important Matters

As a radical and a well-seasoned journalist George fired broadsides at unscrupulous people, social injustice, and the nagging problems of his time. The evils he attacked are still alive, though in slightly different form. Some of what George has to say still applies.

These selections bear witness to the unfortunate timelessness of social, economic, and political injustice. They include trenchant commentary on the military establishment, the "throttling" of American freedoms, the degradation of charity, the problem of racism, and the rapine of society by monopolies. Strikes and unionism, for George, would bring about short-term victories, but these, he believed, people should forego for the sake of the larger vision of justice the single tax would bring. This chapter also contains two works on women's rights, an article demanding the abolition of all debts, an attack on the banking system, and an extract on the patent and copyright system.

George regarded free trade as an intrinsic part of his political economy. It was a means to the ultimate goal of land equalization. Free trade also fostered free production with greater opportunities. Barriers between private property within each country and among different lands had to be eliminated. The single tax without free trade (or vice versa) was as unthinkable as a seesaw with only one person.

ON THE MILITARY

"Our Need of a Navy"[1]

. . . What do we want with a navy?

To protect our commerce? We have no sea-borne commerce except what creeps around our coast. Protection has killed our foreign commerce, and on the ocean American passengers and American freight are carried under foreign flags. Yet even if we had foreign commerce, it would need no navy to protect it. We have but to agree to it, to secure to private property at sea in time of war the same immunity that the usages of civilized nations now give to private property on land. And even if this were not so the days of convoys have passed.

To protect our seaboard cities from bombardment? Who is there who wants or is likely to want to bombard our cities? And if such there were, is it not certain that the most effective defense of our seaboard cities from bombardment would not be steelclad ships such as we are now constructiong and that are certain to be antiquated with the first great war that comes, but by balloons, submarine boats, torpedoes, and electrical devices such as American ingenuity, if its springs be kept in strength, will bring forth whenever there is need?

In the beginning of the century, when compared with European powers, we were small and weak; when the black flag was yet known in the gulf,[2] when Barbary rovers yet sailed the Mediterranean and passed beyond the straits; when Eastern seas were infested with Chinese and Malay pirates; when railroad and telegraph were not known, and it took months to communicate between places where now only minutes are required—then there might have been some reason for spending money on a standing navy. But what reason is there now? Pirates have disappeared, barbarism, on the sea coasts at least, has everywhere succumbed to the power of civilization, and all the principal ports of the world are linked in telegraphic communication with New York and Washington. The American Republic, in the beginning of the century, small and weak, is now, all things considered, the strongest nation in the world, while every decade as it passess steadily increases her superiority. Separated by three thousand miles of ocean from the rivalries and enmities of Europe, seated without hostile neighbors on a continent where none would dream of measuring strength with us, what foe have we, what foe are we likely to have, against whom we should need a navy? The notion that any nation on earth would be "tempted by our defenseless condition" to deliberately attack us, is worthy of a lunatic asylum. There is no power or combination of powers that could successfully invade us, and there is no power or combination of powers that could have any temptation to wantonly attack us. So long as we refrain from wantonly attacking others, peace with all the world is in our hands. It is perhaps the very greatest of all the advantages which we enjoy over the other great nations of the earth that so far as the human eye can see we may be assured of honorable peace so long as we perfer it to dishonorable war.

But "war *may* come." Yes; war *may* come. No one could deny that any more than any one could deny that Mrs. Toodles' daughter *might* marry a man named Thompson. But what is there in keeping up an expensive navy to meet that possibility? The possession of steelclad fleets and navy yards and foundries based on government contracts does not mean maritime strength. We may build and maintain a navy as great as that of England, but so long as we have no mercantile marine—so long as England carries our passengers and transports our freight on the high sea—we shall not rival England's maritime power.

The robbing system of protection has reduced us from the first rank of maritime peoples to the maritime rank of the Turks or the Japanese, and now the advocates of this same system, as one of the excuses for keeping up the blighting taxes from which some few monopolists profit, insist on giving us a "modern naval establishment." It will no more make us a naval power than the purchase of ironclads by Turkey and Japan make those countries naval powers. A navy without a merchant commerce is an exotic that may make a brave show in time of peace if money enough be spent on it, but that will surely wither in the blast of war with a commercial nation. To become strong on the seas again—to have again the American flag floating over the swiftest ships and the best seamen that any nation can boast, it is only necessary to give freedom to American enterprise and American ingenuity—to abolish the taxes that have driven them from the ocean. The millions that we are spending on this infant "modern naval establishment" of ours, if left to private enterprise by the abolition of duties on everything that enters into the cost of building and sailing ships, would soon give us a mercantile marine that would be a better reliance in time of war than any navy; would soon build up foundries and machine ships able to turn out more and better and quicker works than any establishments that mere government can create.

Standing navies and armies are incongruous with our institutions—they belong properly to monarchies and aristocracies, not to democratic republics. Our standing navy and our standing army are and have been since their organization utterly alien to the true American spirit. In them are perpetuated that caste distinction between classes, the outgrowth of European aristocracy, that the American Constitution aims at in prohibiting titles of nobility. Before the civil law all American citizens stand on the same level. Between the president of the republic and the lowest department messenger the distinction is merely that of place and duty. But between the commissioned officer of army or navy and the enlisted man there is a distinction of kind—a distinction essentially and historically the same as that made in the worse days of European monarchies betwen highborn noble and baseborn peasant. Between the lowest commissioned officer and the highest noncomissioned officer in the American Army or Navy, there exists the same kind of impassable gulf that exists between the son of an English duke and his father's butler—the one is a member of a superior and privileged class, the other is essentially inferior. . . .

All this is utterly opposed to the spirit of American institutions. . . . In the very nature of things standing armies and standing navies are inimical to democracy, and never, save in case of absolute necessity, should those who desire the perpetuity of democratic institutions consent to maintain them. Standing armies and navies have always proved the ready tools of tyranny, and in every country in which they have been suffered to pass a certain point have proved the death of liberty.[3]

This arises from their nature. The great virtue of miltary service is implicit obedience, and the whole military education is directed for its inculcation. In a standing army or a standing navy the citizen is converted into a mere killing machine, which reaches perfection as it becomes ready to kill with absolute indifference anyone whom it is ordered to kill. "Theirs not to make reply; theirs not to reason why; theirs but to do and die," is the spirit and virtue of a standing army and a standing navy.

In the very disposition to strengthen our standing army and navy there is an unconcealed desire to create a force that may on occasion be used not against a foreign enemy, but against the masses of our own people. "There is nothing more timid than a million dollars, except two million dollars," and the millions in ones and twos and tens and scores and fifties and hundreds that are piling together in the United States today are more and more attracted to the idea of a strong government. "Militia can't be relied on to put down labor riots, and we ought to have more regulars," is a sentiment that has greatly grown among certain influential classes during the last ten years, which is not without open expression in the press. It is an indication that should remind us of what the whole history of government attests, that while "a well-regulated militia is essential to the existence of a free people," a standing war establishment is always dangerous. If it is a great one it is greatly dangerous. If it is a little one, it is less dangerous. But big or little, danger to free institutions inheres in its existence. For there is always a tendency for the little to grow into the big in such things.

For the man or boy who has no legitimate use for a revolver, the best sort of a revolver to carry, if he must carry a revolver, is one that won't shoot. On the same principle, the wooden navy which the Republicans left when they went out was a better navy for us than the more efficient one that President Cleveland's administration has left. The old ships that could neither fight nor run, but did possess a marvelous capacity for undergoing repairs, fully served every real purpose for which an American Navy is wanted—an excuse for giving a number of gentlemen pleasant life situations, for fattening a number of contractors, and for enabling the party in power to exercise considerable political influence. As it could neither fight nor run, there was less danger that it might be used to get us into some disgraceful war, such as Mr. Blaine had all but succeeded in getting us into with Chile at the time when his power was terminated by Mr. Arthur's accession. . . . [4]

For us to spend money on a useless navy is only a little worse than throwing so much money into the sea; but to spend money on an efficient navy, when we have no need for any navy, is a great deal worse, since it creates a constant disposition to use it.

This is a real danger. To win a little military glory; to rouse the miserable vanities and vile passions that masquerade under the name of patriotism; to excite the madness that in man, as in some other animals, is worked by blood, is the most potent resource of a governing class who wish to divert attention from home matters and secure an unreasoning and unquestioning support. God forbid that the lust for power should bring the curse of another war of any kind upon the United States. It is the only thing that can. But just as we add to our military establishment, so do we increase the danger.

. . . we in the United States have developed the beginnings of a great "modern naval establishment." Is this a thing to be proud of? Is it not like rejoicing that the beginnings of leprosy have been developed among a people that might be clean and whole?

. . . all forms of tyranny—are born of war and the war spirit. Democracy, on the contrary, is the child of peace, and can only really grow and advance in times of peace.

Trace to their root all forms of tyranny and enslavement, all the widespread curses that the world over have degraded and embruted men and made the masses but hewers of wood and drawers of water; ask how slavery, serfdom, cannibalism, private property in land, and national debts came to be; how savage superstitions were engendered and how the slavish reverence for ruling families and classes has been developed and perpetuated—it will be found to be war and preparations for war. Civilization, in what does it essentially consist, but in the art or condition of men living civilly and peacefully with each other? In our most highly civilized society individuals no longer go constantly armed. Why should not nations also become civilized, and discard their war establishments?

Most advantageously situated of all the nations, it might be the grand destiny of the American Republic to lead the world to peace. Not to a "Roman peace" gained through blood and destruction, held by massive legions and carrying in its heart the seeds of its own decay, but a Christian peace, based on mutual respect and forbearance—a living, deepening, growing peace, having for its foundation that golden rule that teaches us that we should act toward others as we would have others act toward us.

Some glimmering recognition of the true place of the American Republic is shown in the proposal that has been made in her name that the nations should agree to settle disputes by arbitration. But how much more effective than any precept would be the example that would set before the world the spectacle of a great nation without a standing navy and without a standing army!

Of all the nations, ours is the one that can most easily and most safely set such an example. Too strong to fear injustice, we ought to be too proud to do it. What do we want with a "modern naval establishment"? In the quick brains, the strong arms, the loving hearts of self-reliant independent citizens who have really "a stake in the country," the republic will find her only sure defense. Building and maintaining "modern naval establishments" can only divert us from securing that.

The real dangers that menace the Republic are not from without, but from within. Standing armies and standing navies, heavy armor plates rolled by Bethlehem Iron Works and big guns made by the Hotchkiss Arms Company cannot guard against these dangers; they can only intensify them.

Bethlehem! The very word recalls the sweet story, radiant with a light that has glimmered down through centuries of iron and blood. Bethlehem, over which the star of a world stood hope, and angels sang of cheer to men of good will; where long seeking wise men bowed in joyful reverence before the lowly cradle of the Prince of Peace, who should turn sword into reaping hook and spear into plowshare! Is it not suggestive of our so-called "Christian civilization" that iron works of this name should have taken the contract to roll armor plates? Many are the stautes of Mars and Pluto that have Christ's name painted on them.

Instead of aping European monarchies, why should not the American Republic take her proper place and lead the way? The millions we have spent on a useless navy and are now likely to spend on a worse than useless one, what might they not have accomplished if intelligently devoted to the advancement of science and the kindly arts. Only a small part of it might ere this have made aerial navigation practicable, and relegated European steel-clads to the junk shop, and pointed fifty telescopes greater than the Lick nightly to the stars.

ON FREEDOM OF CONSCIENCE

Letter, "My Dear Sir"[5]

. . . And last, but to my mind not least, Mr. Hill was the sponsor of that worse than the "alien and sedition acts," the anti-anarchist bill which was carried through a ring-ruled Senate in the closing days of the last session, and beaten in the House by the sturdy opposition of a true Democratic representative, whom the Democratic machine has refused to renominate, John De Witt Warner. This bill, a fitting climax to the shameful Russian treaty ratified by a Democratic President and Senate,[6] (it is said through the influence of the Standard Oil trust) which binds us to the extradition of political offenders, was not aimed at action, but at opinion. It was the most flagrant violation of the freedom of thought ever proposed in this country by any person or any part—an attempt to make the American Republic an active and most efficient member of the league of European despots in an effort to stamp out those political opinions termed anarchistic, which hold that no government at all is better than that prostitution of government which is used but to throttle natural rights and to starve, enslave and torture the masses. Under it $60,000 was appropriated to send spies abroad to obtain information from the political police of the [European] Continent, of the coming to this country of persons holding or charged with holding such political opinions. Had it become law such a man as Prince Kropotkin,[7] the distinguished student and investigator, now enjoying the asylum of England, [and] the distinguished geographer, Élisée Reclus,[8] now enjoying the hospitality of Switzerland, or anyone accused by the foreign political police of anarchistic opinions could on arrival here be subject to questioning [regarding] his "opinions [relating] to government" and subject to search of his person for marks inflicted on the victims of Old World political tyranny, and, by "the orders, depress or judgments of foreign governments and police notifications" be taken "as prima facie evidence"; [he could also be] refused permission to land and sent back to the country from which he came. . . .

"Editorial"[9]

Tuesday of last week was the Hebrew Day of Atonement.[10] Some anarchist Hebrews in Brooklyn proposed to emphasize their dislike for their religion by making the most solemn night in its calendar a time of feasting and merrymaking. For this purpose they hired the Brooklyn Labor Lyceum, and announced an entertainment, to terminate with a supper and ball, in which John Most[11] was to make a speech, the existence of God was to be denied, all government was to be denounced, and the ceremonies of the Day of Atonement parodied.

Some Orthodox Hebrews, taking offense at this, applied to Judge Pratt of the Supreme Court for an injunction restraining the Labor Lyceum from granting the use of their hall for the meeting. They were very properly refused. Thereupon, application was made to the Mayor of Brooklyn,[12] and under pretense of preventing a riot, the hall was surrounded with police and the meeting suppressed as effectually and as arbitrarily as could have been done in Germany or Russia.

That the great majority of the people of Brooklyn approve this action is doubtless true, and it is doubtless true of the great majority of the people of the country. But this is all the more reason why it should not be suffered to pass without protest. The guarantees of liberty are not needed for majorities, but for minorities, and the more unpopular—whether justly or unjustly makes no difference—any set of men may be, the more scrupulously should their legal rights be respected.

The line is perfectly clear.

If men thrust obnoxiously opinions on others; if they assault others with their opinions in places where those others have equal right to be, they are beyond their right, and ought to be restrained or punished.

But in places where they have an exclusive right to be, and in presence only of those who choose to hear them, they are within their right in expressing their opinions, no matter how obnoxious those opinions may be to others—"being responsible," as the Constitution of the State of New York has it, "for the abuse of that right."

In this case the anarchists were clearly within their right, as guaranteed by the Constitution of the United States and the Constitution of the State of New York. They did not propose to go out on the streets or into any place of general concourse to proclaim opinions obnoxious to others, but to express them in a hall to which they, for that evening, had the exclusive right; to which no one was called to go who did not wish to hear them, and to which even no one could go to hear them without paying for the privilege.

That they proposed to deny God, to revile the Hebrew religion, or to denounce government has nothing whatever to do with the matter. In a democratic state, where belief or disbelief is acknowledged to lie entirely within the jurisdiction of individual conscience and government draws its title only from the consent of the people, it is not the business of the magistrate to take care of God, to protect any form of religion, or to silence any objection to government that does not take the form of an overt act. And the reason for this is to be seen in all the annals of persecution, in all the records of oppressive tyrannies. Jewish persecution of Christians, Christian persecution of Jews, the suppression of antislavery meetings by proslavery mayors, had all the same motive and justification as the suppression of this anarchist meeting.

What we of the American Republic need most of all is a higher respect for the rights of the individual. For not only is it true that there is no real freedom where the rights of the minority are not respected, but it is also true that unless the rights of minorities are respected the rights of the majority cannot be long preserved. . . .

ON CHARITY

Letter, "My Dear Mrs. Lowell"[13]

It is so ordered—by natural laws—that over and above the return to the productive exertion of the individual in society there is a value or return, collectively created. If we differ at all it is only as to the disposition of what may be left of this fund after the simple expenses of government are paid out of it.

If I understand you aright you think the distribution of this remainder would entail demoralization by giving to people what they did not directly work for, and would therefore leave it in the hands of the few instead of dividing it among all, in order to minimize the demoralizations.

But by the same reasoning it would be better to give it all to one person or one family, to still further minimize the demoralization, or still better, to destroy it.

But would it not be even better to use this surplus of a common fund for common purposes?

I believe with you that charity demoralizes. The reason is that it lowers and finally destroys self respect, the foundation of all the robust virtues. But it seems to me too sweeping a generalization to infer from this that it demoralizes people to get what they do not directly work for. I do not think that the Astor Library of the Cooper Institute or the Central Park or the British Museum demoralize anybody, or that our people would be demoralized by well-kept streets, an abundant supply of water, better schools, cheap railroad fares, etc., etc. And if you look into the lives of men who have done good work, especially literary men, you will find that in most cases it was some advantage that released them from the necessity of working hard for a living, which enabled them to do good work. The saddest thing to me about this intense struggle for mere existence is the moral loss and mental waste.

However, the question of what we shall do with the surplus will not come up practically for many a day. I do not think, any more than did your father, that such a tremendous revolution can be easily accomplished or even get to the simplification of taxation. The struggle must be hard, bitter, and long.

"The Church's Attitude Toward the Labor Question" and "Dr. Huntington's Proposed Prayer"[14]

Nor am I insensible to the usefulness of little things. The circular of the Church association for the advancement of the interests of labor, I think extremely useful for bringing before the Episcopal clergy and the general public a most telling fact in regard to the conditions of labor in this city—a fact well calculated to excite the sympathy and arouse the conscience of people whose tolerance of things as they are comes from their seeing the world only through the medium of their own surroundings. And I certainly think that the "little bit of reform" at which the circular directly aimed—the getting for shop girls extra pay for extra work during the Christmas season—a good thing in itself. But I do not think that any such little reforms ought ever to be urged, or even assented to, by those who see the need for larger reforms, without an explicit declaration of their insufficiency—an explicit declaration that what alone can solve the social question is not charity, but justice. And I confess to a feeling akin to disgust at the persistency with which such little reforms (that in most cases amount to nothing at all, even temporarily) are advocated by people who ought to be engaged in larger and better work. They seem to serve in many cases as palliatives for conscience and to divert and waste energies that, rightly directed, would be capable of accomplishing something real. See the tremendous force that has been wastefully spent in the organized labor movements of the United States, by being directed to little things, such as the establishing of bureaus of labor statistics, eight hour laws, inspectorates, and the gaining here and there of a little advance in wages. Something has been gained by all this agitation, to be sure, but nothing compared with what might have been gained had this energy been concentrated on measures capable of largely and permanently improving the conditions of labor. . . .

What Dr. Huntington proposes regarding the church's contribution to the settlement of the labor question is that she should put these two clauses in her liturgy: "Incline the hearts of employers, and of those whom they employ, to mutual forbearance, fairness and good will," and "Suffer not the hire of the laborers to be kept back by fraud." There can be no objection to these petitions in themselves, and in spirit, at least, they are already in the prayers of the Episcopal Church. Mutual forbearance, fairness and good will are good things between everybody, and the keeping back of the hire of laborers, or any other just debt, by fraud, is a bad thing.

But to put forward these petitions by way of asking God to solve the labor question seems to me blasphemous—first, because they do not make an honest presentation of the labor question, but hide and cover up its real root and cause; and second, because they involve the assumption that God has so poorly provided for the great masses of His children that ill will or fraud on the part of a small minority called employers can produce the widespread poverty and suffering which festers through our so-called Christian civilization. I believe as fully as does Mr. Newton[15] in the social power of prayer, and realize what he points out, that to lead men really to pray for the overthrow of injustice, is, at the same time, to lead them to work for it. But what effect would the prayers that Dr. Huntington proposes have in his congregation? Would the prayer for mutual forbearance and goodwill arouse in the fashionable worshippers in Grace Church the slightest suspicion that there is any social wrong that needs righting? "Suffer not the hire of the laborers to be kept back by fraud." To whom would they imagine this to apply, except to some wicked sweaters down in the Bowery, of whom they occasionally hear through the newspapers?

Now the plain, clear, God's truth is, that the labor problem does not spring from the want of forbearance or good will on the part of employers or employed, or from the fact that some employers swindle the employed when they get a chance, and that some of the employed swindle their employers when they get a chance. The labor problem, with all the vice, crime, and greed that grow out of want and the fear of want, springs from the fact that what the Creator has given equally to all His children our laws have made the private property of some of them: Dr. Huntington's proposed prayers are simply an attempt to cover up and lead away from this patent fact.

"Republican Government"[16]

The enormous sums that are dispensed in public and semipublic almsgiving (probably far greater sums are given in private and unrecorded alms), are evidence of a vague feeling of the injustice of existing social conditions. But however amiable may be the motives that prompt it, no form of almsgiving can remedy social injustice. On the contrary, it can in the long run but increase the very evils it seeks to palliate. It is like the giving of a dram to the man who shivers for want of proper clothes.

"Charity and Justice"[17]

I would not be understood as belittling that spirit which finds expression in works of benevolence, and which, seeing suffering, hastens to do what is nearest at hand. In Mr. Keyser's distribution of free soup, now brought to a close; in Mrs. Lamadrid's cheap meals; in Mrs. Lowell's work of unselfish devotion in organizing charity; in model tenements and free libraries and industrial schools, I recognize a quality which in its essence stands perhaps at the very summit of human virtues—a spirit which reaches its highest organized expression in those great orders of the Catholic Church, whose members taking the vow of perpetual poverty have devoted themselves to works of consolation, mercy, and helpfulness, and whose annals gleam with the radiance of lives in which it needs no canonization for all men to recognize the saints of God.

But high as we instinctively hold charity, and beneficent as may be its functions when justice is satisfied, no scheme of organized benevolence can take the place of justice in the social order. The cause of the evils with which charity, organized and unorganized, battles in vain, is that we permit and legalize robbery. If there are thousands of children who must go hungry unless charity feeds them, it is because they are disinherited. If there are stalwart men who must needs beg for a fifty-cent job in a charity woodyard, it is because they are fenced-out by monopoly from work opportunities which are theirs by natural right.

And while this is obviously the case, it is impossible not to see that there is a great deal in all discussions of social problems now going on, and in the advocacy and support of many of the schemes of alleviating poverty by benevolence, something which is really not charity, but the reverse—a conscious or half-conscious desire to use the cloak of charity to hush conscience and still the demand of justice.

"I belong," says Count Tolstoi, "to that class of people who by divers tricks take from the toiling masses the necessaries of life . . . and I imagine that I pity people and I wish to assist them. I sit on a man's neck and I weigh him down, and I demand that he shall carry me; and without descending from his shoulders I assure myself and others that I am very sorry for him and that I desire to ameliorate his condition by all possible means, *only not by getting off of him.*"

This is the fatal defect of all the schemes for alleviating poverty and improving the condition of the working masses by benevolence, with which people who will not listen to the simple remedy of stopping robbery and restoring natural rights so frequently amuse themselves. They are devices to help the downtrodden man without getting off of him.

Mrs. Lowell is correct when she says that I place the blame for the fact that able-bodied men apply for charity, upon the people of the United States. I put it upon the people of the United States because in their hands is the sovereign political power—the power of making and unmaking laws; and in the fact that a country so wide and so rich as this is, swarming with able-bodied men who cannot find work, I see only the result of bad laws. But I am far from believing that the people of the United States are equally to blame. Those on whom the responsibility most heavily rests are those who have talent, leisure, and culture; those who occupy . . . a position that make them teachers, leaders, and directors of thought. What, as a class, are these men doing in the United States today in the face of the steadily increasing pressure of the most stupendous social problem? They are engaged in darkening counsel and stilling conscience, and either treating the great wrong, which must surely wreck society if it continues, with flippant denial, or endeavoring to draw men's minds away from any thought of it by rosewater schemes for ameliorating the condition of labor *"without getting off of him."* And in this they are doing not merely negative evil but positive evil. For in their endeavors to hide and lead away from the obvious cause and the simple remedy of widespread and growing distress and discontent they are sowing the seeds of socialism, communism, anarchism, and blind destruction.

ON RACISM

"Henry George in Memphis: How the Race Problem Can Be Solved"[18]

... The colored people are here, the blacks are among you, and for some time to come, so far as we can see, they must remain. Whatever may be the final solution of the question this thing is certain, the more they advance in intelligence, the more they acquire property, the less is the bitter competition for employment, and the easier all such questions will be solved. Everywhere, all over the world, the bitterness of race troubles is intensified whenever men of different color or tongue have to bid against each other for employment. What we propose would give employment for all. It would raise labor to its true dignity, it would make wages what they ought to be, it would do away with the bitter competition, it would transform them from rivals and enemies to friends and peaceful citizens, and it would bring about a state of things in which passion and prejudice so aroused would die. It would elevate the negro race faster than anything else, because at the same time it would elevate the white race. Underneath the local aspect of that question lies the same problem that we have in the North. Make no mistake about it. In any condition of things where there exists a great body of people too poor to feel any interest in the proper administration of public affairs, whether white or black, there universal suffrage brings on the quicker injuries and disorders.

The idea is rapidly passing away in the march of democracy that men who have no property ought not to vote. There is something in the idea that no man who has not a stake in the country is fit to exercise suffrage. Every man ought to have a stake in the country. Every man would have a stake in the country under the simple measure we propose. In the North we have the same class, the same kind. Why is it? Because of the corruption in our great cities? Simply this, that in these cities there is a class of people who are very rich; there is also a great body of voters to whom it makes no difference whether the governmental affairs are managed economically or extravagantly, whether it be wise or injudicious administration, whether good or corrupt; and a republican government based on universal suffrage must, under such conditions, be corrupt. Take the masses of our people in the cities of the North, men who work for a bare living; what difference does a good or bad administration make to them?

Cheapen their goods, improve your cities, let there be economy where there was extravagance, let there be honesty where there was corruption, and then you will see what is the difference to them. The landowner may increase his rent, but no public improvement interests them or does them any good until they are interested as citizens in the prosperity of the state. Then, and until then, must our democracy have a weak and uncertain basis.

Slavery abolished! Slavery has not been abolished—only that coarse and rude form has. Why did slavery grow up here in the South? Why is it that those negroes were not carried to England instead of across the waters to the South? The answer is, that slaves are never carried where population is dense; slaves are always carried to sparsely-populated countries. Where population becomes dense, if you want to compel the labor of other men it isn't necessary to make property of their bodies. All that is necessary is to make property of the land. Carry slaves to Ireland or England? Why, you can get labor there cheaper than most slaveowners paid for their slaves, without any of the responsibilities. The air of England for a long time could not be breathed by a slave. They were nominally free, but the land by and from which alone they got their living being owned by others, they had to come and beg permission to work, and looked upon the privilege of working as a boon, and gave in return all their labor could produce, save just enough to live. So it is here today. Your ex-slaves are free, but they do not get any more or better living than they did before. Do they not now pay for rents about as much as profits were before? Economically, what is the difference?[19]

REGARDING THE WORKERS

On Labor Strikes[20]

During this tie up [of the horse car lines] New York and Brooklyn have been in a state of mild civil war. The companies have been able to run no cars, or to run but few of them; not from the difficulty of getting men willing to work as drivers and conductors, but from the fear of violence. "Scabs" or supposed "scabs" have been hooted, beaten, and driven away. Obstructions have been placed on the car tracks, stones thrown, and other signs of incipient riot from time to time manifested. It is said, and it is probably true, that there would have been more violence, but for the energy and efficiency of the police. As is the custom in New York, they have acted from the first as though martial law had been proclaimed; or rather they simply administered lynch law. They did not exactly hang everybody that it seemed to them good and wise to hang. But they did, as appears from the newspaper reports, proceed to club everybody they thought it good and wise to club, whether he had committed any overt act or whether they merely thought he looked as if he might commit some overt act if suffered to go unclubbed. They cleared saloons, entered houses, and charged on crowds with their clubs without any such old-fashioned formality as the reading of a riot act. Perhaps this was necessary to prevent the necessity of greater violence. Perhaps this is the only way in which in such times riots can be prevented in New York. Such evidently is the prevailing opinion among the influential classes of New York. But to say this, is to say that constitutional methods of government have become impossible in New York, and that order can only be kept by the stick of Eastern despotism. To all but the lower classes this may be entirely satisfactory for the time. But some day, if this be the only way of keeping the peace, the stick is sure to break.

Like all railroad strikes, these tie ups are but another evidence of the mistake of leaving functions essentially public to private corporations or individuals. No owner of a large building would think of leasing out the privilege of running the elevator necessary for giving access to its upper stories to one who expected to make a profit by charging people for carrying them up and down. Still less would he think of submitting, if only for a day, to a suspension of the accustomed means of getting up and down, whenever there should be a quarrel between the leasee and his employees.

Yet that is what we do with our street cars. What is the difference between the elevator in a building and the street cars of a city, except that one runs perpendicularly and the other horizontally?

When it is understood that the ground values of a city belong rightfully to the whole people, that is to say, to the city itself, then the parallel becomes absolutely complete. Under the single tax it would seem as absurd to put a conductor on a street car to collect fares as it would now seem to put a conductor on an elevator to collect fares. Just as the proprietor of a large building gets back the cost of running a free elevator in the increased value of his rooms, so would the city under the single tax run its street cars free to anyone who wished to ride, [for it would] get back the cost in increased land values.

The comments of the press on such conflicts as these tie-ups would be amusing if they were not something more. One set of papers, utterly ignoring the unnatural conditions in which the mere laborer is placed, denounce the strikers as though they were wanton violators of the right of others to make such bargains as they choose and to do such honest work as they see best. All that such papers say would be very just and very true if there were no such thing as customs duties to interfere with the laborer's right of bargain; if there were no fine and imprisonment for the man who buys a little tobacco and makes a few cigars; if the peddler even did not have to have a license; if the franchises that rightfully belong to the whole community had not been given up to the enrichment of a few; and if the land, the natural soucre of all employment, were not for thousands of miles, (wherever there is any possibility that the laborer can go), fenced in from him him even when lying idle.

And so another set of papers pose as friends of the workingman, and just as carefully ignoring the essential injustice that lies at the root of all these labor troubles, pat the men on the back with words that mean nothing, but strenuously urge them to refrain from violence—just as if force in some of its forms were not the only means by which, with thousands of other men ready to take their places, the strikers can hope to bring their employers to terms.

If anything else were needed the failure of strikes and tie ups ought to convince workingmen that their combinations cannot beat combinations of capitalists, so long as labor is denied the natural right of access to the land. To permanently raise wages, the army of the unemployed must be gotten rid of, and they can only be gotten rid of by throwing open to labor the source of all employment. The single tax is the only remedy for a condition in which the mere laborer is helpless. And it could be carried with one-tenth of the effort that has been expended in hopeless directions.

"The 'Fight in the Dark' "[21]

It is folly to tell workingmen that they ought not to strike because strikes can only injure them. Not only are there many workingmen who have nothing to lose, but it is a matter of fact that strikes and the fear of strikes have secured to large bodies of them considerable increase of wages, considerable reduction in working hours, much mitigation of the petty tyrannies that can be practiced with impunity where one man holds in his hands control of the livelihood of another, and have largely promoted the growth of fraternal feeling in the various trades. The greater number of strikes fail; but even the strike that fails, though its immediate object is lost, generally leaves employers indisposed for another such contest, and makes them more cautious of provoking fresh difficulties. The whole power of the trades union for good or for evil rests on the strike; without that as a last resort it could neither hold its own members together, nor treat with employers.

Nor is it so strange as some pretend that one body of workmen without any special grievance of their own should strike to help another. The immediate purpose of a strike is to inflict damage upon opposing employers, and there are many cases in which employers who could defy their own workmen can be seriously hurt by pressure exerted upon them through the medium of other employers with whom they have business relations. To be sure, third parties, who have no direct interest in the quarrel, suffer, and frequently the greatest sufferers are the men who thus go out to help their fellows. But if the strike would be made more costly, its results, in causing employers to hesitate before engaging in another such contest, are likely to be more decisive and more effective. And men may strike, as men fight, in a quarrel not originally their own, either as a matter of sentiment or from the more selfish consideration that they will make alliances that will render them stronger in any quarrels of their own; or, as is generally the case, from the mingling of both motives.

And when men are willing to stop work and submit to loss and suffering in the effort to aid their fellows, does it not show heroism of the same kind as that which prompts men to risk their lives in battle for those weaker than themselves? Those who condemn the strike of the freight handlers in aid of the coal trimmers must, if they be logical and assume the standpoint of workingmen, condemn the aid which the French gave to the struggling American Republic.

As for the morality of strikes it is precisely like that of any other applicant of coercive force. They who really hold that "whosoever shall smite thee on thy right cheek, turn to him the other also"; and "if any man will take away thy coat, let him have thy cloak also"; they who hold that the command, "Thou shalt not kill," applies as well to the man in uniform as to the man in plain clothes, might with some consistency condemn strikes, but they would be alone. If there are any such people, they are not to be found in the editorial rooms of our great dailies or the pulpits of our fashionable churches. On the contrary, the loudest denouncers of strikes—those who declare that they ought to be put down by force if necessary—are to be found among the class who have grown rich by extortion backed by force.

A favorite platitude, now finding wide expression in the American press, is that although men have an unquestioned right to stop work themselves they have no right to coerce others into stopping work, and the disposition of workingmen to do this when they are on strike is denounced as not merely wicked in the highest degree, but as unAmerican.

This is nonsense. When our forefathers struck against England, they not merely struck themselves, but compelled everyone else they could to join them, first by "moral suasion," which amounted to ostracism, and then by such measures as tarring and feathering, harrying, and shooting; and when they boycotted the East India Company's tea they were not content with simply refusing to drink it themselves, but threw it into the sea, so that nobody else could drink it.

A strike can only amount to anything insofar as it is coercive, and whatever workingmen may say, they must of necessity feel, that a strike can accomplish anything only by exerting some form of pressure upon those disposed to go to work. For the most part, so far, this pressure has been a moral one, and the penalty of being held in contempt as "scabs" has been sufficient to induce men to undergo actual suffering rather than assert what the denouncers of strikes declare to be the inalienable right of every American citizen. . . . there is a growing disposition to resort to more violent measures. And whether right or wrong the growth of this disposition is natural.

"Everyone has a right to work or not as he pleases, but no one has a right to prevent anyone else from going to work." That is true. But is it a truth that applies only to strikers?

The fact is, it is because we ignore this truth that trade unions are made necessary and strikes come. The fact is, that the very men who are now calling so loudly for the maintenance, by the bayonet if necessary, of the liberty to work are the most strenuous supporters of a system which denies the liberty to work.

How is it that a land, like ours, abounding in unused natural resources, is filled with unemployed men? Is it not because of the power which our laws give to some men to prevent other men from going to work?

Let the striking laborers of New York City accept the dictum that no man has a right to prevent another from going to work. Let them turn from attempts to compel their former employers to employ them, and where shall they go to employ themselves? Where can they go that they will not find some one, backed by law and force, who forbids them to work? There is plenty of unused land in the upper part of the city. Let them go upon this land and attempt to employ their labor in building houses. How long will it be before they are warned off? Let them cross the East River, the North River or the Harlem. They will find everywhere unused fields on which, without interference by any men, they might employ their labor in making a living for themselves and all dependent on them. But they will not find a field though they tramp for a thousand miles, on which some one has not the legal right to prevent them going to work. What is left for them to do but to beg for the wages of some employer? And if, to prevent being crushed by competition of others like themselves, they strive, even by force, to keep others from going to work, [are they to] blame?

The very worse the strikers do or think of doing is to prevent others from going to work, so that they themselves may work and earn a scanty living by hard toil. But what are the "dogs-in-the-manger" doing who are holding unused city lots, farmlands, mines, and forests—the natural opportunities, in short, that nature offers to labor?

They are preventing other people from working, not that they may work themselves, but that they may live in idleness on what those who want to work are compelled to pay them for the privilege of going to work. If the freight handlers and coal trimmers and other laborers were to form societies which should prevent by force anyone from going to work without their permission, were to charge the highest price for the privilege of going to work which the necessities of others could compel them to pay, and were then to sit down and live in idleness on this blackmail, they would only be doing to others what organized society permits others to do to them.

It seems hopeless to expect the classes who imagine they profit by this primary wrong to open their eyes to the real cause of these labor troubles, but when the workingmen do so, the day of their emancipation is at hand. Everyone of these strikes ought to show them where the real trouble lies. In the great strikes that have been going on in New York, as in all great strikes, the real difficulty the strikers have had to contend with is the influx of unemployed labor. The men with whom the coal companies and the steamship companies have supplied the places of the strikers in New York and vicinity are men drawn from the country by the prospect of work, or men who, after vainly tramping the country have crowded into the city. If there was a brisk demand for labor in the country there would be no such surplus of labor, anxious for work on any terms, on which employers could draw; and that there is not such a demand for labor is due simply to the fact that laborers are prevented by the monopoly of natural opportunities from employing themselves. . . .

"Mr. Hewitt on Labor Organizations"[22]

. . . Trade unions, and all similar organizations of labor, as I have never hesitated to say when addressing men who belong to them, are in their nature not good, but evil. They involve coercion, and can only be effective through coercion or the fear of coercion. The organization of men into trade unions, like the organization of men into armies, must necessarily be at the sacrifice of individual liberty, and while the methods of the one are those of passive war, and those of the other active war, they are both destructive methods—both aim at the infliction of loss and suffering upon those who oppose them, even at the expense of loss and suffering to those who belong to them. The justification of both trade unions and armies, is not their essential goodness, but the existence of other evils which make them for a time necessary for the maintenance of a partial liberty.

. . . To organize a whole people into trade unions, to pool labor and pool capital in all branches of industry, would result, not in freedom, but in an Egyptian system of caste in which freedom, and the idea of freedom, would utterly perish. Most bitterly unjust as is the denunciation of trade unions without denunciation of the monopolies which provoke and compel workingmen to combine in these defensive associations; the railing condemnation of boycotts on the part of laborers without one word in recognition of the perpetual boycott which shuts labor out from the natural opportunities for labor—it is more likely to carry with it its own antidote . . . than is the declaration by such a man as Mr. Hewitt that trades unionism is the way, and the only way, to the emancipation of labor.

"POLITICAL AND SOCIAL": A RESPONSE TO TERENCE POWDERLY[23]

But it is in the part of Mr. Powderly's letter that some of the newspapers style in their headlines a "refutation of the George theory" that he shows himself most puzzleheaded. He says:

Today in every town and hamlet the land question is being studied, and the simple proposition of the Knights of Labor stands up in giant form before every man and woman who toils or feels an interest in the country we inhabit. Theories are advanced, which in themselves sound very nice as to the ownership of all land by the people in common. Before that object can be attained the people must learn to think "in common." It must first be demonstrated that the idea is practicable. I once believed that the people could own and till the soil in common. I did not believe that it was right for an individual to hold absolute ownership of the soil. Today I know that an individual cannot hold absolute title to the soil if the interests of the people "in common" require that it should be otherwise.

I no longer believe that the people "in common" can till the soil and own it in common. First, because they do not think "in common"; second, because the people are only people and not angels. In other words, the people are not good enough yet to discard the native selfishness which was born in them. We must take men and women as we find them. As we find men and women today, they are selfish and grasping. Each one has a desire to own and control a home of his own, and my efforts will be put forth to the end that each man who wishes to may own his own home. If every man owned his own home, labor would be more appreciated than it is; the desire to reduce the hours of labor would be greater, for every man would have a place on which to expend his spare moments.

In the beginning of his letter, Mr. Powderly says that when he assumed the duties of his position he had no knowledge of the science of the labor question. Judging from this letter he has since that time "progressed backward." In 1879 he was at least aware of his own ignorance.

There is a sublimity of confusion in all this. . . . But even Archbishop Corrigan could have furnished Mr. Powderly with a better argument against the socialist notion which he asyas he once held, than the assertion that only angels can own and till land in common. To say nothing of the history of past times, any Jesuit or Trappist or Carmelite can tell Mr. Powderly of land owned and tilled in common by people who, whatever their hopes for the future, have not yet become angels. Mr. Powderly's pious condonation of the "native selfishness" which induces men and women to want to own and control homes of their own, shows, however, the goodness of his heart. His condescension to this selfish and grasping spirit, which in his queer philosophy seems to be one of the things that distinguish men from angels, not merely goes so far as to lead him to declare that his efforts will be put forth to the end that each man who wishes may own his own home, but even leads him to point out some advantages that will result from this concession to unangelic selfishness and greed. The General master Workman of the Knights of Labor is, it is said, so far giving way to his own "native selfishness" as to be building for himself a new house in Scranton. But when he gets to heaven he evidently expects to board.

ON WOMAN'S RIGHTS

"Various Matters:" On Woman's Suffrage[24]

The International Council of Women which assembled in Washington on Sunday, and the meetings in the previous week of the New York State Woman's Suffrage Society at which the European delegates were present, bring up again the matter of the disfranchisement of that "better half" of mankind, who even in American states, where every tramp can vote, are debarred from the suffrage. The cause of woman suffrage is steadily, though slowly and quietly making progress in public opinion. In a large and ever-widening circle the women who want to vote are no longer deemed masculine nor the men who would have them vote, effeminate. The goal has not been reached and may yet be far off, but since the first woman's rights convention was held in the United States forty years ago, great advances have been made.[25] Much of this is below the surface, and shows in a changed tone of opinion rather than in changed laws, but it is none the less real. The progress of such reforms is not to be measured by the noise they make. It is like the progress of a quiet stream in undermining a massive wall. The stream flows on, month after month and year after year, but the great structure still stands, and to one who looks from a distance seems as strong as ever; until some day—when no one can predict—and as the result perhaps of some immediate cause so slight that no one can precisely tell what it is, the great mass trembles and falls.

Some parts of the wall have already fallen. Already in Wyoming Territory women have the full suffrage. They voted for five years in Washington Territory, until last year the act under which their votes were cast was set aside by the territorial Supreme Court because of a technical informality in its title. They also voted in Utah until disfranchised by Congress in the bigoted Edmunds Bill.[26] In Kansas they have municipal suffrage. Arkansas and Mississippi permit them a vote on the liquor question. And in fourteen states and four territories—viz.: Colorado, Indiana, Kansas, Kentucky, Massachusetts, Michigan, Minnesota, Nebraska, New Hampshire, New Jersey, New York, Oregon, Vermont, Wisconsin, Dakota, Idaho, Montana, and Washington—they have more or less a restricted right of voting on school questions.

The advance of women in respect to higher education, their entrance into the professions, their larger place in literature, their occupation here and there of public positions, such as Josephine Shaw Lowell holds on the New York State Board of Charities, are to some extent results of the agitation in favor of equal political rights, and certainly tend to quietly promote it. And so it is with the increasing employment of women in factories, stores, offices, etc. This is in itself an evil—the result of the growth of unnatural conditions and increasing social pressure. But it furnishes an obvious and strong argument for the extension of the suffrage. When women must work like men, it is clear that they ought to vote like men.

One thing is noticeable in these recent suffrage conventions. Women have learned to conduct meetings without men. In the meetings in this city, and in the larger and more important gatherings at Washington, not a man—either of the long-haired or short-haired variety—appeared on the stage or assisted in the proceedings in any other way than that of listener, with the privilege of putting something in the collection baskets carried around by women. No man was even called on to make a prayer or give a benediction. Six "reverends" assisted at the opening meeting in Washington on Sunday last, but everyone of them was a woman. Nor have the meetings been any the worse on account of this exclusion of the bearded sex. They have shown not only a high order, but a great variety of talent.

The notion of the intellectual inferiority of women is in fact quietly but steadily melting away. That women intellectually differ from men is, of course true, and must remain true. But this difference does not necessarily imply inferiority. "If I cannot carry forests on my back, neither can you crack a nut." And even in matters in which men are generally considered superior, women, with the larger opportunities now opening to them, are constantly giving evidences of their ability. . . .

But the main argument for woman's suffrage, to my mind, is not that it will enable women to vote, but that it will lead women to think. In all questions of politics—that is to say, in all questions of law and government—women have as direct and as vital an interest as men. If times are hard and wages low, must not women stint, strain, worry, and slave? If people are crowded into narrow tenement rooms, and children die by thousands before their time, upon which sex does the discomfort and pain most bitterly fall? It is true that women cannot fight, or, rather, that it is not the custom of civilized nations to drag or bribe them into armies or navies for the purpose of standing ready to wound and kill each other. But for every man who wears a uniform is there not some woman, his natural complement, left at home to get along as best she can? And do the losses, the wastes, and the agonies of war, fall more lightly on women than on men? If one sex must shed blood, are not the tears of the other often bitterer than blood?

But with this direct and vital interest in public questions, women, not being called upon to pass upon such questions, are accustomed to regard them as beyond their sphere, and if they think of them at all, regard them flippantly. And this disposition of one-half of our people must exert a powerful influence upon the other half.

I do not regard women as the downtrodden sex. On the contrary, it seems to me that the influence of women upon men wherever they care to exercise that influence, is a natural fact, and that the power which maintains laws and customs oppressive to women is to be looked for rather in feminine than in masculine opinion. Clearly this is the case with our restriction of the suffrage to male citizens. All that the advocates of woman's suffrage have to do is to convert their own sex. Whenever a majority of the women of the United States want to vote, a majority of the men will vote [accordingly]. . . . But in the mean time, men take a less intelligent interest in public affairs because of the little intelligent interest that women take. The conservatism that springs from the indisposition to think; the neglect of general interests which arises from the failure to appreciate how powerfully general interests affect individual interests, are largely reflected from the opinion of women through the opinion of men. Does not this account for much of the sluggishness and flippancy of our thought upon the most important public questions? Does it not account for much of the difficulty in getting the masses to realize the relation between bad laws and hard times? Does it not largely account for that dull, stolid conservatism which is the greatest obstacle in the wall of all reform? . . .

Here is a point for the consideration of the advocates of woman's rights. Its agitation would have the incidental advantage of calling public attention to the [utter] uselessness of our present division of legislative powers. Our senates and assemblies are in reality copies of the British Parliament, with its House of Lords and House of Commons. Unfortunately for us, however, one house has not dwarfed and absorbed the power of the other, as in Great Britain, but in our states, as in the legislature of the nation, one house can neutralize the other. There is some reason for this division of Congress, the Senate affording an equal representation to the states, irrespective of their population, while the House represents the people. But the inconvenience and injustice of such representation are becoming more apparent as our national government becomes more and more the government of a nation and less and less like a league, as the disproportion between the populations of states steadily increases. In our state legislatures, if any reason at all can be assigned for the division, it is simply that of dividing power and providing a check of one house upon the other. But all experience shows that the result of this is merely a division of responsibility which distracts attention and removes the representative from the control of public opinion, while the difference between the members of the two houses regarding the times of election and length of terms also serves to diminish party responsibility. One of the remarkable things in American journalism today is the little space that is given to the proceedings of our state legislatures and our national Congress. The majority of the people of New York know no more of what is being done in the "law mill" at Albany than the mass of the people of China know of what is being done in the Peking boards, and the American Congress has almost ceased to be a forum from which a statesman may speak to the nation. A bit of scandal or a disgusting crime gets more attention in our daily papers than a congressional debate on the most important subject. Other causes have undoubtedly contributed to this result, but there can be no question that the duality of our legislatures has something to do with it. Every important measure must be fought over twice. Its fate in one house by no means determines its fate in the other. Thus public attention tires in the needless strain of watching struggles that may be of no consequence. A single house would call more attention to its acts, would attach more responsibility to its members and to the dominant party, and would unquestionably tend to bring to our lawmaking a higher standard of character and talent.

But if we must have two houses, then by all means let us adopt the Shaker suggestion and fill one with women and the other with men.

"Henry George in England"[27]

. . . It seems startling to think of woman suffrage becoming an accomplished fact in Great Britain within two or three years. And yet this is one of the things which the present political situation may bring about. . . . The idea certainly frightens many of the radical politicians. With the present electorate they feel certain of regaining power as soon as an appeal to the country is made. But if the women are called in they fear that the new vote may swamp them.

. . . It is certainly more than possible that in the very next general election women may vote as well as men, and that when the next Parliament assembles representatives of the sex who up to this time have only been permitted to look down on the Commons through the bars of a cage may take their seats on the benches of the House. . . .

The bill is not likely to pass at this session, but it begins to look as though the British Empire were within measurable distance of a resolution that, with a woman on the throne and a majority of women in the electorate, would put the ultimate political power in the hands of women.[28]

That the women in their new found power might do some foolish things is probable. But it is certain that they cannot do more foolish things than the men have done. And though at first they may stand in the way of some reforms that are on the verge of accomplishment, it is certain that they will ultimately call for larger reforms. . . .

ON FINANCIAL ISSUES

A Historical Tidbit[29]

If Caesar or Napoleon were to come back to earth again as a citizen of the American Republic in our times, the one would not run for public office nor the other seek a military career. The shortest road to the greatest power here and now is through the control of the corporations which we have allowed to possess the highways of the continent.

"Various Matters:" On the Debt[30]

An interesting paper upon the credit system was read at the recent meeting of the National Board of Trade at Cincinnati by J. A. Price, president of the Board of Trade of Scranton, PA. The ever-increasing national debts of Europe he estimates at $22,500,000,000, imposing upon its people an annual interest charge of some $800,000,000, and in addition to this there are railway, municipal and commercial debts and mortgages to an amount that can hardly be estimated. Of the volume of indebtedness in this country he makes the following estimate:

> Present national debt, Dec. 1, 1887: $1,675,816,680
> State: $226,597,594
> County and municipal: $821,186,447
> Railway: $4,163,640,141
> Banking: $4,581,706,208
> Private banking: $1,500,000,000
> Record: $6,000,000,000
> Mercantile: $3,000,000,000
> Individual, otherwise than above: $6,000,000,000
> Aggregate: $27,969,247,048

Estimating our population at 60,000,000, this would be some $465 for every man, woman, and child in the United States, or over $2,000 for every head of a family. Some of the items in this estimate are of course mere guesses, and some of the debts included are of course offset and cancelled by others; but whatever deductions can be made on these accounts, the result is sufficiently startling. The civilized world—and our own country not last in the race—is rushing forward into a sea of indebtedness that must finally submerge itself into general bankruptcy and repudiation.

Colonel Price advocates the abolition of all laws for the collection of private debts, and he is unquestionably right. There is no more reason why the state should lend its machinery of constables, sheriffs, courts, and . . . its prisons to the collection of the debts of the individual, than that it should undertake to black his boots in the morning or tuck him into bed at night. The abolition of all laws for the collection of private debts would not only free our judicial machinery from a clogging mass of business which to a large degree prevents its performance of proper functions, but it would unquestionably lead to a far higher standard of personal and commercial morality, since character would then be the prime element in credit. If it lessened, as it undoubtedly would, the use of credit in commercial transactions, the result would be to put business upon a far more sound and stable foundation and to lessen the intensity of those commercial fluctuations in which periods of stagnation follow periods of speculation. The curse of credit as a flux of exchanges is that it expands when there is a tendency to speculation, and sharply contracts just when most needed to assure confidence and prevent industrial waste.

The enormous figures that Colonel Price presents are also extremely suggestive in other ways. For instance, they [should be called to the attention of those] who incline to the belief that it is capital that oppresses labor, and that before labor can get its fair reward interest must in some way be abolished. The greater part of this vast volume of indebtedness passes as capital, and on nearly all its payments having the semblance of true interest. . . . Yet the worldwide proclamation of a Jewish jubilee would at the blast of a trumpet sweep away this whole vast mass of indebtedness without lessening the wealth of the world by a single iota. Nor, for the most part, does this volume of debt represent any ownership of real and existing capital. The mortgages, for instance, in greater part, do not represent capital loaned to the users of land, but mere rent charges—payments which the users of land have been compelled to agree to make to landowners as a condition to use land. An Eastern speculator or a foreign investor gets hold of a tract of Western land, cuts it up into farms and sells it out to settlers on mortgage, or a tract of land near a city is cut up and sold in the same way. The seller gets obligations which are counted as capital and receives payments which are termed interest. But in reality there has been no production or transfer of capital, and the payments are not interest for the use of capital, but blackmail for the use of land. So railway indebtedness really represents to a large degree, not capital invested in making railways, but what is suggestively termed "water," and the interest they bear is not payment for the use of capital, but is a monopolistic blackmail upon the public.

As for the gigantic public debts, they represent capital only insofar as there are public improvements to show for them. What they do, for the most part represent, is either sheer public plunder, or capital and labor destroyed and wasted in war or preparations for war. Our own national debt, incurred during the war for the maintenance of the Union, is unquestionably the best and fairest of them all. But it does not represent, as is often assumed, wealth borrowed from foreign nations or for the carrying on of a future war. As a matter of fact, during the war we did not increase our obligations much, if any, to foreign nations, and it is as clearly a physical impossibility to borrow wealth from the future to carry on a war, as it is to get men still unborn to fight in it. The wealth that was used and destroyed during our Civil War was from what then existed. The carrying on of war by means of public debts, which is probably the most injurious and anticivilizing of all modern inventions, is not a device for spreading the cost of present expenditures over future time, but one by which governments may obtain wealth from the classes who have wealth to spare, without exciting their opposition—since in return it gives them a mortgage upon the labor of the future. The United States might have come through the war without a penny of public debt if the government had taken wealth from its possessors as ruthlessly as it took men. Whether the wealthy classes would have submitted to this is quite another question.

But it is instructive to consider how different would have been the existing distribution of wealth if we had done so. And ever since the war, our whole financial policy seems to have been steadily directed to making the taxation for the fulfillment of the obligations then given as onerous as possible. Where we borrow forty, fifty, and sixty cents, we have paid one hundred and even one hundred and twenty cents, with money wrung from the people by the most onerous system of taxation—systems of taxation purposely devised to fatten monopoly and make the rich richer. We have paid off noninterest bearing debt, and by means of the national banking system we have permitted the holders of a large part of the public debt to enjoy the principle while they draw the interest. Through the national banking system the banker was allowed to draw from the government $80,000 in money for every $100,000 in bonds he deposited, and then to draw interest on the whole $100,000. This proportion was subsequently increased to ninety per cent, and now a bill is pending in Congress to allow the national banks a dollar in money for every dollar in bonds they deposit, while paying them full interest on the dollar. And not content with this, as though from the mere desire of paying as much interest as possible, and making the redemption of our public debt as slow as possible, we are actually buying up enormous amounts of silver, for which we have no more use than for so many tons of cobblestones, and storing them away in vaults. Secretary Fairchild sees the absurdity of coining silver and proposes instead that it shall be stowed away in bars. But why not leave the silver in the ore and the ore in the ground? That would be a far greater economy. As for the silver notes, that would be just as useful and just as readily taken if they promised to pay silver yet to be mined and refined, or if instead of promising to pay anything at all, they were simply made receivable for public dues.

But it is only when we come to think of the public debts of Europe that we realize the full importance of Thomas Jefferson's idea that no generation should have the right to bind a future generation, and that every nineteenth year ought to be a year of jubilee, in which all public debts should be declared void. If mankind would agree on this, the enormous armaments of Europe would be impossible, and there is not a throne in Europe that would not crumble into dust. Colonel Price has opened a fruitful subject by calling the attention of the National Board of Trade to this matter of growing indebtedness. . . .

"Politics that Mean Something"[31]

The [Civil] War brought the nation one good thing—the taxing out of circulation notes issued by state banks, and the substitution for these local issues a currency of uniform value throughout the United States. But the institutions of the national banking system had nothing to do with this beneficial change. That was simply a sop to the banks—the bribing of these powerful corporations, by giving them special privileges at the expense of a people whose patriotism made them for a time careless of how they were taxed. While the ordinary citizen who bought a government bond parted with his money in consideration of the interest he was promised, the favored corporations who took advantage of the National Banking Law[32] were given back in government notes, bearing their names, nine-tenths the face value of their bonds, thus getting back nine-tenths of the money they were supposed to loan the government, while continuing to draw interest on the whole amount.

This virtual subsidizing of the national banks has cost the people far more than the vast sums paid to the national banks as interest on money they never loaned. The influence of the national banks upon our fiscal legislation is largely accountable for a policy which seems expressly designed to make the payment of the debt incurred during the war as costly as possible to the taxpayer. And now that the redemption of the debt threatens the withdrawal of the national bank circulation based upon the deposit of bonds, all sorts of plans are proposed to secure the continuance of the special privileges for the banks.

The proposition of Senator Farwell of Illinois to issue fifty-year two and a half per cent bonds for the use of the banks, on which they are to be allowed circulating notes to full par value, and to permit them to substitute for United States bonds, as a basis of circulation, state, county or municipal bonds at seventy-five per cent of their par value, is the latest of these propositions to perpetuate the national banks. This brings into striking light the preposterous nature of the whole system.

The issuance of bonds mean, or ought to mean, the borrowing of money. Yet under Senator Farwell's proposition the United States is to issue bonds bearing two and a half per cent interest, to hand back to the purchasers all the money they pay for the bonds, and then to go on for fifty years paying them interest on money it has not borrowed or they have not loaned. And then to secure the perpetuity of this system of subsidizing the banks at the expense of the people, Senator Farwell proposes that the United States shall go into a similar one-sided banking business with these corporations on other securities than its own. Reduced to its simplest terms the proposition is that when these favored banks lend a state, county or municipality $100 at four, five or six per cent interest, the United States is to lend them $75 without interest.

If it should do this for the banks, why should it not do this for merchants, and manufacturers, and miners, and farmers, for the publishers of books and newspapers and, in short, for everybody else? Banks are useful things, it is true. But farms, and factories, and ships, and dry goods stores, and carpenter shops, and bootblack stands, and some newspapers, are also useful things. And if the national banks who take good care to charge other people interest when they loan them money, are to borrow money from the federal government without interest; why should not the United States go into this business of lending money free of interest to everybody?

Senator Farwell's preposterous proposition is carrying out only one step further the existing system of bank subsidies. It is but a natural result of the manner in which the people of the United States have for years permitted themselves to be taxed for the benefit of a few favored corporations. There never was any good reason for the institution of the national banking system, and there is not today any good reason for its continuance. Like all special privileges, it is but a taxing of the many for the benefit of the few, and like all use of governmental power for private advantage, it has resulted in governmental extravagance and political demoralization. The pretence that there is some mystery about currency and banking that common people cannot understand, is like the pretence that no one but the members of the protected rings and trusts are competent to say what tariff taxes shall be levied on the people. The pretence that the national banking system rendered necessary aid in putting down the rebellion, and that it has given us a uniform currency, is like the pretence that we owe our growth and prosperity to the tariff. The national bank notes current in the United States fulfill the functions of generally acceptable money, not because they have the name of a bank printed on them, nor because bonds (on which the banks continue to draw interest) are deposited for their redemption, but because they are issued by the general government, bear its stamp, and rest upon its credit. They are in no wise better than the notes directly issued by the government, but derive their security and usefulness from the same source that gives the greenback its security and usefulness—the fact that they are issued by the government and are receivable for its dues. The only reason for continuing them is the enrichment of the few at the expense of the many. Every single dollar of the two hundred and seventy odd millions of national bank notes outstanding represents a dollar on which the people of the United States are taxed to pay interest, but which is loaned by a paternal government to the privileged banks without interest.

There is no legitimate connection between the functions of government and the business of banking.

The proper business of banking is the receiving, the keeping and the loaning out of money, and the facilitation of exchanges by the extension, interchange, and cancellation of private credits. With the issuance of money the paper business of banking has nothing whatever to do.

It is one of the proper functions of the general government to issue money. But with the proper business of banking the government has rightly nothing whatever to do. There is no more reason for national banks to be subsidized by the government by loans of its money without interest, than there is for national grocery stores or national restaurants, for which the government should supply the capital while private individuals took the profits.

Outside the Bank of England there is not one of the many hundred English banks and banking institutions that has anything whatever to do with the issuing of money, and even in the United States, where this monstrous system of national banks has been suffered to grow up, a great part of the banking business of the country is dictated by banks like the Bank of America, Wells, Fargo & Co., and Drexel, Morgan & Co., that have nothing to do with issuing money, and yet discharge all the proper functions of banks as satisfactorily as do the subsidized corporations. To withdraw that national bank currency and to substitute for it notes directly issued by the government would be to save annually for the people millions directly, and still more millions indirectly, but it would not in the least interfere with the proper business of banking. If any of the national banks chose to dissolve their one-sided partnership, private banks would quickly take their places. . . .

"Property in Literary Productions"[33]

[G. of] Norwich, N. Y. [writes:] It is almost a relief to find even a trivial and passing remark of *The Standard*'s to differ with. At the most only three such have refreshed me with a sense of my own superiority of judgment. Postal savings banks (interest paying), and woman's suffrage are two of these, but it is to the third that I propose a protest. I do not believe that there is any natural property in the creations of one's brains, or that a government countenances robbery that fails to enact a copyright law for the protection of foreign authors. If I publish my thought or my knowledge by shouting it on the streets or by printing and hawking it, it is no longer mine, except for the credit of it. If a government conceives it politic to encourage its wise men by granting the statutory monopolies in their writings and inventions, it is well; but justice makes no such demand; and it is difficult to see the policy of protecting the production of that which has its own sufficient incentive in the laws of other countries. The author's cry of "robber" seems to me as impertinent as the manufacturer's demand for protection.

The difficulty for my correspondent arises from confusions of thought, which are so common that it is worth while endeavoring to clear them up. Even the advocates of international copyright seldom put their claims upon true ground, and, with the exception—to her honor!—of the Republic of Mexico, which gives perpetual copyright, the copyright laws of all civilized countries, like our own domestic [one] treats the author's right to control book publication as though it rested on the same ground and nature as patents granted for invention. The Constitution of the United States itself does this by declaring that "the Congress shall have the power to promote the progress of science and the useful arts by securing for limited times to authors and inventors the exclusive right to their respective writings and discoveries."

Nevertheless, though superficially alike, there is an essential difference between the patent for an invention and the copyright for a book. The one, which gives a right of property in the use of a device or process—that is to say, in an idea—rests on no natural right, but can only be upheld as a matter of policy. The other gives no property in ideas. It merely recognizes the right of property in a particular form, itself a product of labor, in which ideas are made tangible; a right which, irrespective of questions of policy, is a natural right—resting on the same ground as the right of the fisherman to the fish he catches, of the farmer to the crop he raises, of the builder to the house he constructs. . . .

But no man can discover anything which, so to speak, was not put there to be discovered, and which someone else might not have discovered in time. If he finds it, it was not lost. It, or its potentiality, existed before he came. It was there to be found.

It is evidently the perception of this truth, that discovery can give no just claim to ownership, that leads my correspondent to think there can be no basis in justice for ownership in literary productions, and gives rise to the common assertion that there can be no property in productions of the brain. He is right enough as to the principle, but he is confused in its application. He confounds the copyright with the patent, just as the framers of our Constitution also have confounded it, and as it is generally confused, and proceeds on the supposition that it involves the right of property to ideas.

In this he is clearly mistaken. The exclusive privilege given by a patent—the exclusive privilege of making a certain kind of machine or using a certain device, or applying a certain combination for a certain purpose, does confer property in an idea, a perception, or the use of a natural law. It prevents all but the grantee from making that kind of a machine or using that kind of a device, or applying that kind of a combination. But the recognition of the exclusive right of the author to reprint his book gives no such exclusive privilege. It prevents no one from writing that kind of a book. It prevents no one from using either his own ideas or even the ideas he may find in the copyrighted book. It recognizes a right of property, not in any facts stated, not in any thoughts expressed, not in any discovery pointed out, not in any moral drawn, but merely in the book itself—in that particular arrangement of words which gives it identity as a particular piece of work and makes it clearly distinguishable from works by other authors, or even

from another work on the same subject written by the same author—should
he try to do the same thing twice.

"If I publish my thought or my knowledge by shouting it on the streets
or by printing or hawking it, it is no longer mine, except for the credit of it,"
says my correspondent. This is quite true in the sense that I am no longer
the exclusive possessor of it—as I might possibly have imagined myself to
be before. But in the sense that publication takes away any right of ownership is not the full truth. To a thought or perception there is no right of ownership either before or after publication. Everyone has a moral right to think
what I think or perceive what I perceive. He may do it independently of me
or he may do it on the hint from me. But in neither case have I any moral
right to forbid him. Nor does a copyright give me any power to forbid him.

No matter how hard may have been the mental process by which I
arrive at certain conclusions, or how laboriously I may have discovered
certain facts, as soon as I publish them—and it is only when I do publish
them that the copyright laws apply—anyone may appropriate them and use
them as his own. All that the copyright law gives me is the right of property
to the particular book i.e., in the particular and identical form in which the
ideas set forth in my book are expressed.

This form is the result of my labor in the same sense and to the same
extent that a coat or a house is the result of labor. And for the same reason,
there attaches to it the same exclusive ownership by natural right.

In the production of any material thing—machines, for instance—
there are two comparable parts—the abstract idea or principle, which may
be usually expressed by drawing, by writing or by word of mouth, and the
concrete form of the particular machine itself, which is produced by bringing
together certain relations, certain quantities and qualities of matter, such as
wood, steel, brass, brick, rubber, cloth, etc. There are two modes in which
labor goes to the making of the machine—the one in ascertaining the
principles on which such machines can be made to work; the other in
obtaining from their natural reservoirs and bringing together and fashioning
into shape the quantities and qualities of matter which in their combination
constitute the concrete machine. In the first mode, labor is expended in
discovery. In the second mode, it is expended in production. The work of
discovery may be effected once for all, as in the principle or idea of the
wheelbarrow in prehistoric times. But the work of production is required
afresh in the case of each particular thing. No matter how many thousand
millions of wheelbarrows have been produced, it requires fresh labor of
production to make another one.

Now the expenditure of labor in the invention or discovery of the idea
of a machine gives no natural right of ownership of the idea. Not only is the
potentiality of such a machine a part of the common heritage to which there

can be no just exclusive claim, but each invention or discovery is usually—perhaps, except in cases of sheer accident, it may be said invariably—only the last step in a series which began with the discovery of fire or the invention of the stone ax. And not only can we confidently say in the case of any device that supplies a need, and is therefore valuable, that if one person had not discovered it, others would have done so; but as a matter of fact it usually appears in such cases that a number of persons have been contemporaneously working toward the same end.

The natural reward of labor expended in discovery is in the use that can be made of the discovery without interference with the right of anyone else to use it. But to this natural reward our patent laws endeavor to add an artificial reward. The effect of giving to the discoverers of useful devices or processes an absolute right to their exclusive use would burden all industry with the most grievous monopolies, and greatly retards, if not puts a stop to further inventions. Yet the theory of our patent laws is that we can stimulate discoveries by giving a modified right of ownership in their use for a term of years. In this we seek by special laws to give a reward to labor expended in discovery, which does not belong to it by natural right, and is in reality a bounty.

But as for labor expended in the second of these modes—in the production of the machine by the bringing together in certain relations of certain quantities and qualities of matter, we need no special laws to reward that. Absolute ownership attaches to the results of such labor, not by special law, but by common law. And if all human laws were abolished, men would still hold that whether it was a wheelbarrow or a phonograph, the concrete thing would belong to the man who produced it. And this, not for a term of years, but in perpetuity. It would pass at his death to his heirs or those to whom he devised it.

Now a book—I do not mean the printed and bound volume which is the result of the labor of printers, bookbinders, and subsidiary industries; but the succession of words which is the result of the labor of the author—if not a material thing, is quite as tangible a thing as a machine. And in the labor that goes to its production there are the same two separable parts. There is what I have called the "labor of discovery," which goes to the idea of the book, and as to which, as in the case of the inventor of the machine, the author must draw on those who have gone before, for a perfectly original literary man would have to begin by inventing letters. There is also the labor of production—labor of essentially the same kind, though it deals not with matter, but with immaterial things, as that which in the case of a machine is expended in bringing wood, steel, brass, etc., into certain proportions and relations. It is this labor of production, which results in a tangible identity, that gives ownership to the author as a matter of natural right. And it is this right of ownership, not in ideas, but in the tangible result of labor expended in production, that copyright secures.

I presume that one of the principle reasons why the real nature and grounds of property in literary productions is so little appreciated, is that what I have called the "labor of production" is hardly understood except by writers. The common idea is that the man who writes a book only has to decide what he wants to say and then sit down and write it out. Nothing could be more fallacious. Over and above any "labor of discovery" expended in thinking out what to say, is the "labor of production" expended on how to say it. Even the most carelessly written works require some of this. But carefully written works, and especially the works on thoughtful subjects that read as though they had flowed from the author's pen as easily and as naturally as water flows down hill, require in the mere labor of production, in the mere choice of words, arrangement of sentences and sequence of presentation, an amount and intensity of exertion that one who has not attempted it can hardly appreciate. If anyone thinks that to write a book is [merely] to get the ideas and then write it out, let him sit down and try. If he has a critical ability to judge what he is doing, he will soon find himself involved in labor to which digging wells or breaking stones will seem easy, and will ere long appreciate the good sense of the man who apologized for the length of a letter on the ground that he did not have time to write a short one. Now, this labor of literary production is essentially the same kind of labor as that which produces houses, crops, clothing, ships, or any of the material things which man makes. It requires the exertion of the same will power and it involves the exhaustion of the same nervous energy. Mental work is no metaphorical phrase. Anyone who has held himself to it knows that it is labor as truly as is physical work.

If my correspondent will think over the matter I am sure that he will see that it is on this firm basis that the right of property in literary productions rests, and that its recognition, instead of being like that system of spoliation called protection (an impairment and denial of natural right), is but the securing to the author of the natural reward of his labor. He will see that in permitting the works of foreign authors to be republished here without their permission we are really countenancing robbery, as truly as if were permitted our own people to despoil foreigners of their watches or their clothes. And if he has any doubt in this, as in other things, that "honesty is the best policy," he will see, if he chooses to trace it, the cramping and degrading effects of this legalization of robbery upon our national literature and national thought.

And this is also worth considering. The right to use an author's work without his consent, [or] any part of it is to mutilate and garble. Many instances of this have occurred to foreign writers on this side of the water, and to American writers on that. Not long ago a friend of mine, a newspaper man, met another newspaper man.

"What are you doing?" said my friend, "and why do you look so mournful?"

"I am editing Dickens, and I don't like the work."

"Editing Dickens! what do you mean?"

"I am editing Dickens for the _____ library. It's my business to cut him down, so that every volume will come to 850 pages."

ON FREE TRADE

"In One Cause: The True Free Traders of England Strike Hands with the Single Tax Men of America"[34]

The Free Trade Principle

. . . When England adopted a revenue tariff it was thought by enthusiastic free traders of the day that the world would soon follow its example. The world has not. The real truth is this, that you have never yet shown the world the full advantages of free trade. You have never carried it out to that point where its influence in the elevation of the working classes would begin to be strikingly apparent. (Applause)

Now see what the argument is. In our country we have a monstrous protective tariff, a system of taxation that is imposed simply for the purpose of making prices high, so that people who have certain things to sell can force the rest of their fellow countrymen to pay higher prices. Our whole system aims at keeping goods out of the country. That is the only way in which it can protect. Now what are goods? Why, they are good things, as their name implies. (Hear, hear) They are the things we all want, we all desire to get. We call that man rich who has or can command many of them. We call that man poor who wants them. And when we say that a nation is increasing in prosperity, we mean what? Simply that its wealth is increasing—not its land, not its population; but that it is increasing in goods, in commodities— that there are more of them in the country. And that is the wealthiest country that has the most of such commodities. It is very stupid to put on a tariff to keep those things out. We ought to welcome men who bring them into the country, instead of fining them. (Hear, hear) There would be a good deal more sense in our imposing a tariff on those who are going to carry goods out of the country than on those who bring them in. Therefore, we ought to sweep away that tariff. And therefore, going further, we ought to sweep away even a tariff levied for revenue, because a tariff levied for revenue necessarily operates in that way, and necessarily it operates unjustly. It is not worth my while going into the argument before you tonight, but whoever goes into it will see that a revenue tax is the most unjust way of raising a revenue. Here, for instance, you raise a great part of your revenue by a tax on tea. Now the poorest working girl drinks as much tea as the finest lady—more I think. There are lots of your population, a great part of whose living consists of bread and tea. Yet you make the poor working girl, the man who has a large family to support, and has hard work to do it, pay as much in that tax as your greatest millionaire or richest duke. (A voice: A hundred per cent more.) And so on through all your indirect taxes. (Hear, hear)

Free trade, in its narrow sense means that there ought to be perfect freedom to exchange. And why? Because exchange is a mode of production. Production is not completed until the man who is going to use the thing gets it, and trade is that mode of production which enables all the other economies. If each man had to make himself everything he wanted he would have to want mighty little. (Laughter) If every man had to be his own tailor, his own clockmaker, his own house builder, his own farmer, his own doctor, his own dentist, and so on, the result would be absolute savagery. Trade permits the division of labor, the cultivation of skill, the development of ingenuity, the acquirement of knowledge. It enables us to avail ourselves, though we remain in one place, of the advantages nature has given to other places, of the special adaptabilities of other people. Thus trade aids production. Now then, if it is stupid to keep things out of the country by taxes and fines, it is clearly as stupid to prevent their production in the country by taxes and fines. (Hear, hear) If you tax houses you necessarily restrict the building of houses, and there will be fewer houses built. If you tax vans and wheels— (groans)—you will have fewer vans and fewer wheels. (Laughter) Therefore the principle of free trade condemns all such taxes. (Hear, hear)

The Moral Side of the Argument

Free trade means free production, and it is essential to free production that no man shall be taxed for having produced a thing. The spirit of free trade condemns all such taxes. It condemns not merely indirect taxes, but from that most important side—the moral side of the question, all direct taxes that fall upon articles of wealth are just as clearly condemned. The question between free trade and protection is a moral question. This whole question of taxation is a moral question. The right to freely trade is just as essential as the right to freely speak. (Applause) A man cannot be a free man when his trade is taxed. We in America are not yet free. Free! Why if I buy my wife a dress over here, as I get to the other side of the Atlantic, and the Statue of Liberty Enlightening the World[35] looms up before me, a customs officer comes up to me and makes me hold up my right hand and call upon the Mighty Father, Creator of heaven and earth, to witness that I have nothing dutiable about me. Well, if I do as most Americans do who are protectionists, and swear that I have not (laughter) I will still have to give the customs officer my keys and he will open my bag or box and look through it, and in all probability he will see that dress for my wife unless I have put a "greenback" on top. (Laughter and applause) So I am fined or blackmailed for having done what I have a perfect natural right to do. Through all its stages, from the rich men who spend, as they have spent in this last American election,[36] millions to debauch and corrupt their fellow citizens, and to prevent the abolition of taxes which are filling our treasury with a worse than useless surplus—down through all its graduations the whole system is corrupt and demoralizing. (Applause) And if you realize the harmony of the natural laws you must know that it must be so, from the fact that it is a violation of justice. It is my right as a man to freely exchange my labor with any other man. (Applause) It is my natural right, and it ought to be my right as an American citizen, to freely bring into the port of the great republic anything I choose that won't hurt anybody else. (Applause) It is perfectly right to enact laws to keep out plagues, to keep out vermin, to keep out bad things; but the enactment of a law to keep out good things, to violate my natural right, must end in corruption. (Hear, hear) So it is with the taxes that we levy, and that you levy upon things that are the product of labor. A man builds a house here, and under your system, as under ours, your rate assessor comes round and says, "How much is that house worth?" and the better the house the man has built the more he is fined for it. (Laughter) Think of the absurdity of it! (Hear, hear) Have you houses enough? Why, look at the 40,000 people living in Glasgow in one room homes; look at the crowded population of London and the slums of Liverpool. The man who builds a house ought to be considered a public benefactor, but by the system of taxation, which prevails on both sides of the Atlantic, he is considered a malefactor, and the bigger and the better house he builds, and the more houses he builds, the more he is fined. (Applause)

Men like me have been taunted by foolish men with not respecting the Eighth Commandment. We are the men who do respect it. (Applause) We are the men who do stand for the rights of property. We are the men who believe "Thou shalt not steal" to be the enactment by a power superior to that of any human legislature. There is in our view a sacred right of property, and the existence and the progress of civilization depend upon the respect for that right. Whatever a man brings into being, whatever human exertion produces from the raw materials of nature—that belongs to the man who has produced it. It belongs to him as against all the world. No other individual has a right to take it from him under any normal circumstances, nor has any government. If a majority of votes do not mark the distinction between right and wrong, no government has the moral right to take from him or to impair his right in it. But this exclusive right of property in things produced by labor is impaired by taxes upon the products of labor. (Applause)

Free Trade Taxes

All these taxes, it is perfectly clear, both as a matter of expediency and of justice, should be abolished. The principle of free trade requires that. Where are you going to get your taxes, then? Easily. There is a fund which grows with the progress of society, a fund which increases with every increase in population and with every public improvement, a fund which no individual can justly claim, but which belongs to the whole community, a fund which can be taken by the community for public uses without putting any burden upon labor, without hampering enterprise, without depriving capital of its just reward. That fund is the value which social progress attaches to land. . . . Every child that is born, every emigrant that comes, every public improvement that is made, adds not to the value of the house, but does add to the value of the ground. (Applause) Take that for public uses and then you could easily abolish all these other taxes that hamper and restrict production, that punish men for enterprise and industry and thrift. (Applause) When you have done that then the principle of free trade is carried out to its full conclusion. (Hear, hear, and great applause) When you have done that you have not only removed all the restrictions upon production that come from taxes levied on production or on wealth, and destroyed the monopolies they create, but you have broken up the most important and fundamental of all monopolies. When you tax the vacant plot just as fully as the plot beside it, with the fine houses erected thereon; when you take the full value that the growth of the community attaches to bare land, then the incentive for holding land without using it is gone. (Hear, hear) Then, not only will the community get that fund that to my mind is clearly the natural basis and source of taxation, intended by the Creator for the social needs of civilization, but you put all men on an equal level with regard to the use of land. The man who is then using land will only pay to his fellows a fair rate for using it, and the man who is not using land will have to give it up when anyone else wants to use it. There is the easy solution of this land question. (Applause) It is a solution we cannot reach all at once. I, for one, would like to reach it tomorrow morning, but I know it is necessarily a series of steps. We must press forward as hard as we can. The other people will do the resisting. (Laughter) But on this line every step that is gained makes easier the next step; on this line there is no point at which men can come in and claim compensation; on this line you get immediate relief with every step, and every step makes it easier to resume the nominal control, if you want to. If you do intend sometime to buy the landlord out, the more you tax land values before that bargain the cheaper to the people it will be. (Laughter and applause) . . .

"For Cleveland and For Freedom: A Rousing Single Tax Ratification Meeting"[37]

Protection! Protection for American labor! Protection to advance wages! The pretense is a sham and a fraud, and a lie that insults labor! (Applause) Monopoly may need protection, and special privilege may need protection, but what is labor that it should need protection? Labor is the producer of all wealth. (Applause) What labor needs, and what alone labor needs, is freedom—the freedom to exert itself—the freedom to enjoy its natural rewards. Protection! (Laughter and cries of "Freedom to starve!")

No! Men never starve because of freedom. (Applause) Starvation comes from restriction; starvation comes from the denial of liberty; from the refusal of natural rights. (Applause) Go over in imagination this vast country today—this broad land, rich in all the natural materials of wealth—sixty-five millions of us only as yet scratching the surface of a country that would support hundreds of millions. Everywhere you see fields untilled, mines unopened, natural opportunities unused; and yet the protectionists actually tell us that in a land like this, our people—a people as a whole, the quickest, the most intelligent, the most inventive and adaptive and self-reliant in the world—can only get a living through baby acts, and that in the midst of all these abundant natural opportunities labor—poor labor—needs the protection of custom houses, also it will starve! (Laughter and applause)

A Response to "Mr. Powderly on Immigration"[38]

. . . Abolish all the duties and taxes that are now levied in any shape on the useful products of labor and put them, instead, on the value of land. What would become of the trusts and the combinations? How long would the "dogs-in-the-manger" keep their hold of natural opportunities they are not using? . . . How long would the builders stand idle? How long would it be before every man in all this broad land who was willing to work would find all the work he wanted to do, and instead of looking with jealous, hateful eyes at our kindred from beyond the sea who seek our shores, the cry would go up, "Come over and help us! Help us subdue a continent; help us build up a republic stronger, greater, richer, purer, than any nation the world ever has seen before—a republic where there shall be work for all, leisure for all and plenty for all."

All Europe would come? What if they did? We would have room for them, and work for them, and plenty for them. But nothing of the kind would happen. The spectacle of such a republic across the western sea; the return visits of those who had come; the letters that went back; the intercourse which a free trade would give, would arouse such a moral force that thrones would totter and fall, and standing armies would disappear, and a United States of Europe, before a generation had passed away, would clasp hands with a United States of America.

Notes

1. *The Standard*, Apr. 6, 1889, GR. This article displays George's pacifism quite succinctly.
2. A reference to the Gulf of Mexico and the Caribbean.
3. During this period the military was used by authorities to quell labor disturbances. The Homestead Strike (1892) and the Pullman Strike (1894) are but two examples.
4. James G. Blaine (1830–1893) was secretary of state under Garfield and later under Harrison. He established the first Pan American Congress. He was also the unsuccessful Republican candidate for the presidency in 1884. Chester A. Arthur was the 21st president (1881–1885).
5. George to A. P. Potter, Nov. 2, 1894, #6, HGP. This letter and the following editorial shows George's concern with individual freedom, a bedrock of his philosophy.
6. A reference to the Russian-American extradition convention of 1893 during Cleveland's administration.
7. Peter A. Kropotkin (1842–1921) was an eminent Russian anarcho-communist theoretician.
8. Jean-Jacques Élisée Reclus (1830–1905) was a noted French geographer and anarchist.
9. *The Standard*, Oct. 1, 1890, GR.
10. Yom Kippur.
11. Johann Most (1846–1906), a German emigré, was a well-known radical writer, speaker, and leader of the anarcho-communists in the United States.
12. Brooklyn became a borough of New York City on Jan. 1, 1898.
13. George to Mrs. James R. Lowell, Oct. 5, 1883, #3, HGP. In George's opinion, charity was degrading for the individual and for society. It was merely a poor palliative and a sop from the upper classes and hid the true need for reform. See Geiger, *Philosophy of Henry George*, 336–337.
14. *The Standard*, Jan. 8, 1890, GR. William R. Huntington (1838–1909) was rector of the well-endowed Grace Church (Episcopal). Again, George shows his

desire to reform society as a whole rather than by miniscule gestures that would cover up its major problems.

15. Rev. R. Heber Newton was a lifelong friend of George.

16. *The Standard*, Dec. 10, 1887, GR.

17. *The Standard*, Jan. 28,1888, GR.

18. *The Standard*, Nov. 19, 1890, GR. Here we see George championing a cause that unfortunately still poses problems for many people of both races.

19. Elsewhere George wrote: "But the race question still lies a black cloud on our southern horizon, a cloud that at any time may deepen and spread" (*The Standard*, Aug. 24, 1889, GR).

20. *The Standard*, Feb. 9, 1889, GR. George considered strikes much like charity. They may produce short-lived gains but problems would still persist unless the bigger picture of total social justice and equity are confronted. Most of George's works are concerned with the plight of the working man and labor issues, but his *Social Problems*, merits especial attention.

21. *The Standard*, Feb. 12, 1887, GR.

22. *The Standard*, Oct. 27,1888, GR. Abram Stevens Hewitt (1822–1903) was an industrialist and politician who defeated George and Theodore Roosevelt in the mayoralty campaign of 1886. See pages 136, note 2.

23. *The Standard*, Dec. 3, 1887, GR. Terence Vincent Powderly (1849–1902) was the Grand Master Workman of the Knights of Labor during its heyday in the late 1880s.

24. *The Standard*, Mar. 31, 1888, GR. George was quite a progressive thinker relating to the role of women as can be seen by this article and the following one.

25. American women received the right to vote in 1920 with the 19th Amendment.

26. George F. Edmunds (1826–1919), Vermont Democrat Senator and Speaker of the House, spearheaded this anti-polygamy bill in 1882.

27. *The Standard*, Apr. 6, 1889, GR.

28. British women received the right to vote in 1928.

29. *The Standard*, May 14, 1887, GR.

30. *The Standard*, Feb. 11, 1888, GR. The issue raised in this piece would be quite an eye-opener for contemporary credit card companies and banks!

31. *The Standard*, Apr. 28, 1888, GR. A condemnation of banks and a call for monetary reform were part of the Georgist agenda for improving America.

32. In 1863–1864 Congress charted a class of national banks, which were required to invest in federal bonds and were then empowered to issue their notes as currency, up to 90% of the value of their bonds. This arrangement was supplanted by the Federal Reserve System after 1913.

33. *The Standard*, June 23, 1888, GR.

34. *The Standard*, Dec. 22, 1888, GR. The reader should consult George's *Protection or Free Trade* for more details.

35. Designed by F. A. Bartholdi and presented to the U. S. by the Franco-American Union in 1884.

36. A reference to the 1888 campaign between Grover Cleveland and the winner, Benjamin Harrison.

37. *The Standard*, Sept. 1, 1888, GR.

38. *The Standard*, Aug. 18, 1888, GR.

Chapter 7

Views on Religion
and
Personal Correspondence

RELIGION

In nineteenth-century America religion and God were taken more seriously. It was a world of stern moral values. People's sensibilities were jolted by the Industrial Revolution with the exodus to the cities, the rise of factories and science, land monopolies, and other cold but hellish forces.

Among this number was Henry George. Industrial and land slavery had supplanted chattel slavery. Not only material, but spiritual poverty was growing. George's response was a clarion call to return to the land created by God and to His ethical values. Through the Anti-Poverty Society he and the fiery Rev. Dr. Edward McGlynn summoned thousands of people to a nobler existence.

George was profoundly religious. He believed in an intimate relationship between God and Man. But George's faith was simple. It was a belief shorn of any institutionalized dogma or encapsulated in any particular practice or ecclesiastical structure. He looked to an interplay among the spirit of God, the spirit of humanity, and the earth. The land, the divine gift to man, was the conjunction between the spiritual realm and that of daily, worldly activity. George wanted to preserve the integrity and purity of that meeting point, and believed the single tax to be the means, insuring that the land would be held ultimately in common. Thus his political economy—in which the fruits of labor would go to the individual and a just society would flourish—was in essence a spiritual confirmation.

The selections that follow illustrate the religious fervor of George's crusade for a return to the land, as well as the problems he encountered from entrenched church authority. Although he esteemed many doctrines of the

Catholic Church, George was wary of papal influence and its attempts to curb freedom in this country.

"The Case of Dr. Mcglynn"[1]

The case of Dr. McGlynn brings up in definite form the most important issues which have ever been presented in the history of the Catholic Church in the United States. It has in fact an interest far transcending this country [because] it involves the attitude of the greatest of Christian churches toward the worldwide social movement of our times, and its decision will be fraught with the most important consequences, both to the development of that movement and to the church itself. . . .

Christ was cradled in a manger, and came forth from the home of a working carpenter to preach to the tramp and the outcast. Peter was a fisherman, and Paul a tentmaker. It was among the despised and downtrodden and the generous hearted who felt for the oppressed that the gospel of hope for the poor and of menace to the rich made its way. Christ's declaration was that he came not to destroy the law, but to fulfill it; yet to the high priests of Jerusalem, as to the pontiffs of pagan Rome, the gospel of the common brotherhood of man and the common fatherhood of God was rank communism, to be trodden out with anathema, with steel and with fire, because it threatened the privileges of the rich and powerful. Hunted, persecuted, through the toils of its missionaries and the agonies of its martyrs, Christianity made its way, until it had become a power which the greatest of politicians could not despise, and in what is called the "conversion of Constantine,"[2] Roman imperialism, with all it represented, was married in form with Christian truth. From that time, and in every land where it has become a dominant religion, the very powers that at first fought so bitterly against Christianity have sought to use it. This has been true of all forms of Christianity. The Catholic Church has been used to bolster the power of tyrants and to keep the masses quiet under social injustice; the Greek Church to support the absolution of the Tsar.[3] Luther buried his direct anathemas against German peasants driven into agrarian revolt by the unbearable oppressions of their lords; the English Church has been the staunch supporter of regal tyranny and landlord robbery, and Presbyterian ministers have preached to Scottish clansmen that in resisting eviction from their homes they would be resisting the will of God, while in our own day and place the popular preachers of the great liberal denominations, however careless they may be of the charge of heterodoxy, are careful to temper the gospel to their wealthy sheep. . . .

The truth is that having Dr. McGlynn ordered to Rome is a cunning scheme to get rid of him with the least possible remonstrance from his congregation. It would be unpleasant, to say the least, to try to cut off his head here among those who know him and love him, so he is to be sent away to be executed, and time is to be allowed to dull feeling.

But all this is merely in answer to those well-meaning persons who say that Dr. McGlynn should go to Rome. What might happen to Dr. McGlynn in Rome is not in itself a reason that a man such as he might regard. But there are the strongest possible reasons why he should not go to Rome. In this matter a great principle is at stake. Does an American citizen cease to be a citizen when he becomes a priest? Is an American citizen, because he is also a Catholic priest, to be held to answer before a foreign tribunal because of his action in American politics? If this is so, then the sooner we know the better.

The charge is often made that the Catholic Church is the foe of human liberty—the sometimes stealthy, but always persistent, enemy of real progress. This is not true of Catholic doctrine. There is nothing in the Catholic faith which prevents a believer from being a good citizen and a social reformer of the most radical type. But it is too true of those who control the ecclesiastical machinery. And the issue is now made in the case of Dr. McGlynn between the freedom of Catholic theology and the spirit of reaction that controls the ecclesiastical machine.

To say that there is nothing in Catholic doctrines inconsistent with the largest political liberty may seem to many nonCatholics far too strong a statement. But, as understood by intelligent Catholics, the doctrine of papal infallibility means no more than the expression of a trust that when it comes to speaking in his official character as head of the universal church the Divine Providence will not permit any false teaching on matters of faith. In the Catholic view of the pope, in all other capacities and on all other subjects, he is no more infallible than Archbishop Corrigan, and Archbishop Corrigan is no more infallible than the butler who opens the door of his marble palace, or the butcher boy who brings meat to the kitchen.[4]

In matters of faith the Catholic holds that he must submit to his Church (though even in matters of faith Catholic dogma is much more elastic than most Protestants suppose), but in matters beyond the sphere of faith and morals no intelligent Catholic attaches any more importance to the dictum of ecclesiastical authority, be it that of priest, bishop, cardinal or pope, than is due to the character of the man and the reasonableness of the opinion. That there have been stupid and vicious ecclesiastics; that even incumbents of the Chair of St. Peter have been vile and wicked; that Catholic authorities have declared against the rotundity of the earth and its motion round the sun, have instigated wars, massacres, and persecutions— are to him no argument against the Catholic faith, for he sees in them only the aberrations of the human element. That in all ages there have been ecclesiastics or ecclesiastical rings who, prompted by the lusts of the flesh or the desire to please the powers of the world, through ignorance of the limits of their own functions or through a desire to impose upon the ignorance of their flocks, have attempted to stretch ecclesiastical authority beyond its proper domain, any intelligent Catholic will readily concede; but he contends that in all such cases ecclesiastical authority loses its binding force, and that the duty of the true Catholic is to set it at defiance.

No Catholic who really understood his faith would say that the Catholic Irish who fought against the English invaders, armed with the bull of Pope Adrian, incurred any spiritual penalty, or were any the less Catholics.[5] On the contrary, he would say that the very fact of their being Catholics made it the more incumbent on them to resist such an unwarranted stretch of papal power. Archbishop Hughes, in a public speech in this city, gloried in the fact that the Catholic Venetians fought a pope when he tried to use the papal power to destroy their republic, and declared that American Catholics could and would do the same thing if papal aggression ever threatened their liberties.[6]

It is not exactly papal aggression which now threatens the liberties of American Catholics, but it is something which endeavors to shield itself behind the papal authority and to use the machinery of Rome to control American politics. The pope himself probably knows as much of the case of Dr. McGlynn as the new Warden of the Tombs[7] does of the binomial theorem, and the Italian cardinals of the Propaganda can know but little more.[8] Dr. McGlynn has not been summoned to Rome at the instance of Rome, but at the instance of Archbishop Corrigan, prompted undoubtedly by the "Castle Catholics" and the ring politicians of New York.[9]

But whether the Roman ecclesiastical authorities are used through Errington[10] by the British government, or through Archbishop Corrigan by a New York ring, or whether they act in American politics on their own motives and for their own purposes, makes little difference. The prime fact is, that the outrageous claim that the American Catholic clergy, perhaps for their numbers the most influential class of men in the country, are to be in their political action the puppets of a foreign power, four thousand miles distant in space and many centuries distant in ideas; that these men, each of whom may influence hundreds and thousands of votes, are to be subject to disgrace and punishment, to be thrown out of their homes and means of livelihood if their political action does not suit the Italian cardinals of the Propaganda or the worthy gentleman who lives in the twelve-hundred-roomed palace called the Vatican. If American Catholics have not more spirit than to submit to this, then Catholicism is indeed utterly inconsistent with free institutions!

But I am confident that there is too much spirit in American Catholics to submit to such dictation, and for my part I would rejoice to see Dr.

McGlynn make the issue clear and plain by utterly refusing to go to Rome to answer for his conduct as a citizen. In his case the point has long been passed by which endurance ceases to be a virtue. His submission when arraigned for favoring the Irish revolution has merely encouraged ecclesiastical tyranny. The time has come when he ought to make a stand for the sake of his brethren in the priesthood, as well as for the sake of the principles of American liberty.

Even without going into the question of why the government of a worldwide church should be allowed to rest in the hands of a knot of reactionary Italians, it is clear that the organization of the Catholic Church in this country is not such as self-respecting American Catholics ought to be contented with, or as is suited to the genius of our institutions. The organization of the Church in this country is autocratic in the last degree. The American Catholic priest has no such independence as belongs to the priest of Italy, France or Spain. Ecclesiastically he is under martial law, for by a fiction which the ecclesiastical politicians of Rome have seen fit to preserve this country, like Ireland . . . is a missionary country, and is, therefore, under the absolute government of the Propaganda. Some pretence of securing for American priests a little show of independence was made at the council of Baltimore, but what it amounts to may be seen from the fact that there are in New York City only nine pastors who cannot be removed at a moment's notice by will of the archbishop. As for Catholic congregations, they have not only no choice as to their pastors, and no voice in church matters, but have no control whatever over the edifices they build and the property their contributions create. The congregation of St. Stephen's now see their beloved pastor thrown out of the church their contributions have raised and beautified, and they are helpless to prevent it.

However, there is one thing they can do. They can keep a tight grip on their money. That would be the most effective means of bringing the ecclesiastical autocracy to its senses.

In the meantime, American workingmen might as well make up their minds that in their fight for the enfranchisement of labor they must meet the opposition of the Catholic hierarchy.

"Anti-Poverty: A Sentiment that is Rousing New York to Enthusiasm"[11]

Dr. McGlynn (great applause)—Dr. McGlynn (great applause)—in Chickering Hall last Sunday night said it was a historic occasion. He was right. That a priest of Christ, standing on Sunday night on a public platform and addressing a great audience—an audience embracing men and women of all creeds and beliefs—should proclaim a crusade for the abolition of poverty, and call on men to join together and work together, to bring the Kingdom of God on earth, did mark a most important event. Great social transformations, said Mazzini, never have been and never will be other than the application of great religious movements. (Applause) The day on which democracy shall elevate itself to the position of a religious party, that day will its victory begin. (Great applause) And the deep significance of the meeting last Sunday night, the meaning of this Anti-Poverty Society that we have joined together to inaugurate, is the bringing into the struggle of democracy the religious sentiment, the sentiment alone of all sentiments powerful enough to regenerate the world. (Applause)

... This Anti-Poverty Society has no patent remedy for poverty. We propose no new thing. What we propose is simply to do justice. The principle that we propose to carry into our laws is neither more nor less than the principle of the golden rule. We propose to abolish poverty by the sovereign remedy of doing to others as we would have others do to us; by giving to all their just rights. And we propose to begin by assuring to every child of God who, in our country, comes into this world, his full and equal share of the common heritage. Crowded! Is it any wonder that men are crowded together as they are in this city, when we see men taking up far more land than they can by any possibility use, and holding it for enormous prices! Why, what would have happened if, when these doors were opened, the first people who came in had claimed all the seats around them, and demanded a price of others who afterward came in by the same equal right! Yet that is precisely the way we are treating this continent. That is the reason why people are huddled together in tenement houses; that is the reason why work is difficult to get; the reason that there seems, even in good times, a surplus of labor, and that in those times that we call bad, the times of industrial depression, there are all over the country thousands and hundreds of thousands of men tramping from place to place, unable to find employment. (Applause)

Not work enough! Why, what is work? Productive work is simply the application of human labor to land; it is simply the transforming into shapes adapted to gratify human desires, the raw material that the Creator has placed here. Is there not opportunity enough for work in this country? (Applause) Supposing that, when thousands of men are unemployed and there are hard times everywhere, we could send a committee up to the high court of Heaven to represent the misery and the poverty of the people here, consequent on their not being able to find employment. What answer would we get? "Are your lands all in use? Are your mines all worked out? Are there no natural opportunities for the employment of labor?" (Applause) What could we ask the Creator to furnish us with that is not already here in abundance? He has given us the globe, amply stocked with raw material for our needs. He has given us the power of working up this raw material. If there seems scarcity, if there is want, if there are men who cannot find employment, if there are people starving in the midst of plenty, is it not simply because what the Creator intended for all has been made the property of the few? (Great applause)

In moving against this giant wrong, which denies to labor access to the natural opportunities for the employment of labor, we move against the cause of poverty. We propose to abolish it, to tear it up by the roots, to open free and abundant employment for every man. We propose to disturb no just right of property. As Dr. McGlynn said just Sunday night, we are defenders and upholders of the sacred right of property—that right of property which justly attaches to everything that is produced by labor; that right which gives to every one a just right of property in what he has produced—that makes it his to give, to sell, to bequeath, to do whatever he pleases with, so long as in using it he does not injure any one else. That right of property we insist upon, that we would uphold against all the world. To a house, a coat, a book—anything produced by labor—there is a clear individual title, which goes back to the man who made it. That is the foundation of the just, the sacred right of property. It rests on the right of the individual to use of his own powers, on his right to profit by the exertion of his own labor; but who can carry the right of property in land that far? Who can claim a title of absolute ownership in land coming from the man who made it? (Applause) And until the man who claims the exclusive ownership of a piece of this planet can show a title originating with the Maker of this planet; until he can produce a decree from the Creator declaring that this city lot or that great tract of agricultural land, or that coal mine, or that gas well, was made for him—until then we have a right to hold that land was intended for all of us. (Great applause) . . . . The standard has now been raised, the cross of the new crusade at last is lifted. Some of us, aye, many of us, have sworn in our hearts that we will never rest so long as we have life and strength until we expose and abolish that wrong. We have declared war upon it. Those who are not with us, let us count them against us. For us there will be no faltering, no compromise, no turning back until the end. (Great applause and cheering) . . .

"Anti-Poverty; Nearly Six Thousand People at the Academy and Steinway Hall"[12]

. . . I came in when Dr. McGlynn was speaking of the cry that went up from the rabble in Jerusalem, "Crucify him! crucify him!" and it is the history of the world. If poverty meant physical deprivation; if it merely meant hunger and cold, it would not be such a curse as it is. The bitterness of poverty, that which calls on us to exert every effort in this struggle to abolish it, is that it stunts and starves the mental and moral nature of men just as much as it does the physical. (Applause) It degrades, it imbrutes, it corrupts, and that is the very reason that we are always, and in the nature of things always will be, so easily rallied against us. (Applause) And there is, too, it seems to me, in that idea that runs not merely through Christianity, but through so many other religions of God coming down to earth to help men, another deep teaching. They who are degraded can never raise themselves; help comes from above. It is always those who have received power and intelligence and strength who must go and help those who are beneath; and that is the reason why we in this movement have always called on men in the name of duty, in the name of sympathy, have appealed to them not so much on account of what they can do to help themselves, but what they can do to help others. (Applause) And when the spirit of this great movement enters into a man's soul, when its truth enlightens his mind, when its power appeals to his conscience, immediate results are to him nothing. Whether it is 7,000 votes or 700,000 votes or seven votes, he will struggle on all the same. (Applause) Though he may know that victory never can come in his lifetime, yet even during his lifetime his view of life will be higher, his trust in God will be firmer, his assurance of a future life will be stronger, for the faith and hope that he has entertained with regard to this movement. (Applause)

When a man sees and fully realizes that degrading poverty and all the vice and the crime that spring from it are not due to the laws of the Creator, but are due to the selfishness and ignorance of men; when he sees that if mankind would really carry out in their laws those simple precepts taught to fishermen and mechanics by the Sea of Galilee eighteen hundred years ago, then we might all be rich; when he sees that the spring of that bitter struggle for wealth that now debases so much of human life and wastes so much of human power would be gone; when he once realizes that if justice were done, the kingdom of God might indeed be brought on earth, there comes to him a higher ideal of human life; there comes to him a faith, a trust that is more to him than any of the things that the world today counts to be success. (Applause) He knows and feels that though here he may only face disaster; though during the years he has to spend here his path may seem like a road constantly leading up hill; that yet the time will come when he may hope at last to hear the words, "Well done, thou good and faithful servant." (Applause)

And so let us go on, each in our own way spreading the fire and hope of this new crusade, not merely in our meetings, but in our homes and our lives, talking to friends and acquaintances, in asking questions and setting men to thinking. Our work is the work of education—the education of men and women, of graybeards as well as the little children. What we have to do is to awaken thought, to arouse conscience, to get men to see the simple truth that injustice and liberty are the great remedies for all social and political evils. (Applause) . . .

"Ego et Deus Meus"[13]

The letter of Leo, P. P. XIII, to his venerable brother, Michael Augustine Corrigan, archbishop of New York, is, so far as any binding force upon the consciences of Catholics is concerned, of no more weight than a private communication from Mr. Pecci at Rome to Mr. Corrigan of this city. But it is, nevertheless, of the first importance as showing the attitude which this supreme ecclesiastical authority of the Catholic Church has deliberately chosen to take on the most important question of our time, and the nature of the claims which it makes upon the obedience of citizens of the American Republic.

The form and manner of this [letter is] notable. The way in which the Catholics of New York are referred to as "your subjects," and the way in which the pope, styling himself We and Us, with a capital "W" and a capital "U," not only assumes the inflated style of royalty, but appropriates to himself the typographical homage accorded by usage to the Almighty, are extremely suggestive.

Yet the way in which the papers have printed this letter of consolation from the anguished pope to the poor, persecuted archbishop, grieved by the rebellion of his subjects, hardly does justice to this feature of it. Here is the way in which the concluding sentence would appear if printed as it was written in the copies furnished the press from the archiepiscopal palace:

> Meantime WE earnestly pray the God of consolation that He will console you, Venerable Brother, tried by so many cares and as a pledge of His divine favor and a proof of OUR special affection for you, WE lovingly bestow upon you, the clergy, and the people committed to your care the Apostolic Benediction.

The Catholic creed teaches that he who appeared among Jewish peasants some eighteen hundred years ago and spoke as never man spoke, was, under the guise of a simple carpenter, very God of very God—was, indeed, an incarnation of that power which made, supports and orders all things that be. He had but to will it and mighty armies would have started from the dust or winged legions flashed from the skies, and all the kings of the world crawled prostrate at his feet. He had but to will it and palaces grander and fairer than mortal eye has ever seen would have risen from the ground, and all earth's treasures [would have] been gathered for his service. Yet he chose to live [like] a workingman among workingmen; a poor man among the poor, and scorning the pride of wealth, and the pomp of power, to cast in his lot with the disinherited children of God, who though the foxes have holes and the birds of the air have nests, have no place on the earth's broad surface where they can lay their heads without paying some landlord rent. Associating with the robbed, the despised, the outcast, he wore the simple raiment of the common people, ate their simple fare and partook of their joys and sorrows. He called Peter, Peter; John, John; and Mary, Mary; and in return was greeted and treated by them with the affectionate familiarity of favorite scholars toward a loved teacher. Though at his touch the blind saw, the sick became well, devils departed, and the dead came forth, he never suffered his disciples to address him with any of those man-worshipping titles which both indicate and beget servility of soul. Though he fed the multitude he never permitted men to abase themselves before him. Though he walked upon the waters, the only time we hear of him riding was upon the back of the homely ass. For the Pharisees and Scribes—for those who sat in high places and clothed themselves in rich raiment and had men call them holy and eminent—he had nothing but words of bitterest scorn. The whole burden of his teaching was of human equality—of the common brotherhood of men, the common fatherhood of their Creator. And for the coming of the kingdom of God on earth—the kingdom of justice and peace and plenty, the kingdom of liberty, equality and fraternity, he taught men to work and to pray. It was for these "vicious seeds of doctrines scattered under pretext of helping the masses" that he was crucified between two thieves.

When Christ declared that it was easier for a camel to pass through the eye of a needle than for a rich man to enter into the kingdom of God; when he declared that they who would lead should serve; what did he mean? Did he not mean that it is not good for men to be exalted above their fellows? Did he not mean what all history and all observation teaches to be true—that the pride and ostentation of wealth and power deaden the spiritual nature and dull the sympathy of men with their fellows?

The Catholic Church consists of two things—a soul and a machine. The soul is the spirit of Christ's teachings; the machine is the machine of the Scribes and Pharisees and High Priests. The one is typified by the long line of martyrs and confessors, by the Vincent de Pauls and *soggarth aroons* who have made the Church dear to the poor oppressed.[14] The other is represented by forty-thousand dollar archbishops, and the pomp and pride and circumstance of royalty that surround the pope. Catholics believe that the soul of the Church will always have during important emergencies the divine guidance, and that, however weak or wicked or corrupt a pope may be, when acting as the "servant of the servants of God," and speaking ex cathedra on questions of faith or morals to the universal church, Divine Providence will not suffer him to teach fake doctrines. But Catholics—intelligent Catholics at least—recognize in the pope himself nothing more than a man, subject to all the frailties and conditions of other men. And it is a significant fact that, though the Catholic Church has never given up the belief in miracles, and the annals of her saints, down even to recent times, are filled with them, no pope, since the popes began to assume the power and pomp of kings, is credited with a miracle. So instinctively does the soul of the Church feel that that which pertains to Caesar cannot pertain to the kingdom of God.

It is natural to look to the declared representatives and followers of the Nazarene who eighteen centuries ago was crucified for teaching the equal rights and common brotherhood of men, for active hearty support of every movement to elevate the masses by securing social and political justice. But it is unnatural to [give] this aid to men, whatever they may [believe] themselves, who are gorged with wealth and surrounded by pomp. Men who live in palaces and are clothed in purple and fine linen, and associate with the rich and powerful, are, with rare exceptions, now, as in Christ's time, the defenders of "things as they are," the upholders of the social injustice that, to pamper the few, robs, degrades, and imbrutes the many. Nominally shepherds of Christ's sheep, and using his name as a means of gaining wealth and power, their interests and associations make them the friends and supporters of the wolves that prey upon the fold. Among the poorer clergy of the Church of England are many devoted men whose whole lives are given to efforts for the elevation of the masses, but the holders of the rich livings of the Church of England have, as a class, preached a gospel of servility to power and of contentment under injustice infinitely more degrading than the worship of Odin and Thor; while the English bishops, with their stately palaces and princely incomes and titles of "my lord" and "your grace," have been to a man the most bigoted and uncompromising defenders of every hoary wrong, the bitterest opposers of every step in the advance of freedom and the emancipation of labor.

"It is easier for a camel to go through the eye of a needle than for a rich man to enter into the kingdom of God." What, then, can any movement which aims at restoring to the disinherited their equal rights in the bounties of their Creator, and thus abolishing poverty and bringing the kingdom of justice on earth, expect from those circumstanced as are the man who gives this letter to the press and the man who signs it? The one lives in a marble palace in that quarter of New York where the millionaires live, and draws for his own private purse a princely income of over $40,000 a year from the hard earnings of his poor "subjects," who live in crowded and squalid tenements—an income largely made up by a tax upon the burial of every dead Catholic in consecrated ground. He is the center of the most fulsome flattery and abject servility. Though living in a democratic country, whose very constitution prohibits titles of nobility, he is addressed by the title given in monarchical countries only to the highest order of nobility, has a lot of "my lords" to do his bidding, and his "subjects" salute him by falling down on their knees and kissing his hand.

The other lives in the largest and richest palace in the world—a palace so extensive that it is said to contain seven thousand rooms. He is surrounded by the pomp and circumstance, not merely of European monarchs, but of Asiatic despotism. He wears on state occasions, not one crown, but three. He is surrounded by guards, not of common soldiers, but of nobles, clad in steel helmets and white buckskin breeches, and of Swiss mercenaries garbed in all the colors of the rainbow. He is habitually addressed as "Your Holiness," and to exalt him as far as possible above human kind, men are turned in his service into beasts of burden, and he is carried on the shoulders of a corps of trained bearers, while peacock fans, the symbols of oriental grandeur, are borne above his head. He has a court composed of "eminences," and "illustrisimos," and "my lords," and those who approach him kneel down and kiss his foot. The rich are constantly bringing him offerings, and on every occasion the kings of the earth, even to the Sultan of the Turks and the Emperor of the Chinese, send him kingly presents. What sympathy can a man who lives in such an atmosphere have for democracy? "Do men gather grapes of thorns or figs of thistles?" What can the cause of the oppressed masses expect from him? "It is easier for a camel to go through the eye of a needle than for a rich man to enter into the kingdom of God."

It is well to look facts in the face. This letter is enough to undeceive any who have supposed that some sort of a truce might be patched up between Roman ecclesiasticism and the spirit of liberty and progress. Between absolutism and democracy there can be no peace. It is in the nature of things that no one can serve both God and Mammon.

The attitude of the American press and of American Protestants on this question is very significant.

Archbishop Corrigan, the "sentinel on the ramparts" that guard the ill-gotten wealth of the rich, has set up a claim to control the political action of his "subjects," and has removed from his pastorate, deprived of his accustomed livelihood, and ejected from his home, a priest who dared to claim the rights of an American citizen. There has been in the whole matter, from first to last, no question of creed or of personal conduct. Dr. McGlynn's character is as white as the snow. His long years of service as a priest have been marked by unflagging devotion to his spiritual duties and by tireless charity. He has observed the Church's discipline; he has questioned no article of the Church's creed. Not the faintest suspicion of heresy could be attached to any of his teachings. The congregation committed to his charge loved him as no other priest in the diocese was loved.

But he has refused to take political orders from the marble palace; he has claimed the right to advocate such changes in the laws of his native land as he felt to be best for the whole people; he has declared that in becoming a Catholic priest he "did not evade the duties nor surrender the rights of a man and a citizen"; he has denied the right of bishop, propaganda or pope to punish him for his actions in American politics, or to censure him for his opinions in political economy, unless they could show such opinions to be contrary to the teachings of the Christian religion, and he has denied their authority to order him to Rome to answer to Italians for the political acts and the political opinions of an American citizen.

This is what Pope Leo XIII, in his letter of condolence to his afflicted venerable brother, styles "the contumacious disobedience of one of your subjects, not only toward yourself, but also toward this apostolic see," and which he elsewhere styles "the rebellion which has arisen against your authority in your city."

In plain English, Archbishop Corrigan asserts—and he is now engaged in visiting the churches of his diocese and preaching it—and the pope in this letter endorses the assertion, that the American Catholic is bound by his religion to act in American politics as the servile puppet of Rome; that he must vote and speak and think in matters concerning the government and laws of his native country as an Italian four thousand miles away, or his representative in New York, may choose to order.

If only a few years ago such a claim as this had been so openly made, the whole land would have rung with the "no property" cry; our great dailies would have been filled with denunciations of the aggression upon American liberties, and from Maine to California Protestant preachers of all denominations would have pounded their Bibles in eloquent harangues against the pretensions of the Scarlet Woman.[15]

Now there is not a whisper of this. The very classes and the very organs who, a few years ago would have been loudest in the denunciations of papal pretensions, have nothing but praise of Archbishop Corrigan and laudations of the pope.

What does this mean?

It means that the old disputes about religious dogmas are being stilled in the shadow of an impending struggle that is standing over the world. It means that the wedge of the great social question is driving through the ranks of Catholics and Protestants and Free Thinkers alike. It means that the threatening revolt of "the masses" against the injustice which makes them the serfs of "the classes" has already inspired such terror that the latter are ready to welcome any aid which will assist them in maintaining vested wrongs.

Archbishop Corrigan is popular with the Tammany Ring and the rich men of New York for the same reason that Cardinals Cullen and McCabe were popular with the Castle government and Protestant landlords of Ireland; our secular and Protestant religious press applaud obsequiously the pope's letter for the very same reason that Bismarck, the erstwhile persecutor of Catholicism, has become the friend and admirer of "His Holiness." Their very religious prejudices give them such an abiding faith in the "ignorance and superstition" of the Catholic masses that they believe a word from him can, so far as Catholics are concerned, put an end to the growing demand for social justice.

In this they are mistaken. The Catholic faith is not the slavish creed that they imagine. A man can be a conscientious Catholic and yet be a freeman. He may respect the spiritual authority of the church and yet resent bitterly the assumption of ecclesiastical authority to dictate in politics. And this will be the effect of the pope's letter. It will not strengthen Archbishop Corrigan; it will strengthen Dr. McGlynn. . . .

It is just such men as Dr. McGlynn who are going to avert this danger. The standard which they are lifting is the standard of the hope and faith in which Christianity conquered the world. If forty-thousand dollar archbishops and man-carried popes array themselves against it, so much the quicker will the soul of the Catholic Church cast off the incubus of the aristocratic and corrupt machine.[16]

"Political and Social": On the Catholic Church[17]

. . . [One] writer aptly illustrates the real position of the Catholic Church with regard to private property in land, by likening it to the position of the church with regard to chattel slavery.

The Catholic Church has never condemned slavery. It has never taught that it is wrongful for the individual to hold slaves where slavery is sanctioned by municipal law; it has never even taught that the system of slavery is in itself wrongful. Its teachings would doubtless condemn slave insurrection or incitement to slave insurrection, or any attempt to abolish slavery by illegal and violent means.

But for all this, it has never given its positive sanction to slavery. It has never condemned those who say that slavery is a wrongful system, nor even those who say that the holding of men as slaves is an individual wrong on the part of the masters. It would doubtless condemn the shedding of blood, and perhaps even the appropriation of property on the part of the slave in the effort to obtain freedom. But it has never taught that the slave is bound by the moral law not to run away, or that the only rightful way in which he can obtain freedom is by the payment to the master of his full value. And whatever individuals may have done in the name of the Church, the Church itself has certainly never condemned those who seek to abolish slavery by peaceable and legal means. [It has been pointed out that] the Catholic Church has raised no difficulty when slavery had been abolished with compensation to the owners, as in the British West Indies, nor yet has it raised any difficulty when slavery had been abolished without compensation, as in the United States.

The case of private property in land is not merely analogous to that of private property in human flesh and blood; it is another form of the same thing. The two systems are but different modes, adapted to different degrees of density of population and different stages of social development, by which one set of men are clothed with authority to appropriate to themselves the benefits of other men's labor.

The one mode makes property of the active factor of production— labor. The other mode makes property of the passive factor—land. The one is better adapted to that rude state of society in which population is sparse and the productive arts are simple. The other is better adapted to that state of society in which population is dense and the productive arts have become complex.

The position of the Catholic Church with reference to these two forms of oppression, as with reference to all similar evils which derive sanction from municipal law, is simply this: She teaches certain spiritual truths and certain fundamental principles of morals in their application to the individual, but does not enter into the vexed sphere of civil government and civil legislation. Beyond these limits of individual action and relation, she is "all things to all men." The aristocrat and the democrat, the proslavery man and the abolitionist, the protectionist and the free trader; the believer in the divine right of kings and the most ardent republican—all these the Church herself, as intelligent Catholics understand the Church, welcomes alike to her altars. If one man robs another of his own volition, or if one man kills another of his own volition, the Catholic Church condemns these acts as crimes: but if one man robs another with the permission of the laws of his country, or if one man kills another by authority of the commission and command of his prince or legislature, the Catholic Church holds such an act beyond her tribunal. This may or may not be Christianity as it was taught by Christ, but it certainly is a clear, consistent and defensible policy which enables the Church to freely address herself to her special work among all manner of men under all social and political conditions. . . .

On Religious Education[18]

... Nothing can be more pernicious in a country with a popular form of government than religious schools; and this not because they teach religion, but because, necessarily, and totally irrespective of what is taught in them, they foster bigotry and engender prejudice. The great merit of our public schools, and the great necessity for public schools in a country like ours, is that they bring together children of all creeds and classes and thus wear away the prejudices that must inevitably arise where children of one creed or class are kept from association with children of other creeds or classes. People hate each other and despise each other just in proportion as they are kept separate from each other; and the most important lesson which many a boy and girl learns in our public schools is that children of other faiths, which the narrower teachings of home and Sunday school might lead them to despise, are just as intelligent, just as conscientious, just as kindly, and just as lovable as anyone else. To our public schools more than to any other of our institutions is due the growth of that spirit of tolerance between various creeds which is so marked in the United States. And the effect of religious schools may be seen in Ireland and Canada, where the line of creed marks a clear political and social distinction, and religious prejudice is almost, if not quite as rampant as in the days when men burned each other for religious differences and murdered each other for the love of God. The great political weakness of Ireland today is the religious prejudices which have been largely perpetuated by the separate education of religious schools. Had it not been for the feud between Protestant and Catholic, England could not have kept Ireland in subjection; and this feud is at the present time the great force which enables the British oligarchy to deny home rule to Ireland. So in Canada, the distinction of religion fostered by separate schools, which also perpetuate a distinction in language, constitutes the greatest political difficulty of the present and the greatest political danger of the future.

The evil of religious schools lies not in the religious teaching. Neither in Catholic schools, nor in Protestant schools, nor in Jewish schools, does the religious teaching given inculcate prejudice against those of other religious beliefs. But the evil lies in the separation of children of one faith from children of other faiths; in the promoting of that segregation which causes the spontaneous generation of prejudices, and in the restraint upon that intercourse which is the best solvent of prejudice. If we were to maintain separate schools for red-headed children, white-headed children, and brown-headed children, they would infallibly give rise to a certain amount of red-headed, white-headed, and brown-headed clannishness and prejudice, and perhaps at length to red-headed, white-headed, and brown-headed politics. How much stronger, then, are the clannishness and prejudice which arise from the gathering into separate schools of children of different religious beliefs?

As for the notion that children are to be made religious, or even moral, by getting doses of religion with their reading, writing, arithmetic, and geography, it is preposterous in theory and disproved by fact. Creeds, catechisms, prayers, and Bible readings mixed up with study and play, and forced on children when they are in no mood for them, have the effect sought in those curative establishments where to disgust the drunkard with liquor everything he can eat, drink or smell is flavored with it. And it is in clannishness and prejudice, in enmities of race and nation and locality and class and creed that despotism always finds its best tools. Here is the depth of Christ's teaching that men should love, not hate, one another. For it is through their hates that men have everywhere been enslaved.

The honors paid to the flag of the temporal sovereignty and the survivors of the Papal Legion at this meeting, which, ostensibly held in the honor of Pope Leo XIII, was virtually a demonstration against our public schools, are significant. There can be no doubt that the great majority of American Catholics are opposed to the temporal sovereignty of the pope, and would be today in sympathy with the demand of Italian patriotism for the unification of Italy. They are constantly put in a false position in this respect by hierarchical authority and the small but active ultramontane faction.[19] It is the same influences which are constantly stirring up Catholics to war against our public schools.

But, on the other hand, the bigotry of Protestants has largely aided the Catholic hierarchy. Here in New York, for instance, the spirit of our institutions and of religious fairness is violated by the rule which requires the reading of a chapter from the Bible at the opening of the public schools. This is a relic of Protestant bibliolatry that ought to be suppressed. The Bible has no more business in our schools than has the Koran or the Book of Mormon. The grand lessons and inspiring truths that are to be found in its pages fall flat and meaningless when read by an indifferent teacher to careless pupils; and it serves but as a stumbling block and rock of offense to those who prefer another version or do not believe in the Bible at all. The state ought to have nothing whatever to do with religious observances, and religion will be all the purer and all the stronger the less it is meddled with by the state.

Piety Without Feeling[20]

Here is the great, deep, open wrong—the flagrant violation of God's law which lies at the bottom of all the social evils which Dr. Huntington would pray to God to redress. He has but to look around him to see there is no niggardliness in God's bounty. There is land enough and to spare for all our present population, and all who can come. But human laws disinherit God's children on their very entrance into the world. Dr. Huntington has but to look around and to ask who have the legal right to use the land which his Bible and his common sense must alike tell him God made for all, to see that of the great community of which he is a part and in which he is a minister, not one in a thousand have any legal right whatever to what God gave them.

If he ignores this wrong and robbery and yet prays to God to relieve injustice and want, his prayer is an insult to God and an injury to man.

PERSONAL CORRESPONDENCE

Most of George's speeches and literary works, although they originate in private vision, were written with an audience in mind. It was different with George's intimate correspondence to family and friends, which reveal not so much his ideas as his genuineness of purpose, spirituality, and sense of mission. They can therefore be naturally juxtaposed with his public pronouncements on religion for greater insight into his thinking and crusading fervor. This section contains a number of George's letters. They have been only slightly edited and are presented chronologically.

Letter, "My Dear Sister"[21]

I have been very dilatory about writing and more especially [so] about answering the long letter I received from you about two weeks ago, but now I will try to make amends for it, if I can. In the first place I have been working quite hard and from morning to night without any intermission and it is quite a strain. In fact, to sit down and write after the day is over, is but a continuation of the exercise of the same faculty which—in my trade—has been so heavily drawn upon during the day. And though I might at any time send you a few lines, yet I wanted to write you a good long letter, such a one as I used to write and such as you sent me. Again, I have felt unsettled and worried about business—hoping that each day would make some change that I might tell you of. In fact, until a few days past, [I] hardly knew whether our paper would get through the next day, as I heard something would occur to bring it to a close—and, in truth, feeling something like the sailor in a calm, when wishing for even

> "Storm or hurricane,
> anything, to put a close
> To this most dread, monotonous repose!"

But the days have followed each other, and pretty much like each other, too, and nothing has happened—no prospect of war with European powers, no uprising of Seresainesto, no appearance of the Sheriff's officers—nor even of that individual with more money than brains, with an exceedingly strong desire to go into the newspaper business in a small way, whom I have been hoping would come along and buy me out. So we go—what a constant reaching this life is, a constant stretching forth, and longing after something. You know what Emerson in the "Sphinx" makes his "Oedipus" say:

> "The friend that man harries
> Is love of the best—
> Yawns the pit of the dragon
> Lit by rays from the blest."

And so it is—and so it will be until we reach the perfect and that, you and I, and every son of Adam and daughter of Eve, each for himself knows we are very far from.

> "For the longing I feel is a part
> Of the hunger and thirst of the heart—
> The frenzy and fire of the brain—
> That yearns for the fruitage forbidden,
> The golden pomegranates of Eden,
> To ease off its hunger and pain."

Truly it seems that we have fallen upon evil days—a little while ago all was fair and bright, and now, the storm howls around us with a strength and fury that almost unnerves one. Our country is being torn to pieces, and ourselves [and] our homes filled with distress. As to the ultimate end I have doubt, if civil war should pass over the whole country, leaving nothing but devastation behind it, I think my faith in the ultimate good would remain unchanged, but it is hard to feel so in our individual cases. On great events and movements we soon philosophize but when it comes down to ourselves to our homes to those we love, then we can only feel—our philosophy goes to the dogs, and we can but look prayerfully, tearfully, to Him who hath more care for us than for all the sparrows. And courage, He will not forsake us. It is no darker now, than it was that night on the Sea of Galilee when the poor fishermen cowered despairingly in their little bark! Let us hope and pray!

In the meantime, we eagerly wait the arrival of each pony. Twice a week it arrives, and from the outer telegraph station in Nevada Territory, the news is flashed to us in San Francisco. The last two or three times the news has seemed to me rather more encouraging, not so much by reason of anything that has been done, as by the evident determination of the loyal North to see the thing through.

I do not get much time to read now—in fact, I have read very little for eighteen months—hardly more than the newspapers, certainly not enough to keep posted on the current literature of the day. How I long for the Golden Age—for the promises of the Millennium, when each one will be free to follow his best and noblest impulses, unfettered by the restrictions and necessities which our present state of society imposes upon him when the poorest and the meanest will have a chance to use all his God-given faculties, and not be forced to drudge away the best part of his time in order to supply wants but little above those of the animal. . . .

I had a dream last night—such a pleasant vivid dream, that I must tell you of it—I thought I was scooping treasure out of the earth by handfuls, almost delirious with the thought of what I would now be able to do, and how happy we would all be, and so dear and distinct that I involuntarily felt my pockets when I got up in the morning—but, alas! with the usual result. Is it an indication of future luck? or do dreams always go by contraries, and instead, finding I am to lose? But the latter supposition will not worry me, for "he who lies on the ground cannot fall very far." Nor, I suppose I dreamed as starving men are said to, of splendid feasts or thirsty desert wanderers, of shady brooks, and spray-flinging fountains. "Lust for Gold!" Is it any wonder that men lust for gold, and are willing to give almost anything for it, when it covers everything—the purest and holiest desires of their hearts, the exercise of their noblest powers! What a pity we can't be contented! Is it I who knows? Sometimes I feel sick of the fierce struggle of our highly-civilized life, and think I would like to get away from cities and businesses, with their jostlings and strainings and cares, altogether, and find some place on one of the hillsides, which look so dim and blue in the distance, where I could gather those I love, and live content with what Nature and our own resources would furnish; but, also, money, money, is wanted even for that. It is our fate—we must struggle, and so here's for the strife!

What a glorious thought it is, that at last all will be over—all trial, all care all suffering forever finished; all desire filled, all longing satisfied—what now is but hope become reality—perfect love swallowing up all in one boundless sea of bliss. How the old hymn that we used to sing in the Sunday School swells and peals through the mind, when one thinks of and realizes its meaning as a living truth, like a glorious burst of the heavenly music, telling of the joys of the redeemed and freed.

"Oh, that will be Joyful—
Joyful, Joyful, Joyful

Oh, that will be Joyful!
   To meet, to part no more!
To meet, to part no more,
On Caanan's happy shore,
To sing the everlasting song with those who've gone before."

What a thought, what a picture! With all we love or have loved here "to meet, to part no more—one unbroken family around His Throne!" Can we be unhappy long, if we believe this?

I long much to be at home—to see you all. So much during the day, and the drudgery, and the whirl and jostle—but at night when I lie down and think of the old times—when I wake sometimes at midnight, and can almost feel the kisses that seemed to press my brow a minute or two before, and the voices that I heard in my dreams seem to linger in my ears, yet I almost cry with mingled pleasure and pain. If I could only kiss Pop, Ma, and Aunt Mary, good night once, what a weight it would seem to take away. But it will yet be, and not so very far off either, I hope, though at present I cannot count the time. God is good, and he will yet give us this great Joy!

Letter, "My Dear Father"[22]

It is with a deep felling of gratitude to Our Father in Heaven that I send you a printed copy of this book [*Progress and Poverty*]. I am grateful that I have been able to live to write it, and that you have been able to live to see it. It represents a great deal of work and a good deal of sacrifice, but now it is done. It will not be recognized at first—may be not for some time—but it will ultimately be considered a great book—[it] will be published in both hemispheres and [will] be translated into different languages. This I know, though neither of us may ever see it here. But the belief I have expressed in this book—the belief that there is yet another life for us makes that of little moment. Whatever may happen, the Eternal Providence and the Infinite Many will yet reunite us, with those who have gone before.
    Thanking the Almighty who has us, I am
        Your affectionate son,

Letter, "Dear Sir"[23]

. . . But now, I really, and for myself, believe with you. Out of the brain of thought which is set forth in that book, out of my earnest burning desire to do what I might to relieve human misery and make life brighter has come to me a faith. [T]hough it is not as definite and vivid and firm as must be the Christians' Father where it is really felt, [it means] very much to me. The opportunity to write that book came to me out of crushing disaster, and it represents more than labor. But I would not forgo this satisfaction for any success. And I feel that there is much, very much of which I get only vague glimpses or rather suggestions of glimpses.

Letter, "My Dear Sir"[24]

. . . But it is not this of which I speak so much as the sympathy and interest which your letter expresses and which makes me feel that the book has spoken to you as I knew there would be some men to whom it would speak. This is my reward—the verification of my faith. It [means] very, very much to me—more than profit, more than fame. I knew when I wrote it that my book would sometime find such men, but whether I should ever know it, that I could not tell, for many a man does his work and in this life sees no result. And no matter how much of a success the book may become in my lifetime, I do not think I shall be proud of it, as men are proud of writing a successful history or novel. The feeling is one of deep gratitude that [I have] been permitted to do something. And this, already, I know, for your kind letter is one of the proofs of it, that . . . here and there is a man with whom these ideas have taken hold, as they have taken hold of me, and who in his turn will be a fresh center.

Letter, "My Dear Doctor"[25]

. . . And now let me tell you about the book. At last, it begins to look as though it has really taken hold. When I came East I found that it had hardly got started here. And during the campaign and until the last two weeks in Dec. it went very very slow. But then a moment began, and in the last day of the year my copy of the precious edition and every copy of the 1,000 of the cheap edition were gone, and orders and inquiries came piling in from every quarter. As I began to realize for the first time that I have been telling them the truth, and that they have got hold of a book capable of an enormous sale, the more they are beginning to open out. I had a first class ad in the *Herald* this morning, and will have another in the *Sun* tomorrow. This is the beginning. For every day shows me that wherever the book goes it does attract attention. Every reader means more readers, and every buyer more buyers.

Comparatively speaking the success of the book is already tremendous—for so far as I can learn no book on political economy has ever yet been published in the United States, or (to my astonishment in England either) that has ever yet sold a 1,000 copies in the first year. (Unless forced into the schools), and in fact the entire sales of most of them are to be counted in hundreds not thousands. My book is getting to be regarded here as the phenomenal one, and such publishers as Holt are already regretting that they did not take it when they had a chance.

And today I get the first inquiry note from the Radicals of England in a copy of the *Leeds Independant* which declares it a book which every English workman ought to read and propose to receive subscriptions for it. Pretty soon the economists will be forced to notice it. The future of the book is, I think success. . . .

Letter, "My Dear Taylor"[26]

. . . I see a great work ahead of me—it opens longer and longer; but sometimes I fear that I can't hold out. God knows I try my best. . . .

Letter, "My Dear Father"[27]

There is something else I wanted to say to you that I can only write with my own hand. Don't be disturbed because I am not a Catholic. In some things your Church is very attractive to me; in others it is repellant. But I care nothing for creeds. It seems to me that in any church or out of them one may serve the Master, and this is also that faith that is the soul [which] your Church holds. And in my way, in the line that duty has seemed to call me that I have tried to do. Because you are not only my friend, but a priest and a religious I will say something that I don't like to speak of—that I never before have told to anyone. Once in daylight, and in a city street there came to me a thought, a vision, a call—give it what name you please. But every nerve quivered. And there and then I made a vow. Through evil and through good, whatever I have done and whatever I have left undone, to that I have been true. It was that that impelled me to write *Progress and Poverty*, and that sustained me when else I would have failed. And when I had finished the last page, in the dead of night, when I was entirely alone, I flung myself on my knees and wept like a child. The rest, was in the Master's hands. That is a feeling that has never left me; that is constantly with me. And it has led me up and up. It has made me a better and a purer man. It has been to me a religion, strong and deep though vague—a religion of which I never like to speak, or make any outward manifestation, but yet that I try to follow. Believe this, my dear Father that if it be God's will I should be a Catholic he will call me to it. But in many different forms and in many different ways men may serve him.

Please consider this letter to yourself alone. I have only said this much to you because you wrote my wife hoping I would become a Catholic. Do not disturb yourself about that. I do not wish you not to be a Catholic. Inside of the Catholic Church and out of it; inside of all denominations and creeds and outside of them all there is work to do. Each in the station to which he has been called, let us do what is set us, and we shall not clash. From various instruments, set to different keys comes the grand harmony. And when you remember me in your prayers, which I trust you sometimes will, do not ask that I shall be this or that, but only [that I may have] grace and guidance and strength to the end. And believe me, in spite of all [the] differences [that there may] be.

Notes

1. *The Standard,* Jan. 8, 1887, GR. The excommunication of McGlynn became a cause célèbre. The struggle between this priest and Archbishop Corrigan of New York was a watershed in the development of the Roman Catholic Church in the United States and even the world. It represented two distinct viewpoints (free speech, civil and political freedom, and social justice versus hierarchal control) fighting for ascendancy. It also signifies the concern of the Vatican over the Georgist assault on private property in land. Scholars (and George himself suspected) regard the Leo XIII's *Rerum Novarum* of 1891 as a direct attack on his political economy. Consult Bell, *Rebel, Priest, and Prophet* and Geiger, *Philosophy of Henry George,* 336–380 for more information. For a copy of the *Rerum Novarum* (Encyctical Letter of Pope Leo XIII, *On the Condition of Labor*) and George's rebuttal (*The Condition of Labor*) see the last two selections in George's *The Land Question.*
2. Constantine I (274?–337) became the sole emperor of the Roman Empire after his victory at Milvian Bridge (312) where he had purportedly seen a flaming cross in the sky. He was baptized just before death.
3. To be more precise, the Russian Orthodox Church, which is an independent part of the Orthodox Eastern Church. Greek Church is a term used in the West to collectively refer to the latter.
4. Papal infallibility relating to matters of faith was declared in 1870. Archbishop Michael Corrigan of New York was a major opponent of McGlynn and con-demned George's ideas. See note 1.
5. The only English pope, Adrian IV (1100?–1159) was originally named Nicholas Breakspear. The reference is to the "Donation of Ireland." He gave Ireland to Henry II of England as a papal fief.
6. John Joseph Hughes (1797–1864) was the first archbishop of New York.
7. The Tombs refers to a prison in New York City.

8. The Congregation for the Propaganda of the Faith was established by Pope Gregory XV in 1622. It is a committee of cardinals overseeing the training and implementation of foreign missions by priests.
9. Probably a reference to well-placed prelates of the Catholic Church with close ties to New York politicians. The Castle Garden was a hall used for fancy receptions and shows.
10. George Errington (1804–1886) was an English Roman Catholic archbishop.
11. *The Standard*, May 14, 1887, GR. This speech and the next one are potent examples of the mingling of social justice and a religious spirit.
12. *The Standard*, Nov. 19, 1887, GR.
13. *The Standard*, May 28, 1887, GR. The Latin title is translated as "My God and I." In this article and the next one George attacks the Catholic Church as an institution, but not for its divinely-inspried beliefs.
14. St. Vincent de Paul (1576–1660) was a French priest imprisoned by Tunisian pirates, who later worked to better the lot of galley slaves. He organized many charities, and founded two orders (Congregation of the Mission and Sisters of Charity). *Soggarth aroon* is Irish for "the good priest."
15. A female in Revelations 17, who has been interpreted as representing pagan Rome, or the Roman Catholic Church by its detractors.
16. Elsewhere George wrote: "We have no sovereign in this country, but we do have rotten political rings and great corporations who pack the bench and fill even our highest legislative body with paid attorneys, and there is impending a great revolt—peaceable, as we trust—on the part of honest citizens against the moneyed powers which are sapping the very foundations of the American Republic with their corruptions. If the Roman diplomats could intrigue with the oppressors of Ireland, why may they not in the same way intrigue with scheming politicians and the moneyed rings of the United States?" (*The Standard*, "The Case of Dr. McGlynn," Jan. 15, 1887, GR).
17. *The Standard*, Dec. 3, 1887, GR.
18. *The Standard*, Jan. 21, 1888, GR. This opinion would even be considered quite radical in the America of today with a religious moral majority and a growing fundamentalism!
19. Ultramontane literally means beyond the mountains or south of the Alps (Italy), but usually refers to the belief that the pope is the spiritual leader of the Catholic Church in every country.
20. *The Standard*, Jan. 1,1890, GR.
21. George to Jane George, Sept. 15, 1861, #1, HGP. George lived in California from 1858 to 1880. It was here that he married, worked in various capacities on different newspapers, and wrote *Progress and Poverty*. See George, Jr., *Henry George*, 53–334 and Barker, *Henry George*, 34–325.
22. George to Richard George, Sept. 15, 1879, #1, HGP.
23. George to Charles Nordhoff, Dec 21, 1879, #2, HGP.
24. George to A. J. Steers, Apr. 4, 1880, #2, HGP.
25. George to Dr. [Edward Taylor?], Jan. 4, [year?], #2, HGP.
26. George to Dr. Edward Taylor, Mar. 14, 1881, #2, HGP.
27. George to Rev. Thomas Dawson, Feb. 1, 1883, #3, HGP.

Bibliography

Presented here is a selected list of pertinent works. It contains material relating to Henry George and the Single Tax. Although not exhaustive, it is somewhat extensive and includes a number of graduate papers. It is hoped that some of these selections will be of use for future inquiry. Only English sources are listed, except the *Complete Works of Tolstoy* and the biography by Gusev.

Allen, Henry W. *Prosperity in the Year 2000 A.D.* Boston: The Christopher Publishing House, 1936.

Andelson, Robert V., ed. *Critics of Henry George.* Rutherford, NJ: Fairleigh Dickinson Press, 1979.

————. *Commons Without Tragedy.* London: Shepheard-Walwyn, 1991.

————. *Henry George and the Reconstruction of Capitalism.* American Institute for Economic Research, 1992.

————. *Msgr. Ryan's Critique of Henry George.* New York: American Journal of Economics and Sociology,1974.

————. *A Capitalist Theology of Liberation.* Boston: Lincoln Institute of Land Policy, 1933.

————. *From Wasteland to Promised Land.* London: Shepheard-Walwyn, 1992.

Argyll, Duke of; Campbell, George D. *Property in Land: A Passage-at-Arms Between the Duke of Argyll and Henry George.* New York: Sterling, 1894.

————. *The Peer and the Prophet.* London: Reeves, 1884.

Barker, Charles A. *Henry George.* New York: Robert Schalkenbach Foundation, 1991.

————. *Henry George and the California Background of "Progress and Poverty."* San Francisco, 1945.

Beggs, George H. *"The Fairhope Single Tax Corporation: An Analysis of the Efforts of a Single Tax Colony to Apply the Ideas of Henry George."* Ph.D. diss., The University of Arizona, 1967.

Bell, Stephen. *Rebel, Priest and Prophet: A Biography of Dr. Edward McGlynn.* New York: Robert Schalkenbach Foundation, 1968.

Bengough, J. W. *The Whole Hog Book.* Boston: American Free Trade League, 1908.

Benz, George A. *"The 'Single Tax' as a Means of Support for a Local Government, Edmond, Oklahoma."* Ph.D. diss., University of Oklahoma, 1969.

Bernstein, William S. *"Lewis Henry Morgan, John Wesley Powell, and Henry George: A*

Study in the Relation Between Nineteenth Century Intellectual Thought and Social Reform." M. A. thesis, Brown University, 1978.

Berry, Brian J. *America's Utopian Experiments.* Hanover, NH: University Press of New England, 1992.

Birnie, Arthur. *Single-Tax George.* London: T. Nelson & Sons, 1939.

Bonaparte, Tony. *Henry George: His Impact Abroad and the Relevancy of His Views on International Trade.* New York: Pace University, 1985.

Bramwell, George. *Nationalisation of Land: A Review of Mr. George's "Progress and Poverty."* London: Liberty and Property Defense League, 1895.

Brann, Henry A. *Henry George and His Land Theories.* New York: Catholic Publication Society, 1887.

Briggs, George. *Comment on Henry George's Definitions.* San Diego: Henry B. Cramer, 1950.

Briggs, M. C. *Regress and Slavery vs. "Progress and Poverty."* New York: Hunt & Eaton, 1891.

Brooks, Noah. *Henry George in California.* New York: 1899.

Buurman, Gerritt. *"A Comparison of the Single Tax Proposals of Henry George and the Physiocrats."* M. A. thesis, Western Washington State College, 1971.

Candeloro, D. L. *Louis F. Post: Carpetbagger, Singletaxer, Progressive.* Ann Arbor, MI: University Microfilms, 1981.

Cantwell, Harry. *The Philosophy of Henry George.* St. Louis: Kenmore Press, 1901.

Cathrein, Victor. *The Champions of Agrarian Socialism: A Refutation of Emile de Laveleye and Henry George.* Buffalo: P. Paul & Bros., 1889.

Christian, R. F., ed. *Tolstoy's Letters, 1880–1910.* Vol. 2. New York: Charles Scribner's Sons, 1978.

Clancy, Robert. *The Story of the Georgist Movement.* London: Land & Liberty Press, 1950.

———. *A Seed Was Sown: The Life, Philosophy, and Writings of Oscar H. Geiger.* New York: Henry George School of Social Sciences, 1954.

Coleman, James. *George and Democracy.* Georgetown College: By the author, 1887.

Collier, Charles. *"Henry George's System of Economics: Analysis and Criterion."* Ph. D. diss., Duke University, 1976.

Cord, Steven B. *Henry George: Dreamer or Realist?* New York: Robert Schalkenbach Foundation, 1985.

———. *The Ethics of Land Reform: A Trialogue Between Adam Smith, Karl Marx, and Henry George.* New York: Pace University, 1985.

Croft, Albert. *"The Speaking Career of Henry George: A Study in Ideas and Persuasion."* M. A. thesis, Northwestern University, 1952.

Crump, Arthur. *An Exposure of the Pretensions of Mr. Henry George as Set Forth in His Book "Progress and Poverty."* London: E. Wilson, 1884.

Davidson, John. *Concerning Four Precursors of Henry George and the Single Tax.* London: Labor Leader Pub. Dept., 1899.

de Mille, Agnes George. *Henry George: Citizen of the World.* Chapel Hill: University of North Carolina Press, 1950.

Dewey, John. *An Appreciation of Henry George.* New York: Robert Schalkenbach Foundation, 1927.

———. *John Dewey on Henry George and What Some Others Say*. New York: Robert Schalkenbach Foundation, 1927.

Douglas of Barlock. *Social Science Manual, Guide to the Study of Henry George's "Progress and Poverty."* London: Henry George Foundation of Great Britain, 1937.

Dixwell, George. *"Progress and Poverty:" A Review of the Doctrine of Henry George*. Cambridge, MA: J. Wilson & Son, 1882.

———. *Premises of Free Trade Examined*. Cambridge, MA: J. Wilson & Son, 1882.

Dudden, Arthur P. *Joseph Fels and the Single Tax Movement*. Philadelphia: Temple University Press, 1971.

Easterly, John. *"Louis F. Post 1849–1928: The "Henry George Man" as Progressive and Reformer."* Ph. D. diss., Duke University, 1976.

———. *"Louis F. Post: Popularizer and Propagandist for Henry George and the Single Tax, 1849–1928."* M. A. thesis, Duke University, 1970.

Ely, Richard T. *Land, Labor, and Taxation*. Baltimore: Cushing & Co., 1880.

Faidy, Joseph. *The Political Economy of Henry George*. Cedar Rapids, IA: Why, 1903.

Fillebrown, Charles. *Thirty Years of Henry George*. Boston: By the author, 1917.

———. *The Catholic Church and Henry George*. Boston: By the author, 1917.

———. *Henry George and His Single Tax: An Appreciation*. Boston: By the author, 1917.

———. *Henry George and the Economists*. Boston: 1960.

Flaherty, John. *Henry George: Motivating the Managerial Mind*. New York: Pace University, 1985.

Flattery, Hugh. *The Pope and the New Crusade*. New York: Thomas R. Knox & Co., 1887.

Gaffney, Mason and Harrison, Fred. *The Corruption of Economics*. London: Shepheard-Walwyn, 1994.

Geiger, George R. *The Philosophy of Henry George*. New York: MacMillian Co., 1933.

———. *Henry George: A Biography*. London: Henry George Foundation of Great Britain, 1939.

Genovese, Frank. *Henry George and the Labor Unions*. New York: Pace University, 1985.

George, Henry. *Progress and Poverty*. New York: Robert Schalkenbach Foundation, 1992. First published in 1879.

———. *Social Problems*. New York: Robert Schalkenbach Foundation, 1992. First published in 1883.

———. *Protection or Free Trade*. New York: Robert Schalkenbach Foundation, 1992. First published in 1886.

———. *The Land Question*. New York: Robert Schalkenbach Foundation, 1982. First published as *The Irish Land Question* in 1881. Included are other works dating from 1884 to 1891.

———. *A Perplexed Philosopher*. New York: Robert Schalkenbach Foundation, 1988. First published in 1892.

———. *Our Land and Land Policy*. Vol. 8 of *The Complete Works of Henry George*. New York: Doubleday, Page & Co., 1904. This compilation of works was first published in 1900. It includes the pamphlet *Our Land and Land Policy* (1871) and speeches from 1877 to 1894.

———. *The Science of Political Economy*. New York: Robert Schalkenbach Foundation, 1988. First published posthumously in 1898.

————. *Causes of Business Depressions.* New York: Robert Schalkenbach Foundation, 1930.

————. *The Wisdom of Henry George: Excerpts from Social Problems.* Girard, KS: Haldeman-Julius Pubs., 1947.

————. *Verbatim Report of the Debate in St. James Hall, July 2, 1889.* [with H. M. Hyndman]. London: Justice, 1889.

————. *The Land Question: What It Involves and How Alone It Can Be Settled.* New York: D. Appleton & Co., 1881.

————. *Gems from Henry George.* London: Henry George Foundation of Great Britain, 1930.

————. *More Progress and Less Poverty: A Businessman Reviews Henry George.* New York: Robert Schalkenbach Foundation, 1942.

George, Jr., Henry. *Henry George.* American Men and Women of Letters Series, Ed. Daniel Aaron. New York: Chelsea House, 1981.

Green, Charles. *The Profits of the Earth.* Boston: Christopher Pub. House, 1934.

Green, James J. *"The Impact of Henry George's Theories on American Catholics."* Ph. D. diss., Notre Dame University, 1956.

————. *"First Impact of the Henry George Agitation on Catholics in the United States."* M. A. thesis, Notre Dame University, 1948.

Grigg, Kenneth. *Sun Yat Sen: The Third Alternative for the Third World.* Melbourne: Henry George Foundation, 1983.

Grinell, Judson. *Henry George.* Judson Papers, 1919.

Gronlund, Laurence. *Insufficiency of Henry George's Theory.* New York: New York Labor News, 1887.

Gusev, N. N. *Lev Nikolaevich Tolstoi: materiali k biografii s 1881 po 1885 god* (L. N. Tolstoy: material for a biography from 1881 to 1885). Moscow: Izdatel'stvo "Nauka," 1970.

Hackner, Willibald. *Socialism and the Church, or, Henry George versus Archbishop Corrigan.* New York: Catholic Pub. Society, 1887.

Harriss, C. Lowell. *Taxation: Today's Lessons from Henry George.* New York: Pace University, 1985.

Hawks, Charlene M. *"Herbert Quick: Iowan."* Ph. D. diss., Universtiy of Iowa, 1981.

Hazleton, Ralph L. *"Henry George's Social Economics."* Ph.D. diss., University of Utah, 1973.

Heath, Spencer. *Progress and Poverty Reviewed and its Fallacies Exposed.* New York: Science of Society Foundation, 1952.

Hellman, Rhoda. *Henry George Reconsidered.* New York: Carlton Press, 1987.

Higgins, Edward. *Fallacies of Henry George Exposed and Refuted.* Cincinnati: Press of Keating & Co., 1887.

Howell, Sarah. *"Scholars of the Urban-Industrial Frontier: 1880–1889."* Ph. D. diss., Vanderbilt University, 1970.

Hubbard, Elbert. *Little Journeys to the Homes of Great Reformers.* E. Aurora, NY: The Roycrofters, 1907.

Hughes, B. F. *The Basis of Interest (A Reply to Mr. Lowery).* New York: Kraus Reprint.

Johnson, Edgar. *"The Economics of Henry George's 'Progress and Poverty.'"* Ph. D. diss., University of Chicago, 1910.

Jones, Peter. *Henry George and British Socialism*. New York: Garland Pubs., 1991.

Jordan, David S. *The True Basis of Economics*. New York: Doubleday & McClure Co., 1899.

Jorgensen, Emil O. *Did Henry George Confuse the Single Tax?* Elkhart, IN: James A. Bell Co., 1936.

————. *False Education in Our Colleges and Universities*. Chicago: Manufacturers and Merchants Federated Tax League, 1925.

Kindleberger, C. *Henry George's Protection or Free Trade*. Williamstown, MA: Williams College, 1987.

Lawrence, Elwood. *Henry George in the British Isles*. E. Lansing, MI: Michigan State University Press, 1957.

Lewandowski, Eric. *"The Great American Paradox: Tom L. Johnson and the Controversy Surrounding His Role in History."* M. A. thesis, Ohio State University, 1980.

Lindner, Eileen W. *"The Redemptive Politic of Henry George: Legacy to the Social Gospel Christianity, New York City."* Ph.D. diss., Union Theological Seminary, 1985.

Lissner, Will and Dorothy, eds. *George and the Scholars*. New York: Robert Schalkenbach Foundation, 1991.

————. *George and Democracy in the British Isles*. New York: Robert Schalkenbach Foundation, 1992.

Love, James. *Japanese Notions of European Political Economy*. Philadelphia: By Kuya Shihosho, 1899.

————. *A Correspondence Between an Amateur and a Professor of Economics*. Philadelphia: J. B. Lippincott, 1897.

Lowrey, Dwight. *The Basis of Interest. A Criticism of the Solution Offered by Henry George*. Philadelphia: American Academy of Political and Social Sciences, 1892.

Madison, Charles A. *Critics and Crusaders: A Century of American Protest*. New York: Henry Holt & Co., 1947.

Mallock, W. H. *Property and Progress or, A Brief Inquiry into Contemporary Social Agitation in England*. New York: G. P. Putnam's Sons, 1884.

Marx, Karl and Engels, Friedrich. *Letters to Americans: 1848–1895*. New York: International Publishers, 1969.

McMillion, John L. *Henry George on Land and Liberty."* M. A. thesis, Bowling Green State University, 1975.

Miller, Bleecker J. *Trade Organization in Politics*. New York: The Baker & Taylor Co., 1887.

————. *Progress and Robbery: Two Americans Answer to Henry George, the Demi-Communist*. New York: Cherouny, 1886.

Moffat, Robert. *Mr. Henry George, the "Orthodox."* London: Remington & Co., 1885.

Muirhead, James. *Land and Unemployment*. London: Oxford University Press, 1935.

Nitoche, Charles G. *"Albert Jay Nock and Frank Chodorov: Case Studies in Recent American Individualist and Anti-Statist Thought."* Ph. D. diss., University of Maryland, College Park, 1981.

Nock, Albert J. *Henry George*. New York: W. Morrow & Co., 1939.

Noyes, Richard, ed. *Now the Synthesis, The New Social Control*. London: Shepheard-Walwyn, 1996.

Oser, Jacob. *Henry George*. New York: Twayne Pubs., 1974.

Padover, Saul K. *The Genius of America: Men Whose Ideas Shaped Our Civilization.* New York: McGraw-Hill Book Co., 1960.

Pedder, Digby C. *Henry George and His Gospel.* London: A. C. Fifield, 1908.

Portner, Stuart. *Louis F. Post: His Life and Times.* Ann Arbor, MI: University Microfilms, 1963.

Post, Louis F. *The Prophet of San Francisco: Personal Memoirs and Interpretation of Henry George.* New York: Vanguard Press, 1930.

————. *Henry George's 1886 Campaign.* Westport, CT: Hyperion Press, 1976.

————. *Taxation of Land Values; An Explanation.* Chicago: The Public, 1912.

————. *The Single Tax.* Cedar Rapids, IA: F. Vierth, 1899.

————. *Outlines of Lectures on the Taxation of Land Values.* Chicago: The Public, 1912.

Quinby, Laurie. *Henry George's Progress and Poverty.* Los Angeles: Chimes Press, 1925.

Ralston, Jackson. *Confronting the Land Question.* Bayside, NY: American Association for Scientific Taxation, 1945.

————. *Open Letter Concerning Tax Reform.* Cincinnati: Joseph Fels Fund of America, 1909.

————. *What's Wrong With Taxation.* San Diego: Ingram Institute, 1931.

Ramhurst, Robert. *"The Single Tax and Its Practical Modifications."* M. A. thesis, University of Arizona, 1953.

Rather, Lois. *Henry George–Printer to Author.* Oakland, CA: Rather Press, 1978.

Redfearn, David. *Tolstoy: Principles for a New World Order.* London: Shepheard-Walwyn, 1992.

Ring, Henry F. *The Case Plainly Stated.* New York: Henry George, 1887.

Rose, Edward J. *Henry George.* New York: Twayne Pubs., 1968.

Rutherford, Reuben C. *Henry George versus Henry George.* New York: D. Appleton & Co., 1887.

Saldji, Victor. *Is "Progress and Poverty" Outdated?* London: Land & Liberty Press, 1959.

Salter, William. *Progress and Poverty: Rev. Dr. Salter's Sermon at the Congregational Church.* Burlington[?], IA: 1884.

Sawyer, Rollin. *Henry George and the Single Tax: A List of References to the Collection in the New York Public Library. New York, 1926.*

Schubart, Richard D. *"Ralph Borsodi: The Political Biography of a Utopian Decentralist, 1886–1977."* Ph. D. diss., State University of New York at Binghamton, 1984.

Scott, William. *Henry George and His Economic System.* 1898.

Scudder, Moses L. *The Labor-Value Fallacy.* Chicago: Jansen, McClurg & Co., 1884.

Shafer, Robert E. *The Philosophy of Henry George.*

Shearman, Thomas G. *Free Trade.* New York: The American Free Trade League, 1883.

————. *Henry George's Mistakes.* New York: Henry George, 1889.

————. *Objections to the Single Tax.* New York: Henry George, 1889.

————. *Taxation and Revenue: The Free Trade View.* New York: Appleton & Co., 1892.

————. *National Taxation.* New York: G. P. Putnam's Sons, 1895.

————. *Shortest Road to the Single Tax.* Cedar Rapids, IA: Frank Vierth, 1910.

Sheilds, Charles H. *Single Tax Exposed.* Seattle, 1914.

Sinclair, Stanley. *Reform For Our Time.* New York: Center for Land Economics, 1972.

Stebbins, Giles. *Progress from Poverty. Review and Criticism of Henry George's "Progress and Poverty" and "Protection or Free Trade."* Chicago: C. H. Kerr & Co., 1887.

Suit, William W. *"Tom Loftin Johnson, Businessman, Reformer (Ohio Progressive)."* Ph. D. diss., Kent State University, 1988.

Sutton, P. M. *Work's Dialogue With Henry George.* Marshalltown, IA: Marshall Printing Co., 1887.

Swinerton, Steven. *"The Jeffersonian Civil Revolution of 1886: Henry George's First New York City Mayoral Campaign."* M. A. thesis, Northeast Missouri State University, 1993.

Teilhac, Ernest. *Pioneers of American Economic Thought in the Nineteenth Century.* New York: The MacMillon Co., 1936.

Thomas, John L. *Alternative America: Henry George, Edward Bellamy, Henry Demarest Lloyd, and the Adversary Tradition in America.* Cambridge, MA: Belknap Press, 1983.

Tipple, John O. *Andrew Carnegie/Henry George: The Problems of Progress.* Cleveland: H. Allen, 1960.

Tobin, Francis. *Notes on "Progress and Poverty," A Reply to Henry George.* Welsh, 1887.

Tolstoy, Lev N. *Polnoe sobranie sochinenii* (Complete works). Moscow: Gosudarstvennoe izdatel'stvo khudozhestvennoi literatury, 1928–1964.

Tribe, Henry F. *"Disciple of 'Progress and Poverty:' Robert Crosser and Twentieth Century Reform: Robert Crosser, Congressman, Ohio."* Ph.D. diss., Bowling Green State University, 1991.

Toynbee, Arnold. *"Progress and Poverty:" A Criticism of of Mr. Henry George.* London: Kegan Paul, 1883.

Tucker, Benjamin. *Henry George, Traitor.* New York: By the author, 1896.

Wedgwood, Josiah. *Henry George for Socialists.* London: Independent Labour Party, 1908.

Wray, Charles R. *"The Theories and Tactics of Henry George: 1886–1888."* M. A. thesis, Notre Dame University, 1958.

Wynns, Peyton L. *"Henry George, the Single Tax, and the Economic Rent of Land During the Twentieth Century."* M. A. thesis, Florida State University, 1965.

Yanosky, Ronald W. *"Seeing the Cat: Henry George and the Rise of the Single Tax Movement, 1879–1890."* Ph. D. diss., University of California at Berkeley, 1993.

Yardley, Arthur ed., *Addresses at the Funeral of Henry George.* Chicago: The Public Pub. Co., 1905.

Young, Arthur N. *The Single Tax Movement in the United States.* Princeton: Princeton University Press, 1916.

Zimard, Savel. *Modern Social Movements; Descriptive Summaries and Bibliographies.* New York: The H. W. Wilson Co., 1900.

No author. *Henry George Memorial Meeting.* San Francisco, 1897.

———. *Tributes at the Funeral of Henry George.* New York: Robert Schalkenbach Foundation, 1939.

———. *Henry George Centenary Conference 1939.* London: Vacher & Sons, 1939.